616.89   Love, Patricia
Lov   The Emotional Incest Syndrome

THE EMOTIONAL INCEST SYNDROME

THE EMOTIONAL INCEST SYNDROME

What to Do
When a Parent's Love
Rules Your Life

Dr. Patricia Love with Jo Robinson

BANTAM BOOKS
New York • Toronto • London • Sydney • Auckland

All the characters portrayed in
this book are based upon fact. However,
details and circumstances have been
changed to ensure anonymity.

THE EMOTIONAL INCEST SYNDROME

A Bantam Book / May 1990

BOOK DESIGN BY LURELLE CHEVERIE.

Library of Congress Cataloging-in-Publication Data

Love, Patricia.
    The emotinal incest syndrome : what to do when a parent's love rules your life /
by Patricia Love with Jo Robinson.
        p.   cm.
    Includes bibliographical references.
    ISBN 0-553-05768-5
    1. Emotional incest.   2. Adult children of dysfunctional families—
—Rehabilitation.   I. Robinson, Jo, 1947—   . II Title.
RC569.5.E46L68   1990
616.89—dc20   89-49087
                                                                        CIP

Published simultaneously in the United States and Canada

Bantam Books are published by Bantam Books, a division of Bantam Doubleday Dell
Publishing Group, Inc. Its trademark, consisting of the words "Bantam Books" and the
portrayal of a rooster, is Registered in U.S. Patent and Trademark Office and in other
countries. Marca Registrada. Bantam Books, 666 Fifth Avenue, New York, New York 10103.

PRINTED IN THE UNITED STATES OF AMERICA

RRD-H   0 9 8 7 6 5 4 3 2 1

This book is dedicated to parents,
who do the best they can
with the information they have
and the options they see.

Acknowledgments

There are numerous people I wish to acknowledge and thank, beginning with my husband, Will Ponder, without whose support this book would not have been possible.

Although I have been influenced by too many fine people to mention, I do want to single out Pia Mellody for her fine work in the area of co-dependency, abuse, and neglect; and Harville Hendrix, for his friendship and his immeasurable contribution to the field of marital therapy and theory. I must also thank my dear friend, Anne Worth, for her support and for introducing me to both Pia and Harville!

The theoretical foundation of this book rests on the pioneering work of Salvador Minuchin and his theory of Structural Family Therapy. His research and practice have changed the course of marriage and family therapy.

Leslie Meredith, Senior Editor at Bantam, has earned my respect and admiration for her dedication to this book and her attention to details. I want to thank my agent, Susan Lescher, for her unflagging interest in this project. Sharon Morris, Frances Robinson, and Tamera Allred all contributed invaluable editorial assistance. A special acknowledgment to my coauthor, Jo Robinson. Working together has been both rewarding and fun!

Finally, I want to thank the heroic individuals who allowed their stories to be included in this book. Thank you so very much.

PAT LOVE

Contents

88

Introduction

88

This book describes a syndrome known as emotional incest, a surprisingly common but rarely identified style of parenting in which parents turn to their children, not to their partners, for emotional support. To the casual observer, the parents may appear loving and devoted. They may spend a great deal of time with their children and lavish them with praise and material gifts. But in the final analysis, their love is not a nurturing, giving love—it's an unconscious ploy to satisfy their own unmet needs.

Being a parent's primary source of support is a heavy burden for young children. Forced to suppress their own needs, they struggle to satisfy the needs of the adults. Because of this role reversal, they are rarely given adequate protection, guidance, or discipline, and they are exposed to experiences well beyond their years. In adolescence and adulthood, they are likely to be plagued by one or more of the following difficulties: depression, chronic low-level anxiety, problems with self-esteem and love relationships, overly loose or rigid personal boundaries, some form of sexual dysfunction, eating disorders, and drug or alcohol addiction.

Because few victims of emotional incest can pinpoint what was wrong with their families, they have limited insight into the under-lying cause of their problems. Many have a rosy view of childhood that makes recovery even more difficult. How can they think ill of a parent who showered them with so much time and attention? Breaking through this mythology is a necessary step in the healing process.

Emotional incest is not a new phenomenon. History is full of people who were overly involved with their children. Human beings have an innate need for companionship and intimacy, and when those needs are not met by a partner, the natural tendency is to turn to a child. But the syndrome has become newsworthy for the following reasons:

1. Recent changes in family life—notably the dramatic rise in single-parent households and substance abuse—have dramatically increased the incidence of emotional incest.

2. The adult consequences of the syndrome are more clearly understood.

3. Recent advances in the relatively new field of Structural Family Therapy have made emotional incest a definable, curable problem.

4. The syndrome finally has a name.

I have devoted the past five years to researching this book. The clearer I've become about the nature of the syndrome, the more I see it around me. Fully half of my clients have an overly close relationship with a mother or father as a central issue. When I lecture on the subject, I can always count on a handful of people coming up to me afterward to tell me, "What you're talking about happened to me. You've just described my life. For the first time, I have a name for what's wrong with me."

It is my hope that bringing this problem to the public's attention will help address a severe but often overlooked form of abuse and play a role in creating healthier family relationships.

PAT LOVE, ED. D.
AUSTIN, TEXAS

PART ONE

WHAT IS EMOTIONAL INCEST?

Exploring the Problem

❀

1

Growing Up with an Invasive Parent

❁

"Daddy told me the day I was born he fell in love all over again."

Gwen, 33 years old and a talented graphic artist, came to me with two of the telltale signs of emotional incest—chronic relationship problems and a curious blend of high and low self-esteem. When she first walked into my office, she seemed quite poised. She had a confident stride and a warm handshake. She was dressed in a softly tailored green suit, and her dark, shiny hair was very becoming. If I'd been an employer interviewing her for a job, I'd have been favorably impressed.

At first glance, her family background also seemed fairly normal. "I don't have much to complain about," she said when I asked her about her childhood. "I'm one of those rare individuals who came from a 'functional family.' My parents weren't perfect, but they didn't drink, they didn't divorce, they didn't hit us, and they didn't fight. So why am I such a mess? And why am I about to get my second divorce?"

Over the phone, Gwen had told me she was in the middle of divorce proceedings. The year following her first divorce had been really rough, and she wanted to minimize the pain this time around.

"Now that I know what your parents *didn't* do," I said with a smile, "tell me what they *did* do. What were they like?"

"Well, I was a lot closer to my dad than my mother. In fact, Dad and I were really close. He called me his 'Little Princess.'"

Immediately, a red flag popped up in the back of my mind. "What do you remember most about your father?" I asked.

"One of my favorite memories is sitting on the couch with him listening to music. Dad was crazy about Mozart, and so was I. By the time I was twelve, I could identify just about every piece Mozart wrote—just from hearing the first few bars. He was really proud of that. My brother wasn't very musical. Dad would say to him, 'You have tin ears.'"

"What else did you and your father do?" I asked. I was looking for signs of an overly close bond.

"When it was bedtime, Dad would put me to bed and read to me until I fell asleep. In the morning he would wake me up so we could have breakfast together before he left for work. We're both morning people. My mother and my brother are night owls. He looked forward to that time alone with me each morning. He'd talk about his job, his worries, his plans for the future."

Gwen went on to say that she and her father were avid skiers, jogged together every evening, and often accompanied each other to the symphony. By now the red flags were flying. Gwen and her father seemed more like a happily married couple than a father and daughter. They even operated according to the same biological timetable—just like a couple of newlyweds.

"Did you have many friends when you were young?" I asked. Children who are overly attached to a parent generally spend very little time with peers.

"You know, it's a funny thing to say, but I think Dad was my best friend," she replied. "We did everything together."

"What would your mother and brother be doing while you were spending all this time with your father?"

"Mother would be cooking or cleaning the house or reading. My brother would be watching TV or out with his friends. There's only one thing that bothered me about my dad," Gwen said, switching the conversation back to her father. "He was always complaining to me about Mom. He'd say things like, 'You're smarter than your mother,' or 'I wish your mother had your sense of humor.' He'd even say those things in front of her." As she said this, she turned and looked out the window. I could see it still troubled her.

"How did your mother react when he did this?" I asked.

"She just shrugged it off. Sometimes she'd get a cold look on her face and walk out of the room—slam a few cupboard doors, that sort of thing. But they never fought. I used to think that meant they had a good marriage. Now that I have some idea what marriage is about"—and here she looked at me with a wry smile—"I can see they were just putting up with each other. They had little in common other than my brother and me. They'd go to the company picnics, but that's about all."

I had been hearing this kind of sad story more and more frequently. Gwen's father wanted what we all want in life—someone to confide in, someone to be on his side, someone to share his interests, someone to adore him. Not finding what he wanted in his marriage, he, like so many other parents, turned to the next available resource—a child. He had a void in his life that he tried to fill with his daughter.

"Was it hard for your father when you went away to college?" I asked. "You were so close."

She nodded emphatically. "He was devastated. He was depressed my whole last year of high school. 'You're not going to go away and leave me?' he'd say. I felt guilty for leaving home. He drove me to the campus in the fall so we could have one last day together. When we pulled up to the dorm, he told me that the day I was born, he fell in love all over again. I'll never forget that. He had tears in his eyes."

As our session was drawing to a close, I asked, "What would you like to get out of our work together? Over the phone you talked about wanting help in getting over your divorce. Could you be more specific?"

Gwen tilted her head and bit her upper lip, then reached into her purse and pulled out a notepad and a pencil. "I'm better with a pencil than I am with words," she said. She made a few quick lines and held up the pad so I could see what she had drawn. It appeared to be a large, open-petaled flower with a dark center. She pointed to the fluted edge. "This is how I feel about myself some of the time. I feel powerful, special . . ." she paused for a second, then laughed, "my two ex-husbands might even say grandiose." Then she pointed to the tiny, dense black scribble in the center. "And this is how I feel about myself the rest of the time. Small. Dark. Guilty. Worthless." The contrast between the two parts of the drawing was a graphic depiction of her anxiety. She wasn't what she appeared to be. Beneath her confident exterior she felt like a frightened, guilty child. "I want to know why," she said.

*   *   *

Gwen is a classic example of what I call the Chosen Child, a child chosen by a parent to be a primary source of emotional support. In the broadest terms, there are two ways that a parent-child relationship can be out of line: (1) the parent and child can be *estranged*, which means there is too much distance between them, or (2) they can be *enmeshed*, which means they are too close.[1] Of the two, enmeshment is the more common, and a close bond between a parent and child of the opposite sex is so common that we have everyday words for it: "daddy's little girl" and "mama's boy."

When there is a high degree of enmeshment—as in Gwen's case—it merits a special term: *emotional incest*.[2] These are strong words, I know, but I use them advisedly. Just as children are powerless against a parent's sexual advances, they are powerless against an emotionally Invasive Parent. Their sense of self is so limited and their need to be connected to their parents is so great that adults have total control over the relationship. When a parent takes advantage of this power and turns to a son or daughter for need fulfillment, there is a violation of the intimacy taboo between parent and child.

For the child, the consequences of this violation can be severe and long-lasting. Fluctuating self-esteem, a sense of powerlessness, problems relating to their peers and maintaining friendships, eating disorders, depression, and anxiety are some of the common repercussions. Adult children of emotional incest often have sexual dysfunctions and problems in love relationships.

Unfortunately, public awareness of emotional incest is very limited, so the syndrome often goes undiagnosed and untreated. Gwen, for example, was a well-educated woman, yet she was blind to her father's excessive involvement. Even as an adult, the danger signs that were so obvious to me were invisible to her. All she saw was what she had gained from the relationship—praise and affection, extra privileges, patient tutoring, and shared confidences. Every child secretly wishes to have the exclusive attention of the opposite-sex parent, and for Gwen this wish had come true.

The difficult task I faced in the coming weeks was to help Gwen see the negative consequences of this excessive devotion. It would be unsettling for her to see how she had been harmed by her relationship with her father, but confronting this fact would give her insight into her puzzling emotional problems. For the first time she would understand the underlying cause of her marital difficulties, and she would know why she experienced such dramatic shifts in self-esteem.

✂ Varieties of Emotional Incest

Emotional incest can take many forms. Gwen was allied with what I call a Romanticizing Parent, a parent who turns to a child of the opposite sex for the intimacy and companionship one would normally expect to find in a love relationship. In essence, the child becomes a surrogate spouse. As in the case of Gwen's father, often the parent adores the child. Typically, there is a flirtatious, teasing quality to the relationship.

A variation of the theme occurs when a parent is enmeshed with a child of the same sex. Then the relationship has more of a "best friend" or "buddy" quality and lacks the romantic overtones. Mother/daughter and father/son partnerships are especially common in single-parent or one-child families where the choices are more limited.

Emotional incest takes on a decidedly different character when the child is allied with a Critical/Abusive Parent. Then the child is used not just for emotional support but for the release of anger and tension. The child may be treated kindly one minute and abused or shamed the next. Whatever emotion the parent happens to be feeling may be targeted at the child. When a parent has such little self-control, often the family is dysfunctional in other ways as well. Domestic violence, poverty, alcoholism, drug abuse, or criminal activity may also be part of the picture. These more obvious problems mask the enmeshment. Many people who were raised by physically abusive or alcoholic parents, for example, belatedly discover that they were also the victims of emotional incest.

Although at first glance there may appear to be a great deal of difference between these common forms of emotional incest—one child is treated like a "date," another like a friend, another like a scapegoat—these parent-child relationships have two fundamental things in common:

1. **The parent is using the child to satisfy needs that should be satisfied by other adults.** The parent is turning to the child for intimacy, companionship, romantic stimulation, advice, problem

solving, ego fulfillment, and/or emotional release. The child is not equipped to handle these needs and suffers long-lasting consequences as a result.

2. **The parent is ignoring many of the child's needs.** When a parent turns to a child for emotional support, the child is rarely given adequate protection, nurturing, guidance, structure, affection, affirmation, or discipline. It's a flip-flop of healthy parenting: instead of the parent meeting the needs of the child, the child is meeting the needs of the parent.

Families in which emotional incest occurs are also united by a common family profile. They tend to have the following characteristics:

1. **The parent lacks sufficient companionship and support.** Almost without exception, a parent (or stepparent) who is enmeshed with a child has an inadequate adult support system. The parent is single, divorced, widowed, or unhappily married. The emotional support that should come from a partner or adult friends is missing. To fill the void, the parent turns to the child.

2. **In a two-parent household, the parent who is less involved with the child feels resentful.** When one parent is enmeshed with a child, the other parent will feel jealous or left out. But since there is no recognized taboo against emotional incest, the left-out parent finds no grounds for complaint. How can you criticize your husband or wife for loving a child? Lacking a rationale for this anger, the left-out spouse abuses or withdraws from the child.

3. **In families with two or more children, there is more than the normal amount of sibling rivalry.** Sibling rivalry can be found in any family with more than one child. But when one child is getting a disproportionate share of a parent's love and attention, the rivalry can be long-lasting and severe.

If you are wondering whether you were a Chosen Child, compare your family of origin (the family in which you were raised) to the above list of traits. The first one—a parent with unmet emotional needs—is the most telling. If your parent was single or unhappily married and did not compensate for this lack of support by developing a network of friends, it is likely that some degree of enmeshment occurred. Human beings are compelled to satisfy their emotional needs, and they will do so within the available resources. For all too many adults, the most readily available resource is a child.

In the coming chapters you will learn more about the surprisingly high cost of emotional incest. It's a syndrome that has negative implications not just for the Chosen Child but for every member of the household. And once emotional incest takes root in a family, it sends tendrils into generation after generation.

However, this book is *not* just a description of unhealthy family life. It's a helpful, hopeful book about realigning family relationships. My purpose in writing it is twofold: (1) to help you overcome the numerous problems that come from growing up with an Invasive Parent, and (2) to help you create more fulfilling relationships in the present.

✿ Applying Today's Insights to Yesterday's Families

As you take part in this recovery process, you may begin to see your family history in a harsh, new light. Like Gwen, some of you may need to alter significantly your view of a parent. What looked like normal parenting may in fact have been a disguised form of abuse. Those of you who have children may even begin to question ways you've treated your own sons and daughters.

If you make some unsettling discoveries, keep in mind that *what I am doing in this book is applying today's insights and values to yesterday's families.* Ways of relating that we all took for granted twenty or thirty years ago are now being labeled "dysfunctional." A generation ago, psychologists didn't view the family as a system. They didn't pay a lot of attention to family roles, so they didn't think in terms like "surrogate spouse." They focused on the needs of the individual. Because of this narrower view of human psychology, few people understood the difference between normal parenting and enmeshment. It is only because of recent advances in the relatively new field of Structural Family Therapy that emotional incest has emerged as a definable, curable syndrome.[3]

For this reason, I urge you to look at your family, past or present, with a tolerant attitude. On some level, we are all wounded creatures struggling to satisfy essential needs, and we do this for the most part without adequate guidance, reliable information, good role models, or genuine understanding. Mistakes are inevitable, especially in the formidable job of parenting. Ideally, we should use any new insights we acquire not to blame ourselves or others, but to make our lives healthier and more enjoyable. I hope that this book will guide you in this endeavor.

2

Parents Who Send Mixed Messages: Love, Neglect, and Abuse

❈

When a parent relies on a child for emotional support, the results are not always sweetness and light as in Gwen's story, the example in chapter 1. A parent who is overly attached to a child can also be critical or neglectful, which results in a confusing mixture of love and abuse. Instead of feeling privileged for being a Chosen Child, the boy or girl wonders, *Why me? Why not someone else?*

The Neglectful Parent

I have an added measure of compassion for clients who were enmeshed with an abusive parent, because that was my situation. My mother and father were separated shortly after I was born, and I didn't see my father again for many years. For fourteen years I lived alone with my alcoholic mother. There were times when she was so drunk, she would stay out all night. I would wake up to an empty house and have to get myself ready for school. We had no alarm clock, so I was often late. I remember being called in to the principal's office one day to explain my tardiness, and I quickly fabricated a story. I told her that we lived down by the river and the moisture in the air gave me a sore throat.

Like many children, I became what therapists call a "parentified child"—one who takes on many of the responsibilities of an adult. I was the one who decided what to eat and to wear, when and if I should do my homework, and whether I should visit the man down the block who offered me candy to sit on his lap.

It may seem that I suffered more from neglect than enmeshment, because I was left on my own so much of the time. However, the reality is that I experienced both extremes. When my mother was drinking, my needs were neglected. But when she was sober, she turned her full attention on me. By the time I was 12, I was her confidant, social partner, and adviser. I was there to help her fend off her loneliness and give her a reason to get out of bed in the morning; to joke and laugh with her when she wanted some fun and console her when she was blue. I was the constant in her life—the one person she could count on. She had no husband. Her friends came and went. But I was always there.

Strangely, I was not aware of being burdened by this role. I admired my mother and for the most part felt privileged to be her friend. She was pretty, witty, and fun to be around. She treated me kindly and showered me with praise and devotion. She often told me and everyone who would listen that I was pretty, smart, and reliable. She thought I could do anything, and I believed her. The fact that she had such a high opinion of me helped me screen out her faults.

There was only one incident I recall that got me in touch with my hidden anger. The summer I was 10 years old, my mother didn't come home for three days and two nights. By the third day I was terribly worried. She had stayed away before, but never for that long. That evening, the man who lived downstairs came to the door to tell me my mother had been in a car accident and was in the hospital. "I wish she had died!" I blurted.

After that one outburst, my anger subsided and went back underground. The only aftermath of the eruption was that I became even more self-reliant than before. I'd discovered it was too painful to be vulnerable. If my mother wasn't going to be reliable, I was going to do my best not to rely on her.

My mother remarried when I was in junior high school, and for a short time I was no longer my mother's best friend. I was not perturbed by this, however, because I perceived my stepfather as a pale threat. I was right. He had little presence and virtually no authority. He was such a nonentity that it wasn't long before my mother would have little to do with him, and I was summoned, once again, to her side. From that point on, we were intertwined like braids. We handled all the finances, made all the decisions, and did all the shopping. We ran the house. My stepfather had no legitimate role in our family.

Not surprisingly, my stepfather resented this coalition between his wife and stepdaughter. When he got drunk, he'd yell at me and call me hurtful names. At the time, I didn't understand why. I kept thinking to myself: *I'm not mean to him. I haven't done anything wrong. I'm a good girl.* I had no idea how life looked from his point of view. I had no concept of "family roles," no awareness that I was usurping his place in my mother's life.

When I look back on my childhood, it's as if I spent those early years wandering blindfolded through a maze. I would run headlong into an obstacle and realize I had to turn one way or another, but I had no idea what was obstructing my path, and no idea which way to go. I had no overview. No roadmap. No guide.

It's taken me most of my adult years to gain some perspective. For me, as for most people, the blindfold of childhood was removed layer by layer. The first piece of information to lodge in my consciousness was the fact that although my mother and father cared for me, they both had abdicated their roles as parents—my father by disappearing, my mother by consistently placing her needs above mine. This simple fact, which is now so blatantly obvious to me, was revealed only through therapy. Before that, it had been too painful a reality to absorb.

The revelations continued. With a therapist's help, I realized that my mother's praise and high regard for me was partly an unconscious device to relieve her of the burden of parenting. "You've never caused me a moment's trouble," my mother had told me again and again. Underneath this benediction was a disguised ultimatum: "Don't have any needs, Pat, because I'm not willing or able to cope with them." I did my best to cooperate. I looked around at the little she had to give me and made sure I asked only for that. I repressed the rest of my needs or kept them to myself. I was the Hero Child who was asked to come to her own rescue.

Later I discovered that my mother's effusive praise had another purpose, which was to bolster her fragile ego. If she kept telling me I was an extraordinary child, and if I managed to meet or exceed her expectations, she could look at me and see that she was a good parent—and therefore a good person—despite her many shortcomings. She could continue to drink and stay out with her friends and still feel good about herself, because she was doing such an admirable job as a parent. I was the sole, tangible evidence of her worthiness: I was the college diploma she never got, the career that never got off the ground, the public recognition she never received. My mother lived her life through me, and she ordained that I do a good job.

Finally, a few years ago, I got the last piece of the puzzle: I had been the victim of emotional incest. By default, I had played the role of my mother's surrogate spouse. I had been the faithful, loving, supportive partner she never had. Without knowing it, I had been her only reliable source of intimacy and her primary source of emotional support.

When I was able to work my way through the layers of denial that had veiled my childhood, I finally understood why I had so many problems later in life. I understood why I was drawn to men who were not there for me, why I had difficulty getting close to people, and why I had such a hard time asking for help. I understood why, despite all my accomplishments, I felt inadequate and empty. And I understood one of the reasons I had been drawn to a career as a therapist—to be paid for helping others, something I had done all my life.

器 The Abusive/Critical Parent

"I got the feeling my mother was trying
to live her life through me, only I wasn't
doing a good enough job. . . . She used
love like a club."

Although my mother neglected me, she was never mean to me. She had great affection for me and held me in high regard. Some Chosen Children are less fortunate. David, a successful architect in his mid-fifties, had a mercurial mother who doted on him one minute and attacked him the next. "She wanted me to be with her all the time," he told me, "but she was hypercritical. She made me feel like a failure. I was never good enough. My grades were never good enough. I wasn't clever enough. She would taunt me and ridicule me." David's mother, like mine, tried to live her life through her child, but she decided he wasn't up to the job. No matter how hard

David tried to please her, she was always disappointed in him. She had drawn him into the void in her life, but he was unable to fill it.

This is the sad truth about emotional incest. The only relationship that can come close to satisfying an adult is a loving, intimate relationship with another adult. A child lacks the wisdom, the experience, and the skills to be an adequate partner. And it goes without saying that a child must never be a parent's sexual partner. While a child may appear to be an adequate companion for an adult, there is always something missing, and, tragically, the child bears the brunt of the parent's frustration.

As I listened to David, I noticed some similarities between his story and mine. Both of us had been only children raised by single parents—a classic setup for emotional incest. Also, David's mother and father, like mine, had separated shortly after his birth.

One difference between us, however, was that David had had few playmates. I had been allowed to roam the town as I pleased, and I had drawn a lot of strength from my friends. David's mother had shown a more possessive love. He remembers one snowy day when he was quite young. Some kids knocked on the door and asked him to play. As David walked down the stairs, the children pelted him with snowballs. His mother hurriedly called him inside and told him not to play with those children ever again. "And I don't think I ever did," David said. "I just did everything with her." This lack of contact with other children made life difficult for David. "I never did well in school," he told me. "I was socially immature. I didn't know how to get along with other kids. I should have been held back. I wish someone had been paying attention to me."

When David said those words, I knew exactly how he felt. Even though we both had been entangled with our mothers, our mothers and fathers hadn't looked out for us. Their own needs had gotten in the way. Again and again I hear this lament from adults who grew up in enmeshed households: "I wish someone had been paying attention to me." Although we may have been the focus of our parents' lives, they held us too close to them for them to see what we needed. We had been lost in a nearsighted blur.

When David was 7 years old, his father moved back home. "One night there was a knock at the door," he told me, "and I saw a stranger's face through the window. I ran to my mother and told her there was a man at the door. She invited him in, and I saw that he was carrying a big suitcase. He spent the night. The next morning, I learned he was my father."

David's father turned out to be a depressed, ruined man. "He never had a job all the years he lived with us," David said. "He just hung around the house. He used to be a fairly successful farmer, but four years of drought wiped him out. He never could get over that failure, and he never could adjust to city life."

David's father took out a lot of his frustration on his son, expecting him to do an extraordinary amount of work. In addition to having a paper route, he insisted that David take care of the five-plot family garden and do most of the household chores. David struggled to win his father's approval, but it never happened. His father would say to people, "I have these five garden plots, and they make me so much money a year," but he never mentioned that his son did all the work. One day he told David he was "no better than a pissant." In addition, he seemed to delight in punishing David and denying him privileges. Once David overheard him say to his mother, "You always tell the boy 'yes,' so I tell him 'no.'"

In many families, not just enmeshed families, it's common for one parent to be more strict than the other. One parent is the disciplinarian, the other is more permissive. This behavior is an unconscious attempt to balance the family. But the polarization is often extreme in enmeshed households. The parent who is allied with the child sets virtually no limits, and the left-out parent counters by being abusive. I have heard horror stories of jealous parents pushing their children down stairs, locking them out in the cold, and imprisoning them in closets—behavior that brings to mind the torture meted out by wicked parents in fairy tales. When the parent's anger is this extreme, it's more than an attempt to temporize a spouse's leniency—it's an expression of intense, uncontrolled jealousy.

To see if this was true in David's case, I asked him if his father had ever been jealous of his relationship with his mother. He thought for a moment. "I don't know. I didn't see it that way. But I do know that he wasn't getting much attention from her. They were never affectionate. They never did things together. I remember one day when my father was out of the house, she told me he was a millstone around her neck."

Later, as David went on to describe all the things he had done with his mother, I could see plenty of cause for his father's anger: David had become a surrogate spouse. He went to the movies with his mother; he escorted her to church functions; he was her confidant; he comforted her when she was unhappy; he read her stories at night. A stranger looking in the window might have mistaken them for an older woman and her young lover. His father's anger was not without justification. Unfortunately, the anger was directed at David, not his mother. Like many adults, his father found it easier to confront a child than a spouse.

As I listened to David, I could tell he was having a hard time believing that jealousy had been the cause of his father's anger. He was still seeing his family from his viewpoint as a child, and a child does not attribute complex emotions like jealousy to a parent. A child's world view is simple: "If Mom or Dad is upset, I must be to blame." The fact that his father wanted something he had—in this case, his mother's love and attention—was a foreign concept.

Understanding his father's anger would be a milestone in David's recovery. When he realized that the lack of love between his mother and father had been the source of his father's unhappiness—not something he, David, had done—he would be released from the unnecessary burden of guilt. He would no longer feel like such a failure. He would see that it wasn't *his* fault the family was so out of balance—his parents were the architects of the skewed dynamics. But it would take time for David to come to this awareness. As with me, the blindfold would have to be removed layer by layer.

When David entered high school, he began to spend more time with friends. "For the first time I wanted to feel a part of the group," he said. "To be liked and accepted." This was a natural and healthy stage of his development, but his mother, like many overinvolved parents, tried to bind him to her with guilt. "One time I wanted to go to the movies with my friends, not her, and she said, 'Wait until you have children of your own! They're nothing but a disappointment and a heartache. One of these days I'll be dead, and then you'll be sorry.' She used love like a club."

When David graduated from high school, he tried to escape from the web of enmeshment by enrolling in a college one hundred miles away, not the one in his hometown. This strategy worked well during the week, and he felt happy and carefree. But when the weekend drew near, he felt obligated to drive home to see his mother. "My mother interpreted my going to another city as an act of desertion," he said. "She made me feel as if I were leaving the country. She insisted that I see her every weekend. I would be so angry about having to go home, I would pick a fight with her as soon as I walked in the door. Then I would feel bad about fighting with her, and I would go back to school feeling guilty. I would have five more good days, then it would start over again."

Guilt is a potent weapon of the overinvolved parent. Any time the child's needs conflict with the parent's, the parent can lower the boom: "You only think of yourself." "You're so selfish." "Can't you think of anyone else?" The martyr role is equally effective: "Go ahead. Go out with your friends. I'll be all right. I'll be fine sitting here alone by myself. Don't worry about me!" Thus begins a lifelong association between love and guilt.

As my conversation with David drew to a close, I asked him to tell me a few things about his present life. He is an architect involved in the preservation of historic public buildings. He has been married for twenty years and has two children. He is doing quite well financially and is respected in his community. But underneath this facade—which is how he described it to me—he feels like a failure. He finds his mother's dependence on him and his father's hostility a crushing burden to carry. "I hope that there is such a thing as reincarnation," he said, "because this life is kind of shot. Neither of my parents really cared about me. I was a whipping boy for my father and a playmate for my mother. They're both dead now, but my anger doesn't go away. Most of my life, I feel as if I've been wading in mud up to my armpits."

David's relationship with his mother can be broken down into two separate roles: he was part surrogate spouse and part scapegoat. He was expected to satisfy his mother's need for romantic attachment and absorb her tension and disappointment as well. When she was lonely, she had someone to talk to. When she was angry, she had someone to yell at. When she felt like a failure, she could project her unhappiness onto him. When she wanted more out of life, she could harp on his shortcomings. No wonder she had been so distraught when he went away to college: he was the narcotic that dulled her pain.

A child like David, who is both surrogate spouse and scapegoat, often has a harder time in life than a child who is simply a surrogate spouse. The Scapegoat Child experiences fewer of the benefits of being a Chosen Child and more of the drawbacks. But even people like David can heal the wounds of emotional incest. As you will see in the following chapters, gaining insight into the past and making strategic changes in current relationships can repair much of the damage. I have worked with many clients who had suffered just as much as David and yet went on to live happy and fulfilling lives.

✿ The Sexualizing Parent

"He would show me off to his friends
and brag about how beautiful I was.
It was all very romantic."

The final case history in this chapter is one of the most extreme examples of emotional incest I've ever encountered. Marla, like many Chosen Children, makes a favorable first impression. She has beautiful big blue eyes, dimples, long eyelashes, and delicate features. The first time I saw her she reminded me of the Terry Lee doll that was popular in the early fifties, when I was a child. The only visible sign of Marla's struggle is twenty pounds of excess weight that she alternately loses and regains.

By most people's standards, Marla has been very successful in life. She has a Ph.D. in economics and has worked twelve years in a high-ranking position for the federal government. She is bright, competent, and vivacious. Yet I have seen her in anguish time and time again. I remember once in my office when she was overcome with self-loathing. Her lovely face became contorted, and she leaned forward with her head down, as if the internal struggle were cutting her in two. "Each day I try so hard to love myself, to care for myself, because at the core there is such self-hatred," she sobbed. "I find it so hard to believe that I'm okay. I find it so hard to believe that I'm lovable."

In Marla's family, the conditions that foster emotional incest were evident in the first year of her parents' marriage. As soon as the glow of the honeymoon wore off, her mother and father lost interest in each other, and their relationship was limited to an occasional sexual encounter and whatever mundane interactions were required to run the household.

Unwittingly, each parent tried to find comfort and companionship by bonding with a child. Marla's mother turned to her first child, Derek. When Marla was born, her mother was too wrapped up with Derek to have much energy for a new baby, so Marla and her father had mutual needs: they both needed someone to belong to, to bond with, to love and to be loved by. By the time Marla was 2 years old, she was clearly "daddy's little girl." Now Mother was allied with Son, and Father was allied with Daughter. Families that split up in this manner are quite common. As Lynn Hoffman writes in her book, *Foundations of Family Therapy*, "A boy for you and a girl for me is not just a songwriter's fantasy . . ."[1]

The bond between Marla and her father strengthened with each passing year. "My father absolutely adored me," she said, "and took me everywhere he went. He managed a tennis club, and I spent my early years tagging along behind him at the club. He had a tennis racket designed especially for me when I was four years old and began drilling me on my swings." When she was old enough to go to school, he picked her up at school every afternoon and took her to the club, where he tutored her until dark.

As we've seen in previous examples, when a child is over-bonded with one parent, the child is usually estranged from the other parent. The family forms itself into an isosceles triangle, with the Chosen Child's and the parent's sides intersecting and the other parent's side pushed far away. In Marla's family, the geometry was exaggerated. Her father was totally devoted to her, and her mother was physically and verbally abusive. "When I was with my father," Marla told me, "I felt like Cinderella at the ball. When I was with my mother, I felt like an orphan in rags. I think she truly hated me. She would hit me and call me names. I learned to stay as far away from her as possible. When my father wasn't around, I was either in my room or sitting outside on the steps waiting for him to come home. It was a strange childhood. I didn't learn to roller-skate. I didn't learn to swim. I didn't have any friends. I didn't go to birthday parties. I just spent as much time as possible with my father." Marla saw nothing wrong with this arrangement. In fact, she said, "I loved it! My father called me his 'pretty baby.' He let me sit in his lap and he would hug and kiss me. I thought he was wonderful!"

In many families, emotional incest becomes a vicious cycle. This was true in Marla's case. The more attention she received from her father, the more her mother resented her. The more violently her mother expressed her resentment, the more Marla was drawn to her father. Soon she and her father were so entwined that Marla had little time, opportunity, or desire to play with friends. After all, what playmate can compare with a doting, sophisticated, powerful adult? Her father took her out to expensive meals and bought her beautiful clothes; he even had a tennis court installed in the backyard so she could improve her game! What girlfriend could compete with that?

By the time Marla reached adolescence, she was an expert tennis player. She won many trophies, including first place in a national competition. In the summer she and her father traveled around the country so she could compete in various tournaments. While they were on the road, they went to a lot of parties. "I would be my father's 'date,'" she told me. "I would get all dressed up, and we would dance together. He would show me off to his friends and brag about how beautiful I was. It was all very romantic."

When Marla and her father returned to their motel room, they would sleep in the same bed. "My father never sexually abused me," she told me, "he just held me close. I would fall asleep with his arm wrapped around me."

I have had quite a few clients, both men and women, whose parents walked this fine line between emotional and sexual incest. Their parents didn't touch them inappropriately, but they displayed an unhealthy interest in their bodies. Some had parents who did not allow them privacy in the bedroom and bathroom. Others had parents who openly stared at their bodies, took seductive pictures of them, or made inappropriate sexual remarks. When parents are both sexually and emotionally fixated on their children, the enmeshment is usually more intense and more damaging.[2]

Like many overinvolved parents, Marla's father did not set appropriate limits for her. More a friend than a parent, he made no attempts to discipline her. Further, he exposed her to experiences far beyond her years. For example, he taught her to drive when she was only 14 years old, so she could drive him home from drinking parties. Marla recalled many nights when she drove the car while her inebriated father was passed out in the passenger seat. This didn't bother her. "I thought I was hot stuff," she said. "I thought I could handle everything. I pitied children my age because they seemed so young and silly."

Marla's blithe acceptance of her father's behavior deserves a closer look. While her mother was undoubtedly outraged by his drinking and his irresponsible nature, Marla took it all in stride. She accepted her father for who he was; she made no demands. This is a key difference between a child and an adult: a child is often blind to a parent's faults. With little outside reference, the child simply accepts what is given. A spouse, on the other hand, is likely to have a long list of demands and expectations. For example, a typical wife wants her husband to be sober and responsible and to be accountable for his actions. She wants him to help with the home maintenance and the bill paying and the yard work. She expects him to engage in meaningful conversations and to be a sympathetic, supportive listener. In short, she wants an equal partner in a mature relationship. A child, on the other hand, will settle for an indulgent, adoring companion.

At 17, Marla had grown into a beautiful young woman and began attracting the attention of boys her own age. Her father, acting more like a jealous lover than a father, did not allow her to date. No boy was good enough for his daughter. With no outlet for her emotional needs other than her father, and no sanctioned outlet for her growing sexual needs, Marla began having clandestine affairs. A pattern of promiscuity developed that continued for fifteen years. "From my senior year in high school until I got involved in therapy," she said, "my drug of choice was a man. Nothing ever made me feel as good as Daddy, so I kept looking for more of the same. But the trouble was, no one could ever measure up to him. I kept going from one man to another, searching for the same high I felt as a little girl when my father seemed so powerful and so much larger than life." Not surprisingly, many of her alliances were with older men. When she was 21, for example, she dated a man who was 45. It seemed perfectly natural to her: "Older men had money and power. Just like Daddy."

As a child, Marla saw her father as a hero. As an adult, and after many years of therapy, her childhood myopia was shattered. "My father was a drunk," she said bitterly. "He could be very cruel to people, and he was incredibly self-centered. He acted as if the whole world revolved around him. Anything that got in his way, he destroyed. Although he said wonderful things to me and held me and kissed me and was utterly devoted to me, he didn't protect me. And he didn't allow me to be me—whoever that was. I may never find out. I had to be who he wanted me to be. His champion tennis player. His 'pretty baby.' "

Today, Marla seems a woman of extremes. On one hand, she is very accomplished; she has beauty, friends, money, and professional esteem. On the other hand, she has the classic problem of high/low self-esteem and a talent for picking unsuitable mates. Many people who were overinvolved with a parent make tremendous strides just by identifying what took place. Having a name for what happened to them and a conceptual framework for their childhood experiences makes a big difference in their lives. But for Marla and others like her who were deeply enmeshed with a parent, it can take years of therapy to repair the damage.

In these first two chapters I've described four types of parents who become overinvolved with their children, the Romanticizing Parent, the Neglectful Parent, the Critical/Abusive Parent, and the Sexualizing Parent. Perhaps you have seen glimpses of your own childhood in these examples.

To add to your understanding of your family history, take the following questionnaire. It will help you determine whether you were enmeshed with a parent.

CHECKLIST 1:
Signs of Enmeshment

Directions: Read each of the following statements and put a check-mark by the ones that are true for you. You may find it helpful to put the initials of the appropriate parent or caretaker beside each statement to clarify your response. (In this and subsequent check-lists, the word *parent* can refer to parents, stepparents, or other significant caretakers.)

If you have a complex life history, you may find it helpful to write some additional comments by your responses, such as, "this was true before my father remarried," or, "this was true mainly after my mother died."

Answer these questions from a historical perspective. In other words, try to recall how you felt when you were a child, rather than how you feel now.

Part A. Indication of an Overly Close Parent-Child Bond

1. I felt closer to one parent than the other.
2. I was a source of emotional support for one of my parents.
3. I was "best friends" with a parent.
4. A parent shared confidences with me.
5. A parent was deeply involved in my activities or in developing my talents.
6. A parent took a lot of pride in my abilities or achievements.
7. I was given special privileges or gifts by one of my parents.
8. One of my parents told me in confidence that I was the favorite, most talented, or most lovable child.
9. A parent thought I was better company than his or her spouse.

10. I sometimes felt guilty when I spent time away from one of my parents.
11. I got the impression a parent did not want me to marry or move far away from home.
12. When I was young I idolized one of my parents.
13. Any potential boyfriend or girlfriend of mine was never "good enough" for one of my parents.
14. A parent seemed overly aware of my sexuality.
15. A parent made inappropriate sexual remarks or violated my privacy.

Part B. Indication of Unmet Adult Need's

1. My parents were separated, divorced, widowed, or didn't get along very well.
2. One of my parents was often lonely, angry, or depressed.
3. One of my parents did not have a lot of friends.
4. One or both parents had a drinking or drug problem.
5. One of my parents thought the other parent was too indulgent or permissive.
6. I felt I had to hold back my own needs to protect a parent.
7. A parent turned to me for comfort or advice.
8. A parent seemed to rely on me more than on my siblings.
9. I felt responsible for a parent's happiness.
10. My parents disagreed about parenting issues.

Part C. Indication of Parental Neglect or Abuse

1. My needs were often ignored or neglected.
2. There was a great deal of conflict between me and a parent.
3. I was called hurtful names by a parent.
4. One of my parents had unrealistic expectations of me.
5. One of my parents was very critical of me.
6. I sometimes wanted to hide from a parent or had fantasies of running away.
7. When I was a child, other families seemed less emotionally intense than mine.
8. It was often a relief to get away from home.
9. I sometimes felt invaded by a parent.
10. I sometimes felt I added to a parent's unhappiness.

What can you learn from this checklist? Do you have ten or more checks spread out among the three sections? If so, it is likely that some degree of enmeshment occurred. Next, review the overall pattern of your checks. If your checks tend to be clustered in the first

and second sections, you may have been enmeshed with a Romanticizing or a Sexualizing Parent. If your checks are clustered in the
second and third sections, you may have been enmeshed with a
Critical/Abusive Parent. If you have checkmarks sprinkled throughout the three sections, you may have been alternately loved and
abused by the same parent, or one parent may have abused you while
the other adored you. Reflecting on your life history will help you
sort this out. The following chapter explores the consequences of
emotional incest in more detail.

3

The Adult Cost
of Being a
Chosen Child

❀

For many people, the word *bittersweet* aptly describes their life as a Chosen Child. Pat Conroy captures this two-sided reality in his novel *The Prince of Tides:*

> A portion of guilt is standard issue for southern boys; our whole lives are convoluted, egregious apologies to our mothers because our fathers have made such flawed husbands. No boy can endure for long the weight and the magnitude of his mother's displaced passion. Yet few boys can resist their mother's solitary and innocently seductive advances. There is such forbidden sweetness in becoming the chaste and secret lover of the father's woman, such triumph in becoming the demon rival who receives the unbearable tender love of fragile women in the shadows of the father's house. There is nothing more erotic on earth than a boy in love with the shape and touch of his mother. It is the most exquisite, most proscribed lust. It is also the most natural and damaging.[1]

When I work with adults who were enmeshed with their parents, I am constantly reminded of the "sweet" side of the syndrome. By and large, the people I've counseled were attractive and successful in some aspect of their lives. A significant number have had an unusual amount of talent or charisma and have made outstanding achievements in life. For example, I've worked with highly paid executives, nationally recognized artists, successful entrepreneurs—even a Pulitzer Prize nominee. In a few instances, these achievements seemed to be the result of inborn traits such as physical beauty or unusual intelligence. But for the majority of my clients, their accomplishments appeared to be the direct result of enmeshment. Some had a "Stage Mom or Dad" who pushed them into stardom; their parents badgered or seduced them into abandoning their own goals and adopting the higher standards of an adult. Others succeeded for a less obvious reason: being linked with a parent resulted in a heady sense of entitlement. After all, they had won out in the only competition in life that really matters: the competition for a parent's love and attention. As a result, they felt destined for success. They seized opportunities others passed by and attracted people to them with their winning ways.

But what was so confusing to my clients was that these positive qualities were always offset by negative ones. Strangely, they felt both privileged and victimized, both talented and worthless, both blessed and cursed. For every positive trait, they experienced its polar opposite.

Some of them exhibited these mood swings daily: they were full of confidence one moment and overcome with inadequacy the next. Others had week- or month-long mood cycles. A few had decades of success, followed by total collapse. Some had all their self-confidence boxed up into one area of their lives—typically their careers—and failed miserably at everything else. One way or another, the "bitter" part of being a Chosen Child was known to them all.

Why this contradictory mix of emotions? Typically, there are several factors involved. Part of my clients' confusion could be traced to the fact that many of their fundamental needs had been ignored. Their parents' need for intimacy and companionship had taken precedence over their need for nurturing and independence. Paradoxically, their parents' excessive interest in them had created lifelong feelings of deprivation: "No one is taking care of me!"

Another factor was that while my clients may have delighted in all the parental attention, on a deeper level they felt exposed and confined. They didn't feel free to be who they were or to develop at their own pace. They felt manipulated and controlled.

Finally, many clients discovered that for every privilege bestowed by a parent, there had been a jealous reaction from someone else. The thrill of being "mama's little man" or "daddy's girl" was eroded by the jealousy of a left-out sibling. The status that came from being a parent's surrogate spouse was offset by the resentment of the displaced husband or wife. The alliance with a parent had thrown the whole family out of balance, and the Chosen Child was often the target of the resulting anger.

In this chapter I will explore these repercussions in more detail. Whether you will identify with a particular emotional problem will depend to some degree on the nature of your relationship with a parent. If you were allied with a Critical/Abusive Parent, for example, you may recognize yourself in the passage on low self-esteem. If you were allied with a Romanticizing Parent, the section on grandiosity might command your attention, or you might gain insight from the passages on sexual and relationship difficulties. I urge you to read all the sections, however, even the ones that initially seem not to apply to you: you may stumble onto some aspect of your personality or some truth about the past that you have blocked from your awareness.

🎜 Denial and Family Mythologies

All of us experience denial on some level. It is quite common, for example, to have a distorted or limited view of our childhood. This is understandable given the fact that while we were growing up, we had so little experience outside our homes. Without a basis for comparison, we grew up thinking our families were the norm. Whatever went on in our living rooms became the standard. A client said to me, "I was twenty years old before I realized that my mother was the only one who disinfected new clothes and washed them two times before she'd let them be worn. I thought all mothers did that."

In most families, this lack of objectivity is further clouded by the creation of a family mythology—a collection of lies, evasions, distortions, and half-truths designed to obscure an unpleasant reality. It's a way to go on with life without being constantly reminded of its painful aspects. Part of my family mythology, for example, was that the couple who lived downstairs from us were related to us and were partly responsible for my welfare. My mother encouraged me to call them "Uncle Frank" and "Aunt Babe," despite the fact that they were ordinary friends and not relatives. I suspect that one reason my mother created this myth was that it allowed her to stay out all night and not worry about me. If I got into trouble, I could always get help from my "aunt" and "uncle." I colluded in this fiction, because to be one hundred percent dependent on my mother and to be aware of the fact she was neglecting me would have made me extremely anxious. I blocked out my fear of abandonment with a convenient half-truth.

Most of us have myths in our background. Here are some common ones: "Daddy isn't an alcoholic, he just needs a drink to relax." "Mommy and Daddy don't hate each other, they just have a lot of worries about us kids." "My parents don't play favorites; they love all their children equally." "My needs aren't being ignored; I just don't have any." "My mother isn't angry at me; she just doesn't know how to show affection." "My father isn't abandoning us; his job requires that he put in extra hours." We cling to our family fiction even in adulthood, despite the fact it's outlived its usefulness, because we don't want to awaken the pain that was blocked by the convenient mythology.

As adults, most of us experience denial on another level as well, which is to be unaware of the coping mechanisms we developed as children to survive a less than ideal childhood. We are blind not only to some aspects of family history but to parts of ourselves. For example, when I was young, I used to lie a great deal, because lying served a number of valuable purposes. For one thing, it helped me create a more palatable version of reality. I remember telling a friend that I had to rush home for dinner—even though I suspected my mother was at the tavern, drinking. I didn't want to acknowledge to my friend or to myself what really went on at home. I also lied to get out of trouble. I was on my own at an early age, so I made a lot of errors in judgment. Lying got me out of hot water.

However, in retrospect, I think the main reason I lied was to satisfy my mother's high expectations. Deep down, I felt I had to live up to her high opinion of me, or I'd be abandoned. I had to be her successful, talented daughter, or I would have no legitimate role in her life. Therefore, if I failed at a task or didn't get a high grade on a test or missed out on an honor, I either lied or neglected to tell her about it.

It was only recently that I realized I still had this tendency to lie. I was talking to a workshop group about coping mechanisms, and I described how I used to lie to my principal to avoid getting into trouble for being tardy. I explained to the group that I wasn't being a "bad girl" for lying—even though I thought so at the time—it was just my way of coping with the fact there was no one to get me up in the morning. As I was talking, a light went on in my head. I asked myself, *Could it be that you still have a habit of lying?* I spent the next few weeks checking it out. Sure enough, I often obscured the truth. If someone called me early in the morning and asked, "Oh, did I wake you?" I'd say, "Oh, no!"—even if they'd just rousted me out of a sound sleep. If someone asked me to do something I didn't want to do, I'd make up an excuse: "Well, I'd really like to, but I have to go to the dentist." I had not realized how often I told these white lies, because lying was an ingrained—and formerly useful—part of my character. I was in denial of my continuing tendency to lie.

Armed with new knowledge, I went to my husband and said with some trepidation, "You know, I tend to lie a lot." He looked at me and said complacently, "Yeah, Pat, I know." He told me he was well aware of my untruthfulness and had even tried to bring it to my attention, but I had been unwilling to listen.

Once I was able to accept this side of myself, I gradually became more truthful. I rehearsed saying difficult truths. When I caught myself lying, I went back and corrected myself. Once my eyes were open to this hidden consequence of being a Chosen Child, the door was open for change.

I often find in my clients this same convoluted path to self-discovery and growth. In order to change a negative trait, they first need to break through their denial and acknowledge that it exists; people don't change what they can't see. And in order to break through their denial, they often have to get a clear picture of what was wrong in their families and the techniques they developed for coping with it. For example, they may discover they coped with an Invasive Parent by erecting barriers to intimacy, by lying, by over-eating or not eating, by becoming a parent pleaser, or by becoming a compulsive achiever. One way or another, they developed behaviors that helped them survive childhood and diminish their pain. Understanding the underlying reason for their behavior gives them a more compassionate view of themselves: "Oh, that's why I always came home from school and immediately ate all the food in the house! There was no one there to ask how I was or to care about me. I was expected immediately to listen to my mother's tales of woe." Finally, having this tolerant view of past behavior, they are free to look for remnants of the behavior in the present. "Could it be I still have eating problems? Are my eating binges more frequent and more serious than I would like to believe? Is it normal to eat a whole half-gallon carton of ice cream at one sitting? Maybe I should look into getting some help for this. My eating problems may be more serious than I realized. They've been plaguing me for a long time."

As you read the following material on emotional problems of the Chosen Child, be alert for the possibility of denial. And remember that you may be experiencing denial on two separate levels:

1. You may be blocking out some painful aspects of your childhood.
2. You may be blind to some of the coping mechanisms you developed to diminish your pain.

While reading one section you may be blocking how it relates to your past. For example, you may read the section on low self-esteem and find yourself thinking, "Yes, I often have low self-esteem, but unlike this example, it's not because my parents criticized or abused me. They were always nice to me." Consider the fact that you may be unwittingly perpetuating a family mythology. Ask yourself: "Could it be possible that my parents were more abusive or neglectful than I would like to believe? Was there a subtle way they put me down? Did they praise me, but give me the hidden message that I didn't measure up? Did they say they loved me but paid little attention to my needs?"

Later, you may identify with a particular description of family life, but not the attending emotional difficulties. For example, you may read the section on grandiosity and say to yourself, "My father may have openly preferred me to both of my brothers, but that didn't make me grandiose. I'm always humble and level-headed." In this case, test the validity of your self-perception. Ask yourself: "Do people ever accuse me of being arrogant? Has a friend indicated that I'm a bit full of myself? Have I ever had problems at work that might be attributed to grandiosity?" If you keep an open mind as you venture into this chapter, you may make considerable progress on your road to recovery.

🏠 Guilt and Anxiety

GUILT

"I feel responsible for everything that happens around me—especially

*when things go wrong. I feel especially
guilty when other people are
unhappy. I'm sure I must have done
something wrong or failed to do
something I was supposed to do."*

For some people, the single word *guilt* sums up the negative consequences of growing up with an Invasive Parent. Depending on their circumstances, they can feel guilty for one or more of a number of reasons, including: taking a parent away from a partner, winning out over siblings, failing to live up to a parent's expectations, wanting to break away from an overbearing parent, and participating in a love triangle when they were "old enough to know better." One Chosen Child put it this way: "I go through life feeling as if I've been given too much money at the supermarket and decided to keep the change. I wanted my father's love, but I felt guilty for keeping it." Although she had wanted the exclusive relationship she had with her father, she had witnessed the pain it caused her mother and sister. She carried this burden into adulthood and continued to take on the guilt of others.

Lila, a high school student, felt guilty over "abandoning" her mother. Her family had all the elements of a TV docudrama. Her sister, Bev, became anorexic in her sophomore year of high school, and she soon had to be hospitalized. Lila's father was distraught. He had been extremely close to Bev and found he simply could not cope with her illness. He spent most of his off-work hours alone in the bedroom with the curtains drawn and the door closed.

With the family in turmoil, Lila's mother turned to her for emotional support. She would go into Lila's bedroom at night and cry and cry. She cried about Bev and about how useless her husband had become. Lila spent long hours comforting and listening to her mother. She called her mother every day from school to cheer her up. She stayed home on the weekends so that her mother would not be left alone with a depressed husband.

Eventually Lila rebelled and refused to be her mother's live-in therapist. "When is it going to be my turn?" she wondered. "When do I get a break from all the problems?" Her mother retaliated by accusing Lila of being mean and selfish. They began to have daily fights. The tension escalated until the whole family came to me for therapy.

At first, Lila was filled with guilt for abandoning her mother. "Everyone deserted my mother," she told me. "Even me." But finally she was able to see that she was not responsible for her mother's well-being. She was the child, not the parent. She had a right to a life of her own. Her mother should have other support systems in her life and now would have to make an effort to find them.

CHRONIC LOW-LEVEL ANXIETY

"I worry a great deal—even when
things are going well. It's almost
as if I'm waiting for the other shoe to
drop. There's this vague sense that
something bad is about to happen."

A child who plays the role of surrogate spouse is a likely candidate for anxiety, because the role is always a tentative one. One cause for anxiety is the fact that the parent-child coalition is almost always a closely held secret. No matter how close a parent and child may be, there is never a public acknowledgment of the bond. When the child tries to find some external confirmation of status, there is none to be found. In fact, most family members would deny that any favoritism exists. To admit that a parent and child are allied with each other is to admit that the family is in disarray. "I love all my children equally," says the parent. "I play no favorites." The clandestine nature of the parent-child alliance gives it an ephemeral quality. "Am I Daddy's favorite?" The child is never sure.

In addition to this fundamental uncertainty, there are a number of likely circumstances that threaten to disrupt the parent-child relationship. Following are the ones I see most often:

1. If the parent is married, the spouse will try to claim some rights every now and then. No matter how closely linked a parent and child may be, the Left-Out Spouse still enjoys certain rights. For example, the husband and wife usually share a bedroom and are sexual partners. They make obligatory appearances at family affairs, accompany each other to social functions, and make many of the household decisions together. The child never has an exclusive hold on the parent as long as the marriage is intact. (In some ways, this makes the Chosen Child more like a surrogate lover than a surrogate spouse, because he or she always has to make way for the legitimate marriage partner.)

2. **Over the course of time, the husband and wife may resolve some of their problems and push the child out of the inner circle.** The child's role as surrogate spouse may be a temporary one, filling a momentary void in the parent's life. When the husband and wife resolve their difficulties, the child is summarily returned to the rank and file. Occasionally, this dethronement is the result of shortsighted marriage counseling: a therapist who is not mindful of family dynamics will help the couple come closer together without aiding the child in the difficult transition.

3. **A brother or sister may replace the Chosen Child.** Some parents are fickle, switching their allegiance from one child to the next. I know of many parents who have a special fondness for babies. They give all their attention to the youngest child—right up to the point when another baby is born. Then the newcomer occupies center stage. The older child rarely recovers from this fall from grace. "What's the matter with me? Aren't I still special? What have I done wrong?" he wonders.

The dethronement may occur later in life. It is quite common, for example, for the Chosen Child to go away to college and come home to find that a brother or sister has usurped his place. The parent's need for ongoing emotional support was so strong that a replacement had to be found.

4. **The parent may reject the child as the child physically matures.** For fear of becoming sexually involved, a parent of the opposite sex may withdraw when the child shows signs of sexual maturity. Without warning, the parent spends less time with the child and is less physically demonstrative. Unaware of the parent's reason for retreating, the child feels bewildered and rejected.

5. **Some parents become aware of the inappropriate nature of the parent-child bond and withdraw from the relationship.** Some parents wake up to the fact they have an unhealthy alliance with a child and abruptly cut off the relationship. (Again, this can be an unwelcome by-product of marital or individual therapy.) Not given adequate love and reassurance to ease the transition, the child has every reason to feel abandoned.

6. **Some parents punish the Chosen Child for striving for independence.** Many children who are closely allied with a parent struggle for independence at some time in their lives, quite commonly as they

enter adolescence. A parent who is threatened by the child's emerging sense of self may become critical or punitive. The child, once adored, is now condemned.

7. **In search of a more suitable partner, many parents divorce and remarry, removing the Chosen Child from a position of privilege.** It is quite common for a parent who is enmeshed with a child to fall in love or remarry. This can be devastating to the Chosen Child. Suddenly, "daddy's little girl" or "mama's little man" is on the outside looking in, having to witness the parent in the ecstasy of romantic love. The child's frantic cries for help may further alienate the parent, overwhelming the child with feelings of rejection.

8. **The parent may disappear or die, literally abandoning the child.** The sudden loss of a parent is a traumatic experience for any child, but it can be the undoing of the Chosen Child. Said one woman when her father died, "It's as if the sun were ripped from the sky." One moment she was basking in the warmth of being "daddy's little girl." The next moment she was standing all alone in a cold, hostile world, having no one to protect her from the wrath of her stepmother and jealous siblings.

I counseled a man named Joshua, who had lost his mother when he was 14. As he was growing up, his mother was not only his best friend, she was his *sole* friend. He remembers reading Shakespeare with her, studying Homer, sharing thoughts on classical literature—all before the age of 13. To his horror, she died from a stroke the summer he was entering ninth grade. He was told of her death when he awakened at eight in the morning. As soon as he heard the news, he began screaming at the top of his voice. He did not stop screaming until late that night, when his voice literally gave out. His despair was absolute. A constant fear of displacement accompanied him into adulthood. He was uneasy when things were going well. He didn't trust the good times or the people he shared them with. He became very sensitive to the possibility of exclusion. He had exaggerated fears of death or illness. In all his close relationships, he was terrified of abandonment.

To a lesser degree, Joshua's anxieties are felt by many other Chosen Children who, for one reason or another, find themselves displaced. A child is always dependent on a parent, and when the parent is the child's primary companion, the dependency is greatly accentuated. The loss of this privileged position can set up a lifelong pattern of insecurity.

✤ Self-Image Problems

FLUCTUATING SELF-ESTEEM

*"There have been times in my life
when I've been really full of myself—
almost as if I had superhuman powers.
I'd look down on other people and
feel as if we were operating in
two different leagues. At other times,
I've felt completely worthless—
almost like an imposter. There seemed
to be no middle ground."*

Widely fluctuating self-esteem is a common problem for many adult Chosen Children. For some, the high side of the mood swing can be traced to the euphoria of winning the exclusive love of a parent. Being a parent's favorite can give the illusion of being able to conquer anything and anyone in any setting.

For others, the grandiosity comes directly from parental messages. For example, my mother told me I could do anything. When I was 8 she told me that I had so much musical talent I really ought to be taking piano lessons. That sounded great to me—except for one small detail: we had no piano and couldn't afford to rent one. That didn't bother my mother, however. She assumed I would be able to overcome this minor obstacle through sheer talent and determination. Reality proved her wrong. Nonetheless, the message stayed with me: "I can do anything."

In later years, this exaggerated sense of power got me into lots of trouble. Example: In an emotional moment of feeling close to my friends, I might invite thirty people to a dinner party to take place right in the middle of a demanding work schedule. Why not? I could do anything! As the eve of the dinner party drew closer, I would come face to face with reality: there was no way I could pull off the event without hiring both a housekeeper and a cook! I would either have to cancel the party, reschedule my business appointments, or work myself into a frenzy.

When I began to get my life into balance, I actually missed the highs that accompanied these periods of grandiosity. I missed all that energy and optimism. I missed the thrill of making heady, ambitious plans. But I sure didn't miss the lows that followed. For every euphoric period there had always been a time of reckoning, a depression to bring my mood back into balance.

This dizzy swing of feelings from invincibility to inadequacy is prevalent in Chosen Children. Remember the woman I mentioned at the beginning of the book who depicted herself as a flower with a tiny, black center? Much of the time she felt special and powerful, a state of mind represented by the open petals of the flower. But at her core she felt black and worthless. Through therapy she began to have a more consistent self-image. Her dark inner core began to lighten and her periods of euphoria began to diminish. Eventually, both her self-loathing and her feelings of grandiosity were replaced by a mature self-acceptance. The pendulum ultimately slowed down and stopped. In reality she was an attractive, capable woman with a normal allotment of strengths and weaknesses. Neither her exaggerated sense of power nor her feelings of worthlessness were based on reality—they were illusions brought about by growing up in an unbalanced family.

FEAR OF REJECTION

"There are times when I feel worthless—
totally unworthy of love. I isolated
myself for fear of rejection."

Some Chosen Children are plagued with the feeling that they're unlovable. At first this may seem a contradiction in terms: How can a child be a parent's favorite and still feel rejected? The answer is that being enmeshed with one parent often provokes the resentment of the other parent. It's a decidedly Freudian equation: to win Daddy's love is to risk Mommy's wrath.

The left-out parent's anger can take many forms. Some parents subsume their ire and merely act cool or distant. In later years, the adult child will describe the relationship with the estranged parent in words like these: "My mother and I didn't get along," or "I was closer to my father than my mother." One of my clients used this analogy: "It's as if I was looking at my mother through the wrong end of a telescope. She was so emotionally distant."

On the other extreme, some parents are so threatened by the

coalition between spouse and child that they become physically or verbally abusive. One of my clients was locked in a closet for two days by her jealous mother. Another client told me that when she was 6 years old, her mother kept her imprisoned in her room for hours at a time by convincing her that monsters lived under her bed.

Being rejected by a parent has far-reaching consequences, no matter what form the rejection takes. One tragic outcome is that the child naturally assumes most of the blame. "If only I were smarter or better-looking or a different sex or more talented or less trouble or less evil—if only something about me were different—then both of my parents would love me." Unfortunately, the message that stays with the child is: "I'm dumb," "I'm ugly," "I'm a bother," "I'm unlovable," "I should have been a boy."

There are other consequences as well. A child who is rejected by the opposite-sex parent, as was true for me, might generalize from the experience and in later years will feel unworthy of love. I remember saying to my therapist in the throes of despair: "If my father left me and my stepfather hated me, how could any man love me? I guess I'm unlovable."

A child who is rejected by the same-sex parent, a more common occurrence, might have problems forging a positive sexual identity. I worked with a man named Hal who was his mother's Chosen Child. She was bitterly disappointed by her husband and kept telling her son how totally different the two of them were. "You and your father are as unlike as any two people could be," she would say. "It's hard to tell you're related." Meanwhile, she kept up the stream of complaints about his father. Hal put two and two together: "My father is worthless. Therefore it's good that I am very different from him."

In later years, Hal learned to his dismay that his mother's point of view had been extremely biased. His father had many admirable qualities, in fact qualities that he, Hal, needed in order to get along in the world. His enforced estrangement from his father had kept him from absorbing his father's positive traits. "Deep down," he told me, "I've always felt more like a woman than a man. My mother had too great an influence on me."

The jealousy of siblings can also contribute to the Chosen Child's feeling of rejection. When the Chosen Child is getting extra attention, siblings feel deeply resentful. Typically, to equalize the relationships, they take out their anger on the Chosen Child, because it's far easier to trade punches with a brother or sister than it is to take on a parent.

The anger that siblings direct at the Chosen Child can be extreme. One of my clients was nearly drowned—and then resuscitated—by her older brother. Another client was sexually and physically abused by her older stepbrother. A third was stabbed by his older sister with a pair of kitchen shears, a wound that required twenty stitches. The pyschic wounds endured by these and other Chosen Children are every bit as devastating.

SOCIAL ISOLATION

"When I was growing up, I never
felt like one of the group. Sometimes
I felt I was better than everyone
else; other times I felt inferior. It
was a long time before I had a sense
of equality or belonging."

Spending less time with other kids than does the typical child, the Chosen Child has little opportunity to feel part of a group. The problem is compounded for the only child or for the child who is resented by siblings, for the girl or boy grows up with only a limited sense of kinship and belonging.

As a result of this social isolation, the child is denied the leveling influence of peers. Children are very direct in their feedback; they socialize one another with sledgehammers. While this interaction may be painful at times, it does encourage children to act in socially acceptable ways. A child who is isolated from others may hold on to personality quirks that prove a liability later in life.

People who were allied with abusive, alcoholic, neglectful, or mentally ill parents can suffer from an extreme sense of isolation. One Chosen Child I worked with was the only child of a schizophrenic mother. One day she told me, "If only one person had said to me, 'It must be hard living with your mother. You can talk to me if you need to,' I would have felt a thousand percent better. As it was, I was totally alone in the world." No one outside the family had the courage or wisdom to intervene. Now, twenty years later, there are times when she still feels cut off from other people. It is difficult for her to take part in group activities, and she often feels best when she is alone.

A FEELING OF INFERIORITY

"I feel like a failure. I keep
setting goals for myself and failing
to achieve them. Nothing I do is
ever good enough. Not in my eyes.
Not in other people's eyes."

Children who grow up with an Invasive Parent can have an unnaturally low estimation of their abilities, especially if the parent was critical or abusive. Children believe what they've been told, and if they've been told over and over again that they're in the way or no good, they will take the message to heart.

Surprisingly, children who grow up with adoring parents may also feel that they don't measure up. How could this be? Consider the following two scenes.

Scene 1: A boy is going fishing with a friend. They grab a couple of poles, dig a can of worms, and race each other down to the river. Each boy catches one fish. Then the fish stop biting, so the boys turn their attention to building a mud dam. An hour later they walk home in high spirits, each boy swinging a trout from a forked branch.

Scene 2: A boy is going fishing with his father. The father prepares two fishing poles and carefully ties on leader using an improved, double clinch knot. He chooses lures that were recommended in a recent edition of *Field & Stream*. He drives his son down to the river. The boy catches one fish. The boy loses interest when the fish stop biting and starts building a dam. The father continues to fish with great determination and catches three trout. On the drive home, the father notices the boy is downhearted. "What's the matter?" asks the father. "Didn't you enjoy the fishing?"

"I didn't catch as many fish as you did. I'm not a very good fisherman."

"Of course you are! You caught a beautiful fish."

"But you caught more than I did," he replies. "You always catch more."

Despite the father's reassurance, the boy can't help but compare himself to his father, not only in results but in determination and technique: Why didn't he have the self-discipline to keep on fishing?

Why did his line always get tangled, not his father's? Why did he always catch fewer fish?

In measured doses, sharing activities with his father is good for the boy, because it gives him something to aim for. But if the child spends too much time with his dad, he begins to feel inadequate. "I will never be as good as my father," is the enduring message. This low self-esteem continues into adulthood, and the boy grows into the kind of man who constantly belittles his own accomplishments. No matter what he does, he is never good enough.

Perfectionism

DENIAL OF NEEDS

"It's really strange, but I didn't realize I had any fears or problems until I was twenty years old. I did have them, of course, but I blanked them out. It's almost as if I were two people —one who was always on top of things, and then an inner one that was terrifyingly needy. I didn't let that inner one see the light of day."

It is normal for children to be "trouble" from time to time. They need you when you're busy; they ask questions for which you have no answers; they want love when you feel you have none to give; they go through awkward stages; they mount prolonged campaigns for independence; they are a constant reminder that you don't have a solution to all of life's problems.

The Chosen Child often has to repress these needs. A client nicknamed Sunny told me that she'd gotten her nickname from her mother, who elected her to be her perfect, well-adjusted child. "You're always so happy," she would tell her daughter. "You're always smiling." The hidden message was, "Don't be unhappy or have any problems." Sunny did her best to live up to her name and went through life with a perpetual smile. It was heartbreaking to watch her face during therapy sessions. When she told me about sad or painful moments, her mouth was always fixed in a smile. There were times when tears would run down the smile lines around her mouth. It was months before she could allow herself to make a sad or angry face.

Another client grew up under similar circumstances. "My father saw me as something of a saint," she told me. "He would say to me, 'You are so good. You are always willing to help others, but you ask for nothing for yourself. I am so proud of you!'"

What her father was really saying was: "My life is easier when I don't have to respond to your needs. Therefore, you and I will both pretend you don't have any. Your reward is my love and admiration." As a result, she went through life with a one-dimensional personality, admired by many but loved by few. Few people could get close to her, because she couldn't get close to herself. A part of her psyche was locked away, unavailable for use.

Here are some translations of common parental messages that can lead to perfectionism.

Hidden Messages

- "You've never caused me a minute's trouble."

  Translation: *"Don't rock the boat. If you want something different than I want to give you, too bad. You can want only what I want you to have. Repress the rest of your needs."*

- "You've always been such an easygoing child."

  Translation: *"Be happy. Be pleasant. Don't feel your anger, sorrow, or pain."*

- "You're the only one who truly understands me."

  Translation: *"I would be totally alone in the world if it weren't for you. Therefore, you must sacrifice yourself to be here for me. My needs are what count. Helping me is what's important. If you have needs that conflict with mine, I don't want to know about it."*

- "You are such a special child!"

  Translation: *"Be like I want you to be. I have hidden needs that I want you to satisfy."*

- "Of all my children, I expect the most out of you."

  Translation: *"I've selected you to be the one to make my life worth living. All my unfulfilled desires rest on your shoulders. Give up your playfulness. Sacrifice your own view of the world. Cooperate with my unspoken agenda."*

Typically, when children are given mixed messages such as these, they hear and record the spoken words, but experience the underlying message. This leads to a great deal of confusion: "Why did I grow up feeling so neglected when my mother had such nice things to say about me?" Sorting out the real message from the spoken one is part of the work of rewriting the family mythology.

A COMPULSIVE NEED TO SUCCEED

"I'm one of the most driven people
I know. I once dreamed that I was going
to be killed unless I was promoted to
vice president of my firm. I woke up in
a cold sweat. But that nightmare was
just an exaggerated version of what
I feel every moment of the day."

Many Chosen Children are burdened by the belief that they count only if they are superior. I remember a poignant session with Robert, a construction engineer who made millions during the Texas oil boom from 1978 to 1986. In 1987 he was hit hard by a drop in oil prices. His financial strife brought him face to face with reality. At one point he said to me, "I'm really not all that smart. I am very much like everyone else. I am not brilliant. I am pretty ordinary. And as I say this the pain and humiliation are almost unbearable." Idolized by his mother, he thought he had to be extraordinary to have any self-worth.

As I listened to Robert, I couldn't help but identify with him. I, too, felt that success was not an option for me, it was a necessity. This compulsion was particularly evident when I was a teenager. In my sophomore year of high school, for example, I was an honor student and president of my class. In my junior year, I was a class officer once again. In my senior year, I was nominated for a citizenship award, but, to my surprise, I lost by a margin of four votes. This was a crushing blow. It was the first time in my life I had failed to achieve an important goal. But what put me over the edge was overhearing two girls say they were glad the other girl had won. At that point, I went berserk. The next thing I knew, I was pounding on my locker door and screaming at the top of my lungs. I kept it up for a long time—long enough for someone to go get the principal. The principal finally calmed me down by telling me that if I didn't get myself under control, he would have to write the incident on my permanent record.

It took me many years to get a handle on this embarrassing episode. What I eventually realized was that my compulsive drive to succeed was a direct consequence of my mother's high expectations and of my secret fear of inadequacy. I felt I had no choice but to live up to her unrealistic vision of me. Like Robert, part of my legacy as a Chosen Child was the belief that to be average or ordinary is to fail.

✿ Identity Problems

A DIFFUSE SENSE OF IDENTITY

"I'm never sure who I am or what I want. I keep wanting to know what other people want before I make up my mind. I'm heavily influenced by other people's opinions."

A parent who is too closely allied with a child invariably interferes with the development of the child's sense of identity. Typically, the parent programs the child to have similar tastes and values. In dozens of ways—sometimes with words, sometimes with smiles and winks—the parent says to the child: "You and I are buddies," "We like the same things," or "We're different from the rest of the family." The parent is looking for an ally, a champion, a soul mate. In most cases, the child will comply, because pleasing the parent—and thereby ensuring the parent's love—is more important than developing a sense of self. Survival comes first; self-expression is secondary.

Some parents are more extreme in their suppression of the child's identity. A woman named Ginny told me that when she was young her mother would not tolerate the slightest difference between them. She was expected to like the same colors, wear the same kind of clothes, and respond the same way to daily events. If she had a different interpretation of a newspaper article, for example, it was a traumatic event. If she cried at a different part in a movie, she was ridiculed.

It was only when Ginny left for college that she had the

freedom to express her own desires, and she did so with a vengeance. One of the first things she did was to become an environmental activist. Like many young people, she was concerned about pollution, pesticides, and the burgeoning world population. As a way to live out her beliefs, she became a vegetarian and adopted a very simple lifestyle.

When her mother came to visit, she immediately noticed these changes and became extremely agitated. She saw her daughter's new life as a deliberate indictment of her. For some reason, she was particularly upset by two of Ginny's new behaviors: her vegetarianism and her refusal to use paper towels. For the next few years, whenever her mother came to visit, she came laden with paper towels and red meat, which was her attempt to negate any and all differences between them. She could not allow her daughter to deviate from her model. It's no wonder that a significant portion of Ginny's therapy was devoted to reclaiming her own thoughts and feelings. "It seems everything I did for years and years was either because my mother wanted me to do it or because she *didn't* want me to do it," she told me. "I lost that internal sense of what it was that *I* wanted. I was always reacting to her. I didn't know what made me happy. I didn't know what made me mad. I didn't know what to think. It's strange to be discovering who I am at the ripe age of forty."

Some parents expect their children to mirror not only their tastes and values but their negative traits as well. "We are alike," is the chilling message, "and neither one of us is any good." A 30-year-old man remembers his father phoning him in the middle of a drinking binge and telling him, "You and I are both failures. We'll never amount to anything. That's what binds us together. We're too good for the world, so the world will dump on us." The man tried to brush off his father's comments as the rantings of an alcoholic, but the message stayed with him. Not surprisingly, an inability to succeed plagued him for many years of his adult life.

An equally distressing story was told to me by a woman who grew up enmeshed with a manic-depressive mother. Whenever her mother started going through one of her manic episodes, which happened like clockwork each spring and fall, her mother would zero in on her and say in a melodramatic voice, "What is the *matter* with you? You are going out of control!" In an unconscious effort to banish her irrational thoughts, the mother was projecting them onto her daughter. For most of the daughter's life, she had to struggle with the fear that there really *was* something wrong with her. Her mother's attempts to make her a partner in mental illness had a profound and lasting effect on her self-identity.

Some parents engage in actual brainwashing. I counseled a man who had a very invasive mother. One day, she volunteered to share her secrets of child-raising with him. "When you were little," she told him, "I had a way of teaching you right from wrong. I didn't have to slap you, I just gave you a squeeze on the hand and a look. One day I caught you playing with my fountain pen. I didn't punish you. I just put you on my lap, set my pen and one of your crayons in front of you, and asked, 'You didn't want to play with my pen, did you?' You looked up at my face and said, 'No, Mother.' Then I said to you, 'You really wanted to play with your crayon, didn't you?' You looked up again and said, 'Yes, Mother.' And I could tell you weren't just trying to please me. You really meant it. From that day on, you never played with my things. You were such a good child." As he told me of this account, the man realized that his mother had systematically trained him to disconnect himself from his own desires.

AN INABILITY TO SEPARATE FROM THE PARENT

"My brother is forty-two years old, but he doesn't act like an adult. He avoids making decisions. He relies on Mother for financial support. She even cooks for him and buys his clothes. I think he would be devastated if anything happened to her. He is very much a child."

I have seen many, many instances of parents who don't let their children mature. Determined to make a lifelong career out of parenting, they emotionally disable their children. One way or another, they tell them, "You'll never make it on your own," and their children, like all children, do their best to fulfill the parental prophecy.

Rarely are the parents aware of their role in the drama. The same parent who systematically undermines a child's independence will be the first one to cry out, "When is my child ever going to grow up! I'm tired of being burdened by all these problems!"

A client named Rita told a story about the first night she stayed overnight with her boyfriend, a quintessential "mama's boy". She was awakened by a phone call at six o'clock in the morning. Her boyfriend answered the phone. It was his mother, demanding to talk to her. Somehow his mother had found out that she had stayed the night. Her boyfriend handed her the receiver. "I'm Lenore," intoned the mother as soon as Rita said hello. "Are you having an affair with my son?" The accusatory tone of the mother's voice sent chills up her spine. Rita had no idea how to respond and hung up the phone in confusion. Her instinct was to run out of the apartment and never see her boyfriend again. "I sensed that getting involved with him would bring me nothing but trouble." Later she realized that she should have trusted her instincts, because her mother-in-law dominated her husband's life. She monitored his climb up the corporate ladder. She bought his underwear. She kept track of his income. She watched his health like a hawk. What surprised Rita was that her husband allowed all this. "He acted more like a twelve-year-old than a grown man." Severely enmeshed with his mother, he had never managed to break away. He allowed her the same control over his life that she had exercised when he was a small boy.

PERSONAL BOUNDARY PROBLEMS

Loose boundaries: *"I have the hardest time figuring out where I begin and others leave off. I'm always making decisions for other people or feeling other people's pain."*

Rigid boundaries: *"It's hard for me to get close to people. I'm okay up to a certain point, then I start to back away. This really frustrates people— especially my wife. She says living with me is like living with a stranger."*

People who grow up in enmeshed families are likely to have boundary problems later in life. Some will perpetuate the loose boundaries they experienced as children, never being sure where they begin and others leave off. They may share intimate details of their married life with co-workers. They may feel weighed down by the personal problems of people at work. They may become involved with their children's marital problems. They may demand more time and attention from their friends than the normal friendship role encompasses. Because their boundaries were violated when they were young, they have a hard time resurrecting them as adults.

Others have the opposite reaction: they build a wall around themselves to protect themselves from further injury. These are the people whom you feel you never get to know. They don't ask you about your problems; they don't tell you about theirs. They have few, if any, intimate friends. They are wary of close love relationships and are slow to make a commitment. If they marry, their spouses may feel lonely and alienated. They have compensated for an Invasive Parent by becoming overly protective of their thoughts and emotions.

The other night I saw a clear example of how Invasive Parenting can lead to boundary problems. I went to a basketball game at a local community college and happened to sit next to the father of one of the players. Throughout the evening, the man's attention was riveted on his son. At one point he asked me, a relative stranger, if I would go get him a hot-dog. "I don't want to take my eyes off the game," he explained. "I can tell by the way my son's playing that he's discouraged. His shoulders are all hunched up. He's thinking that he's no good. He's worried about what the coach is thinking. He's going to need me tonight to shore him up. I need to stay and watch so I know how best to help him."

I scanned the group of young men and singled out his son. I observed him carefully, but I detected none of the behavior his father had described. The boy seemed to be having a good time and to be playing just as well as anyone else. If he was indeed discouraged, as his father suggested, he was sending out very subtle cues. At that moment I was struck by the intensity of his father's involvement. The boy seemed to have two choices: (1) accept his father's observations as the truth, opening himself up to the violation, or (2) build a thick wall around himself to ward off the invasion. Either course of action would lead to confused personal boundaries in later years.

Rebuilding the boundaries demolished by a parent is a key part of recovering from emotional incest. I counseled a woman not many years ago who made great strides in regaining her sense of personal autonomy. To help her do this, I invited her intrusive father to take part in a therapy session, to which he readily agreed. "I would do anything for my daughter," he told me. Like many overinvolved parents, he was deeply devoted to his daughter and saw himself as willing to do anything within his power to help her. In the sixty-minute session, it became evident to my client that her father didn't understand her at all. He had no idea what she was thinking or feeling. He kept putting words into her mouth that she never said, and he attributed feelings to her that were completely foreign to her. As soon as her father left the office, she expressed profound relief: "All these years, I assumed he could read my mind, that he knew everything I was thinking. I felt he was inside my head! Now I see that he has no idea who I really am. I can't tell you how relieved I am!"

⌘ Relationship Problems

FEAR OF COMMITMENT

"I do just fine with women right up to the point where the word 'commitment' is mentioned. Then I feel like turning and running away. The thought of living with just one woman for the rest of my life sends me into a cold sweat."

Problems with love relationships are the rule rather than the exception for the adult Chosen Child, and one of the most common problems is a fear of intimacy and commitment. To a person who was bound up with an engulfing parent, any close relationship can feel like an invasion. I see this trait quite frequently in men who were the favorite sons of aggressive, domineering mothers. They want love in their lives, but the thought of a monogamous marriage brings back haunting memories of enmeshment. The notion that there could be freedom within a relationship runs counter to their experience.

Blaine has been married and divorced four times. Each time a marriage ended, he told himself he would never marry again. The experience was too painful. But a year or two after a divorce, he would find himself strongly attracted to a new woman and in a short time he would be married once again. At first he would feel safe with his new wife, then a feeling of suffocating closeness would start to build. He would feel that his freedom had been taken away from him and that his every move was being dictated. He would feel trapped with a woman who seemed to be sucking the very marrow from his bones.

LACK OF ROMANTIC ATTRACTION

WOMAN: *I am married to a wonderful
man. He goes out of his way to please
me. I couldn't ask for anything more.
Yet, I'm always dissatisfied. I keep
wondering, "Where's the magic?
Isn't there more to love than this?"*

MAN: *I've been married three times,
and I'm about to sign up for number
four. I've never found what I'm
looking for in a woman. All of my
wives have disappointed me.*

The normal parent-child bond is powerful in and of itself; when it's amplified by enmeshment, it becomes all-encompassing. Unwittingly, some Chosen Children go through life trying to recapture this intensity. For brief moments of time—typically, during an affair or the romantic phase of a relationship—there may be hints of the longed-for passion. But when romantic love fades, they are confronted with those inevitable periods of boredom, stagnation, frustration, and anger. This is part of the normal progression of a love relationship, but the Chosen Child cannot cope with the deescalation. He or she will either be chronically disappointed in the marriage or will seek some form of escape. Common ways to exit the marriage are: divorce; clandestine affairs; becoming overly involved with a child; abusing drugs or alcohol; and workaholism.

CONFLICTS BETWEEN THE SPOUSE AND THE PARENT

*"Ten years ago, I bought a house with
my mother and moved in with her. At the
time, it made good financial sense.
Now that I'm married, my wife wants us
to move out and get a house of our
own. She hates living with my mom. But
my mother won't buy me out, and she
won't let me buy her out. This dilemma
is ruining my marriage."*

If the Chosen Child remains attached to the parent after marriage, the marital relationship automatically becomes a triangle, with both the parent and the spouse vying for control. This is the stuff of melodrama and TV talk shows.

One couple, married only two years, came to me in a last-ditch attempt to save their marriage. They were having three or four fights a week, each one ending with the husband packing up his clothes and going home to his mother. While he was licking his wounds at his mother's house, his mother would urge him to file for divorce. His wife, meanwhile, felt abandoned and vilified. She felt powerless to effect any change, because her husband's automatic response to conflict was to run to his mother. One note of criticism from her, and he was "out of here."

In order to save the marriage, the husband needed to do two things: (1) reassure his wife of his commitment and availability, and (2) draw a protective boundary around his marriage that excluded his mother. I assured him he would still be able to relate to his mother as a grown son, but he would have to stop being her surrogate spouse. He would have to lop off the intrusive leg of the triangle.

ATTRACTION TO SELF-CENTERED PARTNERS

"I've married a very self-centered
woman. She always puts herself first.
I'm an afterthought in her life."

It is quite common for the Chosen Child to grow up and marry someone who ignores his needs. This is an unconscious re-creation of the dynamics of the parent-child relationship. Although outwardly treated like royalty, the child is in reality a servant, trained to meet the emotional needs of the parent.

Believing that other people's needs are more important, the Chosen Child typically grows up and falls in love with someone who is unavailable or inattentive to his needs. Over time, the partner's lack of emotional involvement becomes a fresh source of pain. What I have observed time and time again is that one or both adults will turn to a child for support, and the whole cycle starts over again.

John has been married to Alicia for twenty years. He is painfully aware that his wife is not interested in meeting his needs.

"She abuses me, just like my mother. There are times when I can't distinguish between the two of them. In fact, I sometimes call her 'Mom.'"

John has tried to find some satisfaction in life by becoming involved in his work. Meanwhile, his wife has managed to meet her needs by bonding with their son. "My wife cares about that boy a hundred times more than she cares about me," he told me. "I don't even think she realizes it."

SEXUAL PROBLEMS

"I've had sex with a lot of men,
but I'm not highly sexed. In fact,
it was many years before I was
able to have orgasms."

Sexual problems are common among victims of emotional incest. Although there is no sexual contact between the Chosen Child and the parent—primarily because of the incest taboo—the two of them have ventured into the realm of intimate partners. Because they are sharing their innermost thoughts and feelings, it is natural for sexual feelings to arise.

This sexual energy must go somewhere. Generally, it takes one of two paths: expression or repression. If the child expresses the sexuality, it may be in the form of excessive masturbation or in promiscuity. If teenage children are not allowed to have a normal dating experience—which is often the case with the Chosen Child— their sexual encounters are likely to be brief, clandestine affairs with relative strangers.

Many children take the opposite path and repress their sexuality. If this repression is reinforced by strict family values or more explicit injunctions ("Stop acting like a slut!"), the repression can lead to sexual restriction, a stiff toll to be exacted on later relationships. The man may be impotent or disinterested in sex. The woman may be afraid of sex or have difficulty achieving an orgasm.

A young woman who had a lot of fear about sex remembers when she was 16 years old and happened to see a boy she knew in front of the local supermarket. It was a hot day, and she was wearing shorts and a tank top. Her father drove by and saw her talking to the boy. Later that day he accused her of acting "like a whore." "You'll get into big trouble if you keep parading yourself around like that, young lady," he told her. "It was really disgusting. I was embarrassed you were my daughter!" The girl said nothing, but inside she was horribly confused. What had she done wrong? What she had done wrong was demonstrate some interest in the opposite sex and wear clothes that revealed her physical attractiveness. Her father had latched on to this normal adolescent behavior and distorted it because of his overinvolvement with her. A perfectly natural encounter between his daughter and a young man was seen as a loathsome act.

There are times when a parent's sexual desires go one step beyond projection: they use the child for sexual stimulation. One man told me that when he was 12 years old, his mother used to open the door when he was taking a shower and say, "Don't forget to dry off well when you're finished." This happened repeatedly despite his protests. A woman said that when she was a teenager her father was fixated on her breasts; it seemed that whenever he looked at her, his eyes would zero in on her chest. A man told me that his mother would crawl into bed with him at night and lie close to him, well into his adolescent years. Another man told me that his mother called him a "stud" and said he was more sexy than his father. A young woman was "kidnapped" by her father and whisked off to the coast for a company conference, where he treated her as his "date" for the weekend. A woman told of her mother lying on her bed openly rubbing her vagina, complaining that her husband was not fulfilling her sexually. A man reported being French-kissed by his mother. A girl talked about sleeping in the same bed as her father well into adolescence; he would go to sleep with his arms and legs wrapped around her.

When children are entangled with a Sexualizing Parent, they have an increased chance of being sexually victimized in later years. Because a parent has violated their emotional boundaries and aroused their sexuality, they are ideal candidates for "date rape" or other forms of abuse. Nona, a bank manager who had been enmeshed with her father, was later sexually abused by her uncle. Her early experience of being "daddy's pretty baby" had taught her to acquiesce to adults. Although her father had never touched her inappropriately, he had set up the preconditions for victimization.

4

The Family Role Call: How Emotional Incest Affects Other Family Members

88

Emotional incest is not a two-person event. It's a family affair, involving every person in the household. To understand fully the role of the Chosen Child, the other family members have to be taken into account. This chapter takes a closer look at all the auxiliary players.

All families are systems, in that every member of the family—whether newborn or grandparent—affects every other. When there is a new addition to the family, perhaps through a remarriage or the birth of a child, the entire constellation is rearranged; new alliances form and old ones disband with little conscious thought or acknowledgment. When there is a departure from the family, such as when parents divorce or a child leaves for college, someone or something fills the void. In this continuing drama, the actions of one family member elicit reactions from everyone else, and every plot development has implications for the entire group. In enmeshed families such as the ones I've been describing, the interplay between individuals is greatly exaggerated. An incident that involves one family member can send shock waves through the whole system.

A client of mine named Ursula spent a weekend visiting an old college friend and saw firsthand how intertwined a family can be.

She was so unnerved by the experience that she used part of her next session with me to debrief. The melodrama began the moment she arrived at her friend Marjorie's house. Her friend opened the door, her eyes red from crying. "Marjorie, what's wrong?" Ursula asked.

"Something awful has happened," Marjorie informed her. "Evie's been turned down by Vassar." Evie was Marjorie's oldest daughter, a talented high school senior and the clear favorite of her two daughters. Marjorie delivered the news as if it were Evie's death sentence.

"Oh, I'm so sorry," Ursula said, struggling for a response that matched Marjorie's grave assessment of the situation. "That must be quite a disappointment for Evie."

"She's devastated. She's up in her room crying."

A moment later, Marjorie's husband marched into the house. His wife had insisted he leave work early to help console Evie. Marjorie's younger daughter trooped home a few minutes later, summoned from a friend's house. Once everyone was duly assembled, Marjorie announced to one and all that their dinner reservations were canceled. Everyone was expected to stay at home and commiserate.

Plans were disrupted Saturday as well. The younger daughter continued to be roped into the drama by not being allowed to leave the house. "That would seem heartless," Marjorie informed her. Even Ursula was put on notice: she was not to talk about their college days when Evie was around. "It might hurt Evie's feelings," Marjorie informed her.

Amid this upheaval, Ursula struggled for a sense of proportion. Having a daughter turned down by her number-one college is indeed a cause for disappointment, but Marjorie had turned the rejection into a dirge. Her insistence that all parties share in her tragic assessment indicated the family's degree of enmeshment. Marjorie was so wrapped up in Evie's life, she decreed that everyone else be equally involved. She had lost all perspective. She drew the whole family into her web of enmeshment, wiping out the normal boundaries between individuals.

88 Blood Ties

Salvador Minuchin, a noted family therapist, has devoted his career to exploring the interplay between family members, and one of his experiments sheds some light on highly enmeshed households such as Marjorie's. The stated purpose of the experiment was to get some measurable data on how children absorb family tension. A four-member family volunteered to participate in the study: Mr. and Mrs. Collins, their 17-year-old daughter, Dede, and their 12-year-old daughter, Violet.[1]

When the experiment began, a team of researchers determined the baseline anxiety level of each of the family members by measuring the amount of free fatty acids (FFA) in their blood. (FFA is an indicator of emotional stress; the more FFA, the more stressed the individual.) Then the parents were separated from the children and ushered into a conference room equipped with a one-way mirror. An interviewer skillfully induced an argument between the adults, while Dede and Violet were instructed to watch through the mirror. Although the girls could not interact with their parents, tests showed that their FFA levels rose significantly just from viewing the conflict.

Sixty minutes later, the girls were reunited with their parents, and the interviewer asked them to work as a team to resolve the parents' ongoing argument. "It became evident," writes Minuchin, "that they [the two girls] played very different roles in this family. Dede was trapped between her parents. Each parent tried to get her support in the fight with the other parent, so that Dede could not respond to one parent's demands without seeming to side against the other. Violet's allegiance was not being sought. She could therefore react to her parents' conflict without being caught in the middle."

This difference between the girls' roles was clearly reflected in their test results. Although both of them became more anxious when they were brought into the room with their parents, Dede's anxiety level rose significantly higher than Violet's. When the interview was over, Violet quickly regained her equilibrium, but Dede remained anxious for the next ninety minutes. Because she was more enmeshed with her parents, she suffered more from the interaction. Consistent with what we know about the Chosen Child, a child who is asked to solve the emotional problems of adults invariably experiences a lot of stress.

However, I contend that if the experiment had been set up a different way, with different underlying dynamics, another family member might have exhibited the most tension. For example, if Minuchin had devised the experiment so that the parents were encouraged to display their affection for Dede—rather than ask her to come to their aid—sister Violet might have felt left out, and her blood test might have indicated more stress than Dede's. And in another variation of the experiment, one in which the researchers cleverly manipulated the situation so that Dede was allied with her father against her mother, I suspect it would have been the mother who experienced the most tension. I have ample evidence from my practice that when there is a cross-generational alliance in the family, the excluded family members suffer as well.

In chapter 3, I explored the high cost of being the Chosen Child. Now we'll look at the other family members: What price do they pay for *their* part in the drama? What is it like to be a parent who is overly involved with a child? What is it like to be a Left-Out Child? A Left-Out Spouse? Reading the following profiles may help you rewrite some family mythology and gain greater insight into *your* family members.

⅏ The Invasive Parent

Viewed from the outside, the Invasive Parent—the one enmeshed with a child—appears to be in an enviable position. As we've seen, the parent gets many of his needs met by the Chosen Child, who—unlike a spouse—rarely makes demands, criticizes, or challenges the parent to "relate." The child merely accepts what is given. If Daddy is a little self-centered or irritable or hits the bottle once too often—so be it. That's the way Daddy is. The child has no basis for comparison.

An Invasive Parent who is married also gets to enjoy the convenience of having a spouse. Even though there is some unresolved tension in the marriage—otherwise the parent would not turn to a child—there is a semblance of a relationship. For example, the couple may have sexual relations, share household and parenting responsibilities, and have occasional moments of intimacy. When there is more substance to the marriage, the Invasive Parent appears to be sitting in the catbird seat. He or she basks in the adoration and companionship of a child and reaps many of the rewards of being married as well.

Crystal married a man in his late forties who seemed to be in this enviable position. "He was snug as a bug in a rug before I came along," she told me, the resentment evident in her voice. "He and his daughter were living by themselves in a beautiful house with a pool.

She never asked him for anything but money, and he had lots of that. They had the same opinions, the same politics, the same tastes and values. She cleaned house, cooked all the meals. I feel that if our relationship falters in any way, he will go running back to her. And I know that she will welcome him with open arms." Aware of her husband's dual options, Crystal was wary of putting any pressure on him. "He's in a no-lose situation," she told me. "He either has my love and affection, or he has his daughter's, and my fear is that when push comes to shove, she will win out. She makes a lot fewer demands than I do."

At first, it may look like this man has the best of both worlds. But it must be remembered that he, like all parents who are overly bonded with a child, initially turned to his daughter because of a lack of more suitable companionship. After his divorce from his first wife, he turned to his daughter to help ease his pain and loneliness. And even though living with his daughter seemed to satisfy his needs, it was not fully rewarding to him, or he would not have remarried. Like all parents who are enmeshed with a child, he had an unsatisfied desire, whether conscious or unconscious, for a more encompassing union with another adult. But when he acted on this desire and married for the second time, he had to contend with his wife's jealousy. He was being forced to choose between the two people he loved most in the world. He was sitting in the hot seat, not the catbird seat!

I have counseled numerous adults who were overbonded with a child. One such client, a woman named Dot, was three years into her second marriage. Enmeshed with her oldest son, Rudy, she felt like "the frayed rope in a game of tug-of-war." She had been blissfully happy the first year of her new marriage because, in her words, she "finally had it all." She had a special relationship with Rudy, and, for the first time, she had a husband she could love and respect. For a short time she was able to luxuriate in both relationships.

But then Dick, her second husband, began to resent the unusual degree of closeness between Dot and her son. In the second year of their marriage, his resentment caught fire. "He turned into a person I had never seen before," Dot told me. "It's like I had never known him. He and Rudy would get in these horrendous physical fights. Then both of them would come running to me to referee. Dick insisted that I side with him. Rudy demanded that I see his side.

Now, at the end of three years, I'm worn out. I love them both, but at times I wish they'd both disappear."

Besides juggling competing claims from the spouse and the child, the Invasive Parent ultimately faces a greater trial—the loss of the child, for in all but the most ingrained parent-child relationships, there comes a time when the child moves away from the parent. It can happen abruptly or it can happen over time, but either way the loss is often heartbreaking.

A very kind gentleman named Theodore came to me for therapy some years ago complaining of depression. I learned that the depression had begun two years previously, about the time his youngest child, Robin, was 12 years old. At first Theodore failed to see any connection between the onset of his depression and his daughter's coming of age. He thought his problems were work related. But as I listened to his account, I began to see that Robin's twelfth birthday marked the beginning of the end of a very special relationship for him. Prior to this time, he and Robin had been real buddies. They had played tennis together, shared confidences, and crewed their sailboat in weekly races. They had taken daily walks, eaten their meals together, and stayed up late watching the TV.

At the fateful age of 12, however, Robin found her relationship with her father less compelling. She began to spend hours on the phone with friends, and she spent more and more time away from home. The summer she turned 13, she went away to summer camp for a month while her father wandered aimlessly around the house. When she came home, she had less time for her father than ever.

Theodore's depression deepened over the next few months. But, like most overinvolved parents, he wasn't aware of the pivotal role his daughter played in his life, so he couldn't pinpoint the cause of his unhappiness. His wife, who had learned to cope with the exclusive father-daughter duo by becoming active in local politics, backed further away from her husband because of his moodiness. Her complaint: "I can't relate to him because he's so depressed. I don't want to go anywhere with him or include him in my plans because he's like a dark cloud over my head." His wife's rejection made him long for his daughter's companionship even more, but by then Robin had a steady boyfriend. This loving, good-hearted man no longer occupied a position of prominence in anyone's life.

Fortunately, Theodore had the good sense to seek professional help for his depression and was able to make some dramatic changes. In six months, he had a clear picture of how empty his life had become. He broke free from his inertia by getting his neighbor involved in sailboat racing. He realized that he didn't have to give up his love of sailing just because his daughter was no longer willing to be his first mate. A few months later, he joined a health club and started working out every morning, which gave him more energy and self-esteem.

As his depression lifted, he gained some interest in working on family relationships. At my suggestion, he asked his wife and daughter to join him for a few sessions, to which they both agreed. We spent the initial group session mapping out their family dynamics on my chalkboard. When Robin realized that her growing independence had coincided with her father's depression, she had the expected reaction—guilt. She turned to her father and said with tears in her eyes, "I'm sorry, Daddy. I didn't mean to hurt you. I just wanted to spend time with my friends." Both Theodore and I assured her that her actions had not been harmful—in fact, they had been the catalyst for her father's growth. If she had continued to play the role of "daddy's little girl," the two of them would have blindly pursued the same narrow course, becoming more and more enmeshed. By moving away from her father, both of them had been freed up to live fuller, more rewarding lives.

During the second family session, it became clear to Theodore and his wife that marriage therapy was in order. Their relationship was badly in need of help. His wife agreed to join him for weekly sessions. The fact that he was now a happier, more alive human being gave her enough motivation to try to work things out.

88 The Left-Out Child

It's a fact of life that parents *don't* respond to their children equally. They may love each and every one of them, but they invariably find themselves drawn to one child more than another. In some families, this natural attraction is not moderated by compassion or fairness but is acted out as favoritism. I know of a family where one child was sent to Harvard while his younger, equally deserving brother had to attend a state college, even though the family could afford to send both of them to Ivy League schools. One client invited his favorite daughter to eat in the dining room with him while the other children ate in the kitchen. In a third family, the middle child was given a generous allowance twenty years after leaving home, while the other children were expected to fend for themselves. Added to these blatant signs of favoritism were tens of thousands of subtle, daily interactions that said to the Left-Out Child: "You are not a priority in my life. You are not as important to me as your brother or sister."

I've just begun work with a young woman named Molly. Molly is well aware that her younger sister, Liza, is her mother's favorite. Molly is about to be married, and a few weeks ago, she and her mother and sister drove to Dallas to shop for a wedding gown for her and a bridesmaid dress for Liza. To Molly's dismay, her mother was less interested in helping her pick out her wedding gown than she was in helping Liza shop for her dress. Molly was left alone in the dressing room while her mother chatted with Liza in the adjoining room. Molly struggled in and out of the elaborate gowns as she listened to the excited, intimate chatter of her younger sister and mother in the next stall. When Molly described this scene to me she cried out in a rare burst of anger: "Dammit! It's my wedding, not my sister's!"

It is difficult to maintain your self-esteem when you grow up in a family in which you don't feel prized or valued, where the laurels always go to someone else. When a sibling gets all the attention, you ache for your share of the love. You want your special gifts to be celebrated and your weaknesses to be met with compassion. You want your parents to acknowledge the fact that you are just as fine and lovable a person as your brother or sister.

The Left-Out Child's goal in life is straightforward: to seek a place in the sun. But the way this is done differs from child to child. Some excluded children try to cater to the whims of the parent. They become highly attuned to the parent's needs and mirror the parent's interests. Many years later, they are often the ones who volunteer to take care of the aging mother or father, trying to return to the well in search of life-giving love.

Madeline was just such a Left-Out Child. She never married, but chose to live at home and take care of her mother, a sour woman who was disabled with arthritis. But no matter how many meals Madeline cooked, no matter how diligently she cleaned the house, no matter how many games of Scrabble she played with her mother, no matter how many hours she patiently sat on the couch as her mother flipped restlessly from one TV channel to the next, Madeline could never compete with her brother, Chris. A phone call from Chris was the highlight of the woman's day. A visit was a state occasion. Meanwhile, Madeline toiled away in the background. She was the classic "old maid," withering away in the shadow of a demanding, self-absorbed parent.

Some excluded children take a different tack and broadcast their frustration: "Pay attention to me, damn you!" They are sullen and uncooperative, venting their rage at both the parent and the favored sibling. Sadly, this approach usually results in further rejection. Insult is added to injury when the parent makes the inevitable comparison—"Why can't you be nice like your brother (or sister)?" In the strange, seesaw dynamics of sibling relationships, the favored child often responds to the insolent behavior of the excluded child by acting even more sweet and compliant. Such a stark contrast between the behavior of siblings should serve as a warning signal to parents: something is out of balance in this family. But the warning often goes unheeded and the Left-Out Child experiences more and more rejection.

Some excluded children seek approval outside the family: "If I can't be on the inside, I'm going to find what I need somewhere else." They cling tenaciously to friends or school, or flaunt their independence by running away from home. In extreme cases, the Left-Out Child is attracted to cults or gangs in order to gain a sense of belonging. Unfortunately, choosing a deviant lifestyle alienates the parent, and the Left-Out Child is pushed even farther away from the inner circle.

Finally, it is quite common for a child who has lost out to a brother or sister to attempt to bond with the other parent. The bond between the Left-Out Child and the Left-Out Spouse makes a lot of sense because they both need love and companionship. The arrangement may even work for a while, because each individual secures a bastion of intimacy. But ultimately this alliance transforms the Left-Out Child into yet another Chosen Child, who then has to contend with all the negative consequences of enmeshment as well.

In large families where one of the children is clearly favored, it is often possible to see a number of these coping mechanisms being played out. One Left-Out Child may be a parent pleaser, another an overachiever, another a criminal, a fourth a member of a religious cult. Outside observers wonder how the same two parents could produce such diverse offspring. What they don't see is that the children are trying to solve the same family problem—parental favoritism—and that they are following one of the unwritten laws of family dynamics: choose a coping mechanism not preempted by other siblings.

✵ The Left-Out Spouse

Of all the members in the enmeshed family, the Left-Out Spouse, the one relegated to the far outpost of the love triangle, is the most commonly misunderstood. Displaced by a son or daughter, the spouse may feel violently jealous. He or she may have a hard time justifying this anger, however, because there is rarely any one incident between the Invasive Parent and Chosen Child that is blatantly wrong: the relationship is inappropriate only when viewed as a whole and *only* when viewed against a backdrop of healthy family dynamics. When the Left-Out Spouse reacts to an isolated incident, the whole thing seems blown out of proportion.

A client named Fran grew ashen as she related the seemingly innocent event that triggered her rage: "It was Lynette's thirteenth birthday, and I was talking to her father about what to get her. I'd seen a beautiful coat I thought would look nice on her, so I told him about it. 'We don't have to get her the coat,' he told me. 'I've already bought her a diamond bracelet. I got it last year in London, and I've been keeping it for her thirteenth birthday.' When he told me about the bracelet, I felt as if he had slapped me in the face. In that one moment I understood why husbands and wives kill each other. I hated him. I hated my own daughter. All of a sudden something blew up inside me, and I heard myself shouting at him. 'Why don't the two of you just move out by yourselves! You should marry her, not me!'"

Fran looked at me, drew in a deep breath, then exhaled in a rush. "How could I say such a thing?" she asked me, shaking her head in dismay.

Fran had been beside herself with rage, but in retrospect, the event seemed not to warrant her explosive reaction. It was true that her husband had spent a lot of money on the bracelet—more than a thousand dollars—but they were a wealthy family and could indulge in such luxuries. So why was she so irate? Shouldn't she be happy that her husband was thinking about their daughter? Many fathers ignore their children's birthdays or begrudge spending money on them. As Fran looked back on the confrontation, her rage seemed totally unfounded. "What is wrong with me?" she asked.

To help Fran comprehend her anger, I got out a piece of paper and asked her to tell me all the little things that bothered her about the way her husband and daughter interacted. Before the end of the session, she had come up with more than twenty items. When the facts of the matter were written down in black and white, she finally grasped the full extent of her predicament. Here is a portion of the list:

• Mark greets Lynette with a kiss when he comes home from work, but only calls out a greeting to me. Sometimes he even forgets to do that.

• When Lynette calls Mark at work, he drops everything to talk with her. I'm put on hold. Or he'll promise to call me back and then forget to do it.

• When we go out to dinner, Lynette and Mark sit side by side. I sit across from them. She leans up against him, and they often talk in such a low voice I can't hear what they're saying.

• Mark is always forgetting my birthday. He has never given me expensive jewelry.

• Lynette still sits on her father's lap. He likes to stroke her hair. He is always telling her she has beautiful hair. My hair is thin and has no body. Hers is like a lion's mane.

• Mark asked Lynette where she wanted to go for summer vacation before he asked me where I wanted to go.

• Mark and Lynette often stop talking when I walk into the room.

• Mark carries pictures of Lynette in his wallet, but none of me.

• Mark has just arranged to have professional photos taken of Lynette to hang in his office. He has none of me.

It was not an isolated comment about a bracelet that led to Fran's violent outburst; it was the accumulation of scores of ego-bruising events. Enduring all these slights had a kindling effect: each minor, seemingly insignificant incident added to the one that preceded it until she was ablaze with anger. Fran's jealousy was not a sign of mental instability, it was a natural and healthy response to a crazy situation. Her intense feelings were a sign that the family was out of balance. Except for one key activity—sexual intercourse—her husband was treating her daughter like a mistress. The expensive jewelry; the petting; the intimate body language; the quiet, seductive conversations; the shared secrets—these are the earmarks of an affair, not a father-daughter relationship. Clearly, the alliance was an unhealthy arrangement that worked to no one's advantage. Fran's instincts were telling her, "This is wrong!" And the intensity of her reaction was an accurate measure of just how wrong it was.

This session was pivotal for Fran. Once she realized the reason for her turmoil, she stopped feeling bad about herself. "I used to think of myself as a witch," she told me as she was getting up to leave, "the one who spoiled everyone's fun. Now I know better. My husband is the one who's out of line, not me!"

Anger is just one way that a Left-Out Spouse can respond to a parent-child coalition. Some parents become depressed instead. In this case, their internal, unconscious dialogue goes something like this: "I'm feeling hurt and abandoned, but I won't show anybody those feelings because I can't justify them. I don't even understand them myself. How can I resent the fact that my husband loves his own daughter? I'm so confused and upset I'll make myself emotionally ill."

Paul was a Left-Out Spouse. He can pinpoint the very incident that shoved him out of the inner circle. He and his wife were having a fight. He doesn't remember what the fight was about, but he will never forget his wife's response. Right in the middle of the argument she picked up their two-month-old son, Isaac, took him away to another room, and quietly shut the door. He stood outside the door and listened to her coo to the baby. He told me, "I've been on the outside ever since."

Some spouses cope with the abandonment in a more active way: they become busy with work, civic activities, or hobbies, or they opt for a less socially acceptable solution and drink too much, take drugs, or have extramarital affairs. "I don't need you," all these activities are saying, "I've got something going for me on the side."

Some spouses link up with a second child. "You've got a child," says the parent, "now I've got one, too." Splitting the family into two separate parent-child coalitions is a common tactic. One child sides with Mom, the other with Dad, and a wide gulf separates the parents. To the casual observer, the family appears intact, but it's really two separate factions.

❀ The Shadow Parent

It may come as a surprise to you that all the while Cinderella was toiling away in the ashes, her adoring father was alive and well, living in the same house. He hadn't died or gone off to France to seek his fortune. He was living right there at home, allowing his precious daughter to be treated like a lowly servant. In the original version, Perrault, the author of the tale, gave this explanation for the father's failure to intervene: "The poor girl bore all this patiently and dared not tell her father who would have scolded her, for his wife totally dominated him."[2] Cinderella's father was the original Shadow Parent.

I use the term *Shadow Parent* to refer not to a discreet role in the family but to a personality type: passive, detached, and noninterfering. Either the Invasive Parent or the Left-Out Spouse can be a Shadow Parent. When the Invasive Parent has a passive personality (as in the example of Cinderella's father), the Chosen Child will have little protection from the scorn of the Left-Out Spouse. Says the Shadow Parent: "Don't upset your mother. Do what she says. Let's let our relationship be our little secret. I won't stand up for you. You'll have to fend for yourself."

If the Left-Out Spouse has a passive personality, there will not be much resistance to the parent-child alliance; a potentially corrective force in the family will be missing. For example, my stepfather was a Shadow Man. Dominated by my mother, he allowed her to call most of the shots. This meant she was free to become overly reliant on me without having to worry about his jealous reaction. It would have been to everyone's benefit had he found an effective way to demand more of his rights as a spouse.

I gained additional insight into the Shadow Parent recently when I worked with Lucy, a placid, likable woman. Lucy's husband and oldest daughter are enmeshed. They share the same interests, sit close to each other as they watch TV, get up each morning to jog together, and share numerous confidences throughout the day. The girl seeks the advice and companionship of her father long before she will turn to her mother. Strangely, Lucy does not object to this. She sees what is going on between them but does not interfere. It's almost as if she has offered her daughter to her husband on a platter: here, take her, she's yours. I've discovered that behind this seeming act of generosity, however, is a hidden fear. My client is secretly relieved that her daughter is satisfying her husband's emotional needs. Her passivity is caused by a fear of intimacy.

✗ The Spouse of the Chosen Child

When the Chosen Child grows up and marries, another person stumbles into the quagmire—the spouse of the Chosen Child. I have a lot of sympathy for a person who marries one of us Chosen Children, because we can be "larger than life." Our joys and problems appear boundless and overrun the concerns of our spouses, and our crazy mixture of high and low self-esteem can drive them to distraction.

I recently interviewed a grown-up "daddy's girl" who made this candid assessment of herself: "I know I'm difficult to live with. There is an all-encompassing quality to me. I take up so much room in our marriage with all my emotions. It's almost like there isn't room for my husband. I swamp him with my needs. When the kids draw pictures of us, they draw me half again as large as they draw him. I'm clearly the star of the family, and he's the supporting actor."

Accustomed to being the focus of a parent's attention, the Chosen Child naturally assumes center stage. A marriage is a relationship between equals, but the Chosen Child has little experience with equality. Being on an equal footing with a spouse feels like a demotion. Without being aware of it, the Chosen Child often dominates the relationship.

If the Chosen Child was allied with a Critical/Abusive Parent, different marital problems can arise. The feelings of inadequacy and low self-esteem that characterize the Scapegoat Child can be difficult for a partner to deal with. The partner may feel the constant need to shore up the Chosen Child's ego and counteract the early years of abuse or neglect. This is a futile task, however, unless the Chosen Child is willing to examine those old parent-child issues. It takes a concerted effort to erase early messages from a parent.

Another spouse who earns my sympathy is the one who marries a Chosen Child who has reacted against an Invasive Parent by developing an impenetrable barrier to intimacy. Although the barrier was erected to keep out an overbearing parent, it also shuts out the marriage partner.

I worked with a man and woman who were contemplating divorce primarily because the husband, a Chosen Child, kept a constant vigil on his boundaries. The smallest request from his wife would trigger a security alarm. For instance, one of her requests was that her husband call her every day when his business took him out of town. She often felt abandoned by him, and this was one way she could feel more connected.

As soon as she stated her request, her husband was up in arms. It was a violation of his rights and his autonomy to agree in advance when and if he should call her. She was asking too much! She was always asking too much! How could he survive if she was always dictating the terms of his life?

This seemingly innocent request for one phone call a day tapped into a lifetime of frustration with an invasive mother. He was willing to make a legal commitment to marriage, but not an emotional one. He was not willing to "couple." He went through life as if he and his wife were two single people living in the same house. This distance kept him safe from his unconscious fear of engulfment.

If a Chosen Child grows up without fully breaking away from the Invasive Parent, the spouse of the Chosen Child has an additional obstacle to overcome: in-law problems. It is not uncommon for the Invasive Parent to dictate how the newlyweds should run their household, to require frequent phone calls or visits, to encourage financial ties between the families, to insist that the couple live nearby—ideally, in the same house—and to dictate the terms of all family gatherings. These demands are a clear violation of the autonomy of the younger couple. If, in later years, the Invasive Parent moves in with the family of the Chosen Child—which often happens—in-law problems occur daily, if not hourly.

The spouse of the Chosen Child appears to have only two ways to handle the invasive in-law: (1) give in to the demands and become an additional source of support, or (2) treat the Invasive Parent as an intruder, a foreign body to be rejected. If the spouse chooses the first option and joins the ranks, the couple will be absorbed into the family and have little personal freedom. Whenever they step out of line, there will be a price to pay. If the spouse chooses the second option and resists the Invasive Parent—watch out: the temperature will rise. Adding an outsider to the boiling pot turns the family into a pressure cooker.

Sometimes the Chosen Child secretly encourages the battles between the spouse and the Invasive Parent, because on some level, the emancipation feels long overdue. But even so, the parent will rarely blame the Chosen Child for the fracas—it's the son-in-law or the daughter-in-law who's considered the outlaw.

Michael was up to his neck in in-law problems. His wife, Jane, was her mother's Scapegoat Child. All the years she was growing up, Jane had been her mother's safety valve. Whenever her mother was sad or angry or lonely or depressed, Jane had absorbed all the fury. Like most children, she put up with her mother's excesses without thinking twice. This was how life was. To protect herself, she escaped into books and fantasies. She grew up to be a kind but shy, introverted young woman.

When Jane married Michael, he quickly became the target of her mother's ire. "That man" was not good enough for her daughter. "He doesn't earn enough money. He's too self-centered. He doesn't show enough respect for me (Jane's mother.)" Every day Jane had to listen to her mother's tirades. Her husband tried to ignore these incursions, but this became impossible when his mother-in-law broke her hip and moved in with them for a summer. Now the enemy was on home base. Fights broke out daily between the mother-in-law and son-in-law. Years of frustration were released on both sides. Jane patiently bore this added tension, trying to cater to her mother without alienating her husband. Eventually, the mother-in-law's hip mended and she moved back to her home. If that hadn't taken place, it is likely that Michael would have ended the marriage just to find some peace and quiet. In many cases, a marriage relationship is less tenacious than an enmeshed parent-child bond.

❦ A Drama Where Everyone Loses

This look at the cast of characters of the enmeshed family shows how every member is adversely affected by an overly close parent-child bond. The family's natural system of support is eroded and each member must find a substitute form of gratification. The Left-Out Child constantly jockeys for love and attention. The Left-Out Spouse either unites with another child, becomes angry or depressed, or tries to find solace in a job, drugs or alcohol, or clandestine affairs.

If the marriage breaks up, the Invasive Parent and Chosen Child often find themselves living together in a single-parent household, where the relationship intensifies like a hurricane tracking over tropical waters. If the Invasive Parent later remarries, the parent-child alliance becomes a major, if not insurmountable, obstacle to the new marriage. If the Chosen Child grows up and marries without breaking free of the entanglement, the spouse of the Chosen Child gets tripped up by the cross-generational ties.

In all of these situations, each individual is struggling to make sense of the situation and to find some measure of happiness, but these measures often are seen as a calculated attempt to deprive others of their happiness, and resentment is the order of the day.

5

Why Do Parents Become Overinvolved with Their Children?

❀❀

At some point in the recovery process, nearly all of my clients ask the same question: "Why did my parent do this to me?" They've come to realize that much of the pain of their childhoods can be traced to one source—growing up with an Invasive Parent—and they want to know why it happened.

Some clients are filled with anger: "Why did the bastard do this to me?" Others are protective of the parent; they want an explanation that allows them to hold on to their high regard for their mother or father. Gayle, a 44-year-old voice teacher, was looking for a nonblaming way to understand her father's excessive involvement with her. They had been close as long as she could remember, but their relationship had intensified when her mother died of cancer. For the next seven years, she and her father had clung together like survivors of a shipwreck. "My father was everything to me," she told me. "He was father, mother, and best friend. We told each other everything."

When she was young, Gayle had seen her father as a gentle, loving, good-hearted man who had a lot to teach her about life. Today she still thinks the world of him, but she now understands that their overly close relationship was the source of many of her problems—including her most vexing one, obesity. "I think I'm avoiding relationships by stuffing myself with food," she told me. "A part of me is still connected to my father. It feels wrong to be with anyone else. So I eat and eat."

At the end of one session, Gayle told me that talking about her father with me sometimes made her feel guilty. "One thing I know for sure," she said, "is that he never meant to hurt me. He thought the world of me. Everything that he did, he did for me. If he knew he had caused me any harm, it would kill him. He was just trying to be a good father."

I reassured Gayle that her perception of her father was probably accurate. Few parents who are guilty of emotional incest realize they are harming their children. In fact, many of them see themselves as devoted, self-sacrificing parents acting in their children's best interests. What they don't realize is that in addition to giving their children love and attention, they are using the relationships to satisfy their own unmet needs. Unconsciously, they're allowing their natural love of their children to swell until it fills the empty spaces in their lives.

Acknowledging the Pleasures of Parenting

Exactly when does a parent's natural affection for a child turn into emotional incest? It's hard to say, because all parents derive some degree of comfort and satisfaction from their children. Parenting is never a totally thankless task. If it were, the human race would have vanished long ago. No one could put up with the late-night feedings, the dirty diapers, the incessant crying, and the constant need for attention if there was nothing to gain from the relationship.

One of the hidden joys of parenting is a simple one: increased physical contact. There is no feeling that can compare to that of your newborn lying warm and content in your arms. The softness of the baby's hair and the creaminess of his skin invite constant touching. The baby thrives on this physical contact, and so do you. As your children grow older, the physical affection continues. You rock your children to sleep, kiss them good-night, hold their hands as they cross the street, hug them as they leave for school, snuggle next to them on the couch. A woman told me that one of the hardest times in her life was when her son turned 12 and no longer wanted to be touched. "My arms would ache for wanting to hug him," she said. At that point, it wasn't the son who was missing the contact, it was the mother.

Another benefit of parenting is increased intimacy. At first, a child's ability to communicate is fairly primitive: "Read to me! Listen to me! Pick me up! Rock me to sleep! Watch me! Feed me!" But when the child reaches 6 or 7, you begin to have thoughtful conversations. You share daily happenings and ponder universal truths. By the time your child is a teenager, your interaction can be almost as enriching and stimulating as it is with an adult. Being a parent has stretched your ability to be intimate, increased your safe harbor from the world, deepened your vital connection with other human beings.

Something else parents gain from their children—and this may seem a bit self-serving—is unconditional love. Children love their parents regardless of what they do. Their need for attachment is so great that they can make a banquet out of crumbs. Imagine this typical scene: A man drags himself home after a hard day at work. He's lost a key client, and his frantic efforts to contain the damage have made him an hour late for dinner. When he gets home, his wife gives him a peck on the cheek and chides him for ruining supper. His 4-year-old daughter, however, gives him a much warmer reception. She vaults across the room, leaps into his arms, and smothers him with kisses. "Daddy's home! Daddy's home!" His late arrival has only heightened her anticipation. Who can blame a parent for reveling in this devotion?

Children can also be a source of pride. I am always pleased when people tell me my children are attractive or well-behaved or talented. Whether I like to admit it or not, there are times when I perceive them as a reflection of my self-worth. This mirroring phenomenon is universal. At any student recital, the spotlight may be on the children, but the faces of the parents are lit up with reflected glory.

✿ Keeping Parental Love within Bounds

When you add to the many pleasures of parenting our inherent drive to nurture our young, the parent-child bond becomes a very strong ✓ one indeed. Marriages crumble. Friendships wither. But children are with you for life. This love is so intense, in fact, that it takes offsetting forces to keep it in line. It is only when parents have other sources of love and intimacy and other interests in life that their love for their children stays within bounds.

A friend of mine, a family therapist named Helena, reminds me of how all-encompassing motherhood can be. When I first met Helena, she was childless by choice. She had a good marriage and a thriving private practice. Her life was full and complete without children. Then she accidentally became pregnant. At first she was apprehensive about all the changes a baby would bring into her well-ordered life. How was she going to find the time and energy to devote to a child? Who was going to fill in for her in her practice? How were they going to live on only one income?

But as her womb started to swell, she began to think more positively about motherhood. When her daughter, Theresa, was born, it was as if she had died and gone to heaven. "I had no idea how much I could love this child," she told me. Instead of cutting back on the number of clients she saw, she closed her practice altogether. The thought of handing Theresa over to a babysitter seemed one step short of child abuse. Now when we go to lunch, it's not psychotherapy we talk about—it's Theresa and her latest accomplishments.

I see nothing wrong with Helena's infatuation with Theresa. In fact, it gives me a lot of pleasure to see her so taken with motherhood. The reason I'm not worried is that Helena has a good relationship with her husband, and her husband has a strong interest in the baby; love moves freely among all three members of the family. Also, Helena has a lot of interests other than parenting. She may be a full-time mother now, but she plans to resume her practice when Theresa is old enough to go to school. Finally, Helena's background in family therapy gives her a definite advantage: she knows that a strong marriage relationship is the foundation for a healthy family, so she is careful to nurture her marriage as well as her child. I doubt that Helena will ever turn to Theresa for emotional support.

❈ A Lack of Love, Information, and Role Models

Many parents have a lot fewer resources than my friend Helena. They are single or are trapped in unfulfilling marriages, and they go through their lives feeling lonely and unloved. The intimacy they share with their children may be the one bright spot in their lives.

Furthermore, few parents have much information about healthy family functioning. They aren't clear about the emotional needs of children, and they haven't learned the all-important difference between parenting and partnering. When I lecture on the roles and responsibilities of marriage partners—discussed in detail in chapter 7—people always pay close attention. They pick up their pens and take notes, because what I am telling them is new information. Somehow, the facts about healthy love relationships have been left out of our curriculum.

When I married for the first time, I too was woefully ignorant about family relationships. I viewed the marriage relationship as a brief hiatus between courtship and parenthood. I thought that as soon as the first baby was conceived, the husband and wife were supposed to spin a domestic cocoon and metamorphose into mother and father.

My naïveté can be explained partly by the fact that I, like so many people, grew up in a dysfunctional family. When I left home and got married, I had no idea how to "spouse." How do husbands and wives treat each other when they're sober? How do they show respect for each other? How do they resolve conflicts without yelling and fighting? What do they say to each other over breakfast when they don't have hangovers?

Without a workable model of family life, I cast about for alternatives, and the TV was a potent source of information. Unfortunately, the programs I watched growing up in the 1950s did more harm than good. One of the fallacies I absorbed was that being a parent was more important than being a husband or wife. Remember *Leave It to Beaver* and *Father Knows Best*? In both of these shows, supposed models of family life, parenting was the primary focus. June never said to Ward, "Honey, let's talk about our relationship." It was always, "Ward, I'm worried about the Beav." And if Father *really* had known best, he would have spent more time with Margaret and less time with Betty, Bud, and Kathy. Remember *Fury*? In this father-son-horse triangle, there was no room whatsoever for Mom; she'd been written out of the script. And in *Bonanza*, the scriptwriters disposed of four wives, not one. For all those years, it was just Ben and the boys. It's no wonder that Adam, Hoss, and Little Joe had so many problems with women: when a parent-child bond is as strong as it was on the Ponderosa, there is no room for lasting love interests.

Ultimately, what I saw on TV confirmed what I was learning at home: the really vital connection is the one between parent and child. A lot of my clients seem to have absorbed this message. A couple who came to me for therapy were overly engrossed in their little girl. There were numerous warning signs: they had gone deeply into debt to purchase a home in a good school district so she would have the best possible education; they both volunteered every week at Anna's school; they gave her expensive private lessons; and every year they threw the best and biggest birthday party in Texas—and believe me, that is BIG (they hired magicians and clowns, ordered two-foot-high cakes, and handed out such elaborate party favors all the other kids thought it was their birthdays as well). Society rewards and sanctions a close relationship between parent and child, so most people who knew them regarded them as model parents.

But the signs of obsessive interest were there to be seen. When Anna was invited to other children's birthday parties, for example, one or both parents were always in attendance—even when she was 9 and 10 years old. "It's easier to hang around than drive all the way back home," they explained. Anna wasn't allowed to go to camp or stay overnight at a friend's house. "She doesn't sleep well away from home," was the explanation. When the parents were invited to social functions, Anna always accompanied them. Once they were invited to a formal dinner for university professors. Instead of hiring a babysitter like all the other parents, they dressed 3-year-old Anna in a long gown and brought her along. Throughout the interminable speeches, Anna sat quietly at her place playing with dolls. Everyone oohed and aahed over her, but I knew something the other guests didn't know: her parents would have been lost without her; Anna was the kingpin that held their marriage together.

Much of my work as a family therapist is devoted to helping couples like this make their marriage relationship more of a priority. By and large, it's an uphill battle. Many parents feel guilty when they hire a babysitter and steal a few hours together to go out to dinner and a movie. When it comes to allocating funds, they perpetually shortchange themselves: they send their kids to private schools and dress them in designer clothes, but they don't set aside enough money to get away by themselves for a weekend. Without realizing it, they are systematically undermining their marriages.

❀ A Lack of Self-Awareness

So far in this chapter, I've mentioned two factors that can transform a parent's natural love for a child into emotional incest: a lack of a strong marriage relationship and a lack of good information about healthy family life. Now I want to add a third factor: a lack of self-awareness. Many people become enmeshed with their children because they fail to see their own lives objectively. They don't see to what extent they are siphoning off their energy to their children. Oh, how clearly they see the mistakes other people are making! But when the curtains are drawn around their own living rooms, they suddenly lose perspective. Ways of relating that seem way out of line to others feel normal—even desirable—to them. If they were able to penetrate their denial and see exactly what they were doing, they might make some immediate changes.

I worked for two years with Helen. For twelve years, Helen was totally dependent on her son, Mathew, for love and support, but she was completely unaware of it. In fact, she considered herself an ideal mother. Her story provides a good example of how oblivious parents can be to their excessive involvement.

Like many women, Helen quit work when her baby was born so she could stay home to take care of him. Her husband, Allan, had a good job and was able to support the family on his salary alone. "I wasn't going to farm Mathew out to someone else," Helen told me. "Why have children if you're not going to go to the trouble to raise them?" She was determined not to make the mistakes others had made. "My friends seemed to ignore their babies. They would plop them down on the floor and let them play by themselves as long as they didn't cry. It seemed heartless to me. I would yearn to pick up their babies and cuddle them." Helen could not tolerate this much distance between herself and Mathew. "I was always holding him. Always talking to him." Helen didn't view her behavior as excessive; she viewed other parents' behavior as negligent.

One by one, most of Helen's friends went back to work, but she chose to stay home with Mathew. She spent her time dreaming up new educational toys for him, reading to him from Newbery Award–winning books, taking him to the zoo and the science museum, and teaching him how to read and write. She decided not to have another baby because she didn't see how she could give this much energy to a second child. As a result of getting so much of his mother's attention, Mathew became quite precocious. For example, he could read fluently by the age of 5. His brightness reinforced Helen's style of parenting. "I felt sorry for other children," she said.

At first glance, you may see little wrong with this family portrait. Helen was content being a full-time mother, and Mathew was reaping the rewards of her single-minded efforts. But there is something missing. As you may have noticed, so far there has been little mention of Helen's husband, Allan. One of the reasons that Helen had so much time and energy for mothering was that Allan was rarely at home. He was an electronics engineer in a start-up computer company and worked long hours. He came home late at night, long after Mathew was in bed, and often left early the next morning. For most of Mathew's early years, he worked Saturdays, too. In essence, Helen was a single parent. Neither Helen nor Allan minded this arrangement, however. Helen was busy with Mathew; Allan was busy with work. The couple had an amiable relationship and rarely fought or disagreed. Because there was little friction between them, they assumed they had a good marriage.

The first sign that the family was in trouble occurred when Mathew went to kindergarten and had difficulty getting along with other children. The teacher told Helen that Mathew spent most of his free time sitting alone reading books. Knowing what we know about this boy's intense relationship with his mother, his lack of interest in group activities is not surprising. For the first time in his life he was separated from Helen and exposed to a group of young children. He must have felt at sea: Where was his mother? Who were all these little people?

Helen got even more disheartening reports from Mathew's first- and second-grade teachers. Mathew still hadn't learned to be part of the group and had grown critical of the other children. By third grade, his alienation from other children was so pronounced that the principal set up a special conference with a child psychologist. Helen left the meeting convinced that the real problem was not her parenting, as the psychologist had seemed to imply, but the school's inability to challenge Mathew intellectually. A week later she took him out of school and began teaching him at home.

When Mathew was 10, Helen and Allan separated. It wasn't a traumatic separation, because they had been living parallel lives for some time. "To be honest," Helen told me, "it was a relief not to have

Allan around. Matt and I didn't have to adjust to his Sunday reentry into the family every week; we could keep on with our normal routine."

For a year, the mother-son household functioned remarkably well. During the days there were school lessons and music practice (Mathew was taking Suzuki violin lessons, a method that requires intensive parent involvement), and during the evenings there were movies to watch and books to read. Many an evening was spent with the two of them curled up together on the couch, reading books or watching TV.

When Mathew was 11, this tidy little world fell apart. Allan filed for a divorce so that he could marry another woman, and to Helen's surprise he asked for joint custody of Mathew. After much negotiation, the judge awarded primary custody to Helen on the inarguable grounds that she had been the primary caretaker. Allan was allowed to have Mathew on the weekends.

On the Saturday morning of the first weekend Mathew was to stay with his father and stepmother, Helen reluctantly drove Mathew to his father's house. On the way home, she felt anxious. She stopped off to check out some library books and rent a movie to play on the VCR. She was determined to keep herself busy. Saturday seemed long to her, but it passed uneventfully.

When Helen awoke Sunday morning, however, she had a suffocating sense of isolation. The house was so quiet that she could hear her watch tick. Her heart began to race. She got out of bed and wandered around the house in a panic. Her anxiety increased, so she forced herself to go for a walk. When she got back to the house, she was strangely fearful of going inside. She grabbed her purse and her car keys and drove to the nearby shopping mall. The mall didn't open until noon, so she drove around aimlessly for an hour. When the doors of the mall finally opened, she shopped for clothes and went to two movies. She didn't return home until it was time for Mathew to be dropped off.

Helen had another, more severe anxiety attack the next time her son spent the weekend with his father. This time she was so panic-stricken that she drove to the emergency room of the nearest hospital. An intern gave her some medication to calm her down and sent her home with the advice that she see a therapist to get to the root of her anxiety. The next week, Helen came in for counseling.

After a few sessions Helen was able to see what had eluded her for twelve years: she was completely reliant on Mathew for emotional stability. She had no close friends and few outside interests to minimize her intense bond with her son. Over the years, he had become her sole source of emotional support.

Toward the end of our first year of working together, Helen deepened her insight. She began to see that the ferocity of her mothering was in part an attempt to make up for the loneliness of her own upbringing. During one session she said, "My mother was a distant, cool woman. I wasn't going to make the same mistake with Mathew." But Helen realized there was more to it than that. Another day she told me, "In a way, I felt as if I were the baby soaking up my own mothering. I didn't feel lonely or abandoned when I was with him. Every moment I spent with Mathew was a convoluted way to mother myself." What looked to the outside world like devoted parenting was in reality a way to satisfy her own unmet needs for attachment. "I was so blind, so totally blind to what I was doing," she cried in anguish. "Where were the warning signs?"

Helen was not a bad person. She did not knowingly become overinvolved with her son. She just didn't have enough information or objectivity.

The same could be said for most parents who are overinvolved with their children: they wouldn't rely so heavily on a son or daughter if: (1) they knew how harmful it was to the child, and (2) they had some awareness of what they were doing.

I reassure victims of emotional incest who are just beginning to come to terms with the past that they don't have to think ill of their parents. It's possible to understand what happened to them without apportioning blame. Their parents, like all parents, were doing the best they could given the information they had and the options they saw. The root cause of their overreliance on them was not maliciousness or selfishness, but a simple and understandable desire to parent their children and satisfy unmet needs for love and companionship.

🕸 Warning Signs of Emotional Incest

Because the difference between affectionate parenting and emotional incest can be difficult to detect, I have developed a list of behaviors that might indicate a tendency toward overinvolvement with a child. This information may give you added insight into your parent's behavior. If you have children, it might also open your eyes to some potential problem areas in your current family. (Healthy parenting will be more fully discussed in chapter 14.)

1. **Wanting a child soon after marriage.** Unless there are extenuating circumstances (age or health, for example), an overeagerness to start a family may be a clue that one or both partners are uncomfortable with the marriage relationship.

2. **Nursing a baby into the toddler years.** Behind a woman's desire to give her child a good start in life and a lot of physical closeness may be her own unmet need for nurturing.

3. **Permitting a child to sleep in the adult bed.** In this culture, it's expected that a young child learn to feel comfortable in his or her own bed. A parent who encourages a "family bed" may unwittingly be encouraging the child's dependency.

4. **Teaching a child at home.** Parents who take their children out of school and teach them at home may be trying to maintain an exclusive relationship, or, like the woman in the last example, trying to hide the fact that their children do not get along well with their peers.

5. **A reluctance to hire babysitters.** Many parents mask their overinvolvement with a child by claiming they can't find acceptable babysitters. They put so many restrictions on suitable childcare that they wind up being the only ones qualified for the job.

6. **A reluctance to let a child spend a night with a friend or go to summer camp.** Going on overnights and camping trips away from the parent is a natural way for a child to start separating from a parent. A parent who discourages this may be trying to delay this healthy stage of development.

7. **Feeling unusually distraught that a child will be leaving home.** It's normal to miss a young adult child when he or she leaves home, but getting depressed about it months or years in advance is often a sign of overdependency.

8. **Setting more restrictions on a child's activities than is common with other parents.** In the guise of being worried about the child's safety, health, or social development, the overinvolved parent may set too many limits on a child's activities. As a result, the child spends too much time at home.

9. **Resenting the time a child spends with friends.** In a healthy family system, the child is encouraged to have a lot of friends. An overinvolved parent may cut down on this interaction or make the child feel guilty for spending time with peers.

10. **Devoting a great deal of time to the development of a child's talents.** A parent who spends hours each day helping a child with his homework, music lessons, or sports activities may be frustrating the child's natural movement toward independence.

It's important to note that any one of these circumstances in itself does not constitute emotional incest. But when a parent displays several of these behaviors and the behaviors are coupled with a lack of a satisfying spousal relationship, the chances are good that the parent and child are enmeshed.

6

Identifying
Families
at Risk

❀

Emotional incest may be a new term, but it's certainly not a new phenomenon. As far back as 700 B.C., the Greek playwright Sophocles was exploring the nuances of obsessive parent-child relationships in his timeless play *Electra*. Electra's extreme attachment to her deceased father and her intense hatred of her mother is a textbook example of emotional incest.

In looking back on our best-known fairy tales, I am amazed at how many of them draw their potency from parent-child alliances. If our fairy tales were stripped of all stories based on kings who try to hold on to their daughters by assigning impossible tasks to their suitors; daughters who choose to stay at home with Daddy, eschewing all the men who come to claim their hand in marriage; and stepmothers who are jealous of their comely stepdaughters, we would have little to read to our children at night.

Emotional Incest and
the Single-Parent Family

In recent years, changes in the way we live have caused a dramatic rise in the incidence of emotional incest. One of the most significant changes has been the unprecedented rise in the number of single-parent families. Currently, one out of every four children (23.9 percent) is being raised by a single parent, and it has been predicted that one out of every two children will live in a single-parent household for some period of time before the age of 18.[1]

When children live in a single-parent household, conditions are ripe for emotional incest, because it takes a strong-willed adult *not* to rely on the ready comfort of a child—especially during the tumultuous years following a divorce. During this trying time, the adult needs a lot of support, but jumping into a new love relationship often feels premature. I have heard many newly divorced people say, "The last thing I want right now is another partner. It's going to be a long time before I am ready to date—let alone get serious with someone." It takes time to recuperate from the trauma of divorce. Meanwhile, a child makes a safe and convenient companion.

The mechanics of running a single-parent household can further contribute to emotional incest. Without a spouse, the single parent is burdened with all the parenting duties and household chores, which leaves little time for entertainment. It's not easy to cultivate friends when you're working all day and halfway into the night—especially when your kids are young and leaving the house means hiring a babysitter. By default, a child becomes a primary form of social contact.

Some single parents try to solve the time and energy crunch by asking the children to do more chores, and many children respond well to the added responsibilities—as long as they are given added privileges and status; they enjoy feeling more "adult." But when a child takes over the responsibilities of the former spouse, the all-important boundary between parents and children begins to blur.

Lack of money, a common denominator of many single-parent households, is another contributing factor. When funds are limited, so are options. With little extra money it's difficult for the single parent to travel, date, take classes, or get involved in a sport or hobby. Emotionally drained, physically exhausted, and financially strapped, the single parent finds that the expedient solution is to stay at home with the child. Without realizing it, the parent turns to the child as the primary source of emotional support.

Children can become enmeshed with the noncustodial parent just as easily as with the custodial parent. In some instances, the noncustodial parent and child were enmeshed before the divorce; custody arrangements do not necessarily conform with existing parent-child alliances. But quite frequently, the close attachment arises after the divorce as a result of the "Disneyland Dad Syndrome," the tendency of parents to go overboard in their desire to make the most of their limited time with their children.

Typically, Disneyland Dads (or Moms) cater to their children's whims by taking them to movies, concerts, and sporting events. They court the children's favor—and assuage their own guilt—by offering them money or gifts. Fearful of spoiling a good time, they are slow to discipline, relegating this unpleasant task to the custodial parent. All of this makes it easy for the child to idealize the noncustodial parent: "But Daddy lets me do it!" If the noncustodial parent is slow to find adult companionship, enmeshment is the likely outcome.

Few enmeshed single parents, whether custodial or noncustodial, are aware of the degree to which they've come to depend on a child. As we've seen, an emotionally needy parent often has a hard time differentiating between normal parenting and emotional incest. A single father named Albert came to me for counseling because of depression. After several weeks, we were able to pinpoint his problem: he was already mourning the fact that his daughter would be leaving for college, even though her departure was two years away. He found it humiliating to admit he was that dependent on her, but when the facts were laid out in front of him, he couldn't deny it. Here's what he was forced to acknowledge: (1) he had been single for seven years and had not dated anyone all that time; (2) he was monopolizing most of his daughter's free time; (3) he was jealous of her friends, whether male or female; (4) once, she had spent the weekend with a girlfriend, and he had retaliated by giving her the silent treatment for an entire week.

Even though Albert finally awakened to the fact that he had an overly close relationship with his daughter, he found it difficult to do anything about it. He was a shy man. His wife was the only person he had ever dated, and the thought of entering the dating scene at age 45 overwhelmed him. We talked over his options, and he decided that he would have to force himself to become more socially involved. He agreed to join a singles' group at a nearby church, but it took him three months to summon enough self-confidence to follow through with this decision.

When children see that a single parent has so few resources, they often feel responsible for the parent's happiness. One teenage son felt so sorry for his newly divorced mother that he stayed home almost every weekend. The few times he went out on dates, he felt terribly guilty. He didn't realize until later in life to what degree he associated women with guilt and responsibility.

❀ Emotional Incest and the Stepfamily

Emotional incest is endemic in stepfamilies, another rapidly growing segment of the population. This is not surprising, because most parents who remarry have been single for some period of time and are likely to have become overly reliant on a child. This secret parent-child alliance is then transported into the new marriage, often producing immediate fireworks. One client told me that on the evening of her wedding, her 15-year-old stepdaughter took her aside and delivered a loaded message: "Daddy and I have a very special relationship, and we have been together a long, long time." My client reported that the way the girl looked at her made her feel as if a loaded gun were being pointed at her head. She could almost hear the trigger being cocked.

When the stepfamily turns into warring factions, it is not uncommon for the biological parent to have a double alliance, one with the new spouse, the other with the child. At first, the new spouse is likely to win out. As long as the parent is "in love," there is little need to rely on a child. But in many instances the parent-child alliance, which is older and stronger, eventually triumphs. This same woman recalls a heated argument with her husband two years after the wedding. At one point she yelled at him, "You always give in to your daughter! She has you wrapped around her little finger! She means more to you than I do!" The man broke down into tears. "When everyone else deserted me," he sobbed, "my daughter was always there. My wife left me. Our friends sided with my wife. My parents died. But my daughter was always there." Shortly thereafter, the marriage dissolved, and the father and daughter resumed their exclusive partnership.

In some stepfamilies, the children live first with one biological parent, then the other, going from household to household in search of happiness. This coming and going tends to destabilize both families, which adds to the likelihood of enmeshment.

I once worked with a stepfamily that had just such a swinging-door policy of child custody. I often felt I had to take notes to keep track of the children's whereabouts. (You may have the same feeling as you read this account. If your head starts swimming, you will have some inkling of what it's like to live in an enmeshed stepfamily.) Isabelle and Bill had two teenage boys, Rex and Jimmy. Both parents favored their older son, Rex, a handsome and outgoing boy. When they divorced, it was decided that Rex was to live with his father. Jimmy, the Left-Out Child, stayed with Isabelle and her second husband, Arendt.

Problems soon developed when Bill began treating Rex more like a buddy than a son. He told the 15-year-old boy all about his sexual escapades, brought his lovers home to the house, and allowed his son to drink beer and stay out all night. Not surprisingly, Rex's grades and attitude reflected this free-spirited lifestyle.

It wasn't long before Isabelle put a stop to the matter by insisting that Rex come back home and live with her. She wasn't going to have her favorite son living in what amounted to a swinging bachelor's pad. However, Rex's return caused problems with his younger brother, Jimmy, who had been enjoying the luxury of having his mother's full attention for the first time in his life. The rivalry between the two boys was so intense that the father, Bill, invited Jimmy to come live with him. By now Bill had remarried and, perhaps because of the temporizing effect of his second wife, was a much better parent to his younger son than he had been to Rex. The threesome got along quite well.

Meanwhile, Isabelle started having problems with Rex, the Chosen Child, who was rebelling against his mother's attempts to rein him in. Ironically, for fear of alienating him, she acquiesced to his demands and started granting him the same kind of liberties he had enjoyed with his father. This infuriated her second husband, Arendt, who was jealous of Isabelle's intense involvement with Rex and justifiably angry at her unwillingness to discipline him. Soon, Isabelle's second marriage was on the rocks.

Part of my job as a therapist was to point out that when there is frequent kid-swapping, children rarely experience consistent love and discipline. I urged Isabelle and Bill to come up with a stable plan for child custody. The bulk of my job, however, was to help Isabelle see that she needed to be more of a parent to Rex and more of a wife to Arendt. Her roles were confused—she paid more attention to her son than to her husband. Unless she redefined her priorities, a second divorce was likely.

❧ The Only Child

One-child families have a higher than normal incidence of emotional incest. With no other child to dilute the intensity of the parent-child bond, the only child stands out in bold relief. Said a mother of an only child: "When you have three children, and one of them has his elbows on the table, it's likely to go unnoticed. A brother or sister is probably doing something far worse. But if you have only one child, both parents are going to jump on him at once." And it's not just table manners that invite this scrutiny—everything about the only child is watched closely, including his health, physical development, school performance, talents, weaknesses, and achievements. This can turn parenting into an obsession.

Another contributing factor in the one-child family is that all the parents' worries and wishes and dreams are channeled into one offspring. In large families, expectations can be parceled out: "Child 1, you be the achiever; Child 2, you be the athlete; Child 3, you be the artist." The only child has to be all things to both parents. "I was told I could do anything," complained an only child, "and I experienced that as a direct order. I was supposed to excel at everything that was laid in front of me."

The lack of in-house playmates further heightens the bond between parent and only child. With no brothers or sisters, the only child may spend hours a day alone with the parent. As a result of all this adult interaction, the only child can become an articulate, surprisingly mature little person. This pseudo-maturity tends to make the only child a favorite of teachers and produce dramatically high scores on achievement tests, but it wreaks havoc with peers. It is not uncommon for only children to: (1) bemoan the immaturity of playmates, (2) reject them, or (3) be rejected by them. This makes the child even more reliant on adults for companionship, increasing the likelihood of emotional incest.

In some families, both parents become enmeshed with the only child. One of the most bitter divorces I ever witnessed was between a husband and wife who were both seeking custody of their only son. Months before the divorce they began "courting" the 11-year-old boy, trying to win his allegiance. Once the divorce proceedings got under way, the competition turned vicious. The mother fabricated a sexual-abuse charge against the father, and the father trumped up a charge of drug addiction against the mother. During the long, drawn-out proceedings, the boy was hospitalized for asthma, perhaps because he had no room to breathe.

🕸 Substance Abuse and Emotional Incest

Alcoholism and drug addiction have become a tragic fact of life in American society. Substance abuse dramatically increases the likelihood of emotional incest because it creates a void in the marriage relationship. A person who has an alcohol or drug problem cannot be a satisfactory marriage partner, because the bottle or the pills or the needle always gets in the way.

The problem is compounded as the addiction progresses and the adult begins to withdraw from co-workers and friends. Then the family is not only fractured internally, it's detached from the larger community. With few outside resources and a sham of a marriage, many addicted adults and/or their beleaguered spouses turn to the one ever-present source of need gratification: a child.

I believe I am uniquely qualified to talk about this subject, not only because of my training in substance abuse but because I come from a family of alcoholics. My mother, my father, my stepfather, my grandmother, my grandfather, and my stepgrandfather were all hard-core drinkers. My mother died from the disease at 45 years of age. I don't believe she would have relied on me so heavily if it hadn't been for her excessive drinking, which destroyed two marriages and made it impossible for her to hold on to challenging work outside the home.

One of my most haunting memories about my mother's drinking comes from the time when I was about 9 years old. To me, it's a clear example of how alcoholism contributes to a parent's reliance on a child. My mother and I were visiting her mother and stepfather in Cleveland. One night, all three adults were drunk and, as usual, a fight erupted. I was awakened by the sound of angry voices. Soon my mother burst into the room and told me to get up and get dressed. She threw our things into a suitcase and told me we were leaving. We walked to the Greyhound bus station, more than a mile, my mother weaving unsteadily. It was winter, and I remember being freezing cold.

When we got to the station, my mother wired a friend for money so she could buy us tickets home. We sat on a couch inside the women's restroom waiting for the money to arrive. It wasn't long before my inebriated mother stretched herself out on the couch and was fast asleep. I, however, was wide awake. A sign above my mother's head said, NO LOITERING. NO SLEEPING. I wasn't sure what *loitering* meant, but I thought it had something to do with not being busy. In desperation, I reached for my mother's purse and began sorting through it so I wouldn't be breaking the rules. I arranged it and rearranged it for what seemed like hours. At one point, a maid came into the restroom and looked over at my mother. "Do you know her?" she asked. "She's my mother," I said. The maid gave me a sympathetic look: it should have been me asleep on the couch, not my mother.

Alcohol was my mother's primary relationship. It was more important to her than being a mother, more important than being a wife. It winnowed her resources to the point where I was the only person she could count on to accompany her on her long journey down into alcoholism.

▓ Mental Illness as a Contributing Cause

Mental illness, like alcoholism, creates a void in the family, making it more likely that one or both parents will turn to a child for companionship. Angelica, a Chosen Child, grew up with a manic-depressive mother. During the many years her mother was emotionally unstable, her father relied on her. Too principled to divorce his troubled wife, he found comfort in Angelica.

For the most part, Angelica's mother's problems occurred during the manic swing of the pendulum, when she would become agitated and unpredictable. Angelica told me about an incident that took place when she was about 11 years old and her mother was driving her home from a shopping expedition in Chicago. Suddenly, her mother slammed on the brakes and jumped out into the middle of a busy intersection. To Angelica's horror, she began cavorting in the street and singing at the top of her voice, "We are the Presbyterian Prancers." People honked their horns and laughed, enjoying the spectacle. Eventually, a policeman drove up and told Angelica's mother to get back in the car and drive home. She refused to listen. Angelica got out of the car, took her mother's hand, and coaxed her back to the driver's seat. She kept saying to her, "We've got to go, Mom. We've got to go." After what seemed like an eternity, her mother pulled herself together enough to drive home.

As outbursts like this became more common, Angelica and her father formed a united front to ward off the woman's encroaching insanity. They created a zone of safety in a crazy, unpredictable world. By the time Angelica was in high school, she and her father were operating as if they alone lived in the house. Once, when Angelica's mother was in a mental hospital for an extended stay, they completely redecorated the house, acting for all the world like a celibate husband and wife.

🎴 The Superchild Syndrome

As families become smaller and couples wait longer to have children, we are seeing the rise of a new phenomenon: the Superchild. This is the child whose conception was orchestrated by basal temperature readings, whose sex was revealed by amniocentesis, who listened to classical music in utero, who at birth was put on a waiting list for private preschool, and who was instructed in linguistics, dance, the martial arts, gymnastics, reading, voice, music, soccer, and/or a foreign language before the age of 6.

A parent who is intent on creating a Superchild is in reality trying to meet his or her own needs, for it is not to the child's benefit to be rushed from one enriching experience to the next. A little girl or boy who is constantly being tutored and entertained doesn't have time to be a child. I almost made this mistake with my daughter. When she was 8 years old, I had her in church choir, Sunday school, a youth group, and gymnastics. When I then wanted to add Brownie Scouts to her crowded roster, she said to me, "If I do that, I won't have time to play." Fortunately, I saw the wisdom in her comment and became a more relaxed mother.

In addition to being deprived of "down time," the Superchild is often given the unmistakable message that self-worth is equated with performance. If I am worthwhile when I excel at a piano recital, am I worthless when I make a mistake? A single parent I know drives thirty-five miles three times a week to take her daughter, Lisle, to ballet lessons—lessons she had to talk her daughter into taking. When I expressed to her my sympathy about how much time she had to spend in the car, she replied, within her daughter's hearing: "I don't want Lisle to have chunky muscles like I do. I want them to be long and stretched out. It's worth the trouble." If Lisle grows up to have short, stocky limbs like her mother—which is likely, given her genetic makeup—won't she feel like a failure? When a parent transfers his or her unmet needs to a child, the child pays the price. The consequences may be self-destructive perfectionism, low self-esteem, and burn-out—yes, even in young children.

✄ Other Families at Risk

Two more families that demonstrate a greater risk for emotional incest are the two-career family and the workaholic family. Why should they be more vulnerable to the syndrome? In a two-career family, there is no one at home to manage the day-to-day affairs of the household. The adults plunge into housework and parenting duties as soon as they come home from work, and weekends are devoted to an enervating game of catch-up. Because time and energy are at a premium, the adults must choose between spending time with each other or nurturing the children. Many make what appears to be the right decision and devote themselves to the children. Unfortunately, this leaves them little time to spend together as a couple, which slowly drains their reservoir of good feelings. Unwittingly, they may rely on their children to replenish their sense of well-being.

Families with a workaholic parent have a different liability. When one spouse is married to a job, the other spouse has to function as a single parent. Resentful of the lack of companionship and burdened by all the household and parenting responsibilities, the left-at-home spouse is likely to be depressed and angry. With many of the disadvantages of being single and without the permission to explore other love relationships, the left-at-home spouse frequently becomes enmeshed with a child.

When families have more than one of the contributing factors mentioned in this chapter—and many do—the probability of emotional incest greatly increases. For example, it is not uncommon for a single parent to have only one child. The one-parent, one-child household is an ideal setup for emotional incest, because neither the parent nor the child has a suitable companion; they are thrown together by default. Two other contributing factors that often go hand in hand are workaholism and excessive drinking: it's not unusual for a weary, overworked adult to reach for a bottle of booze to speed decompression after a hectic day's work. Pressured from work and numbed by alcohol, the parent is an unsuitable marriage partner, and there is a good possibility that one or both adults will turn to a child for the missing support.

It is vital that families at risk have a firm but flexible set of guidelines to follow. They need to make a clear distinction between what it means to be an affectionate, caring parent and what it means to be emotionally dependent on a child, and this distinction must be constantly reinforced. Doing what seems easiest or most natural is rarely the best solution. In most instances, emotional incest is the easy way out. Becoming enmeshed with a son or daughter is an expedient way for an adult to find love and companionship. Until now there has been no taboo against excessive intimacy, no publicly recognized name for the syndrome, and little to discourage the inappropriate bond. As a result, the boundary between parent and child is frequently violated, and every member of the family pays a price.

7

Key Differences Between Enmeshed and Healthy Families

❀

A chalkboard is an indispensable piece of equipment in my office. With virtually every client, I make it a point to draw on the chalkboard a diagram of a functional family—a family that meets the needs of all its members. Then I describe this model family in some detail. Invariably, my clients find the information helpful. Despite all the rash of self-help books in recent years, there has been precious little information about healthy family life. Much of the emphasis has been on what goes wrong.

In one instance, conveying this information came close to being a miracle cure, something rarely seen in my profession. One of my clients, a single mother with parenting problems, watched with more than the usual interest as I sketched out the boundaries of a healthy family. I drew symbols for the parents and children, then separated the two generations by a dashed line. I explained that the dashed line represented a permeable barrier, one that allowed occasional forays over the line (such as when a father and daughter develop a mutual interest in skiing) but for the most part kept parents and children on two separate planes.

As my client listened to my description, a look of comprehension dawned in her eyes. "*That*'s what was wrong with my family!"

she said. "There was no line between me and my father. We were on the same level." She was quiet for a moment. Then she added with a voice filled with regret, "And that's what's wrong with my family today. I've turned my son into a friend. No wonder I have problems controlling him. We live on the same plane." Seeing that parents and children should operate in two different realms was all she needed to understand what had been wrong with her relationship with her father and to begin to realign her relationship with her son. It was a crucial piece of information.

In developing my model of a healthy family, I relied to some extent on the extensive research of family therapist Salvador Minuchin. One of his key observations is the one I just mentioned: in healthy families, there is a clear separation between adults and children. Whether the family has one or two parents and regardless of the number of assorted relatives living under one roof, the adults and children are kept apart by an invisible boundary. This boundary can be likened to a one-way valve. It allows the adults to meet the needs of the children, but it prevents the children from meeting the needs of the adults. Although love and affection flow freely in both directions, the children are not allowed to become part of the adult support system.

To better understand family dynamics, Minuchin has further divided the family into three subgroups: (1) the "spousal unit," which refers to the husband and wife team, (2) the "parental unit," which refers to the caretakers of the children, and (3) the "sibling unit," which refers to the children. Although these terms may seem unwieldy at first, looking at your family of origin in terms of these three subgroups may give you a better understanding of how the system went awry.

The remainder of this chapter is a description of the roles and responsibilities of these three family subgroups. The first paragraph in each section describes a healthy family system; the second paragraph is a contrasting description of an enmeshed family. As you read each section, ask yourself which description best matches the family in which you were raised, the healthy model or the dysfunctional one. (This first part discusses a two-parent household. Comments on single-parent households follow.)

❀ The Spousal Unit: Roles and Responsibilities of Adult Partners

1. **The adult partners respect and support each other.** In a healthy family system, the two partners are "best friends." They are genuinely interested in each other and show this interest on a daily basis. They count on each other when the going gets rough, and they consider each other a buffer against the outside world. They greet each other warmly after a hard day and can say, "I need some sympathy," or, "I need a backrub." They freely share their dreams, their successes, and their frustrations.

In an enmeshed family system, there may be a lack of respect and intimacy between the adult partners. Energy that should be staying within the relationship is diverted to other members of the family, outside activities, or addictive behaviors. In some cases there is open hostility between the adults.

2. **The partners nurture each other.** In a healthy family system, the adult partners take care of each other. They offer encouragement, support, and affirmation. They make each other feel loved and respected. They give each other special privileges and surprises. Hugs, kisses, and nonsexual touching are common forms of nurturing. If one of the partners is sick or disabled, the other gladly lends a helping hand.

In the enmeshed family, children are the main source of affirmation and affection for the adults. Hugs, kisses, and touching are reserved for children, not adults. The adult partners expend little effort making each other feel safe, loved, and appreciated. Insults, slights, or put-downs may be more common than loving affirmations.

3. **The partners practice tolerance.** Happy couples understand that living together requires tolerance and compromise, which helps them overlook benign personality quirks and respect each other's individuality. They are not threatened by each other's need for individual time and space. Mistakes are taken as a part of life, and apologies are freely given and received. The partners have a realistic

view of marriage and are prepared for the fact that there will be boring or difficult periods to endure.

In the enmeshed family, there is little tolerance for differences. Rules are either absent or rigid, leaving little room for mistakes or alternate views. A partner's habits may be under close scrutiny, with little leeway for personal idiosyncrasies. Partners "keep score," and grudges may be harbored for years. An overly romantic view of marriage may be superimposed upon this disheartening relationship, further magnifying its shortcomings.

4. **The partners have fun together.** In a healthy family, the adult partners engage in activities that both individuals enjoy, ranging from passive games such as bridge to physically demanding sports such as tennis. The adults have a shared sense of humor. The more fun they have together, the more spontaneous they become. This spontaneity adds a spark to their relationship and keeps romantic love alive.

In dysfunctional families, there is often little pleasure to be found in the marriage relationship. Instead, the adults become overly reliant on their children, or find stimulation in television, outside activities, drugs, or alcohol.

5. **The adult partners are lovers.** Individuals who are involved in a healthy, primary love relationship delight in their sensuality. They maintain their sexual energy over time by exploring new options, taking risks, and developing different styles of sexual expression. They share intimate details of their sexual relationship only with each other. If any sexual difficulties arise, they work together to resolve them. They adapt their sexual practices to compensate for any changes due to physical ailments, childbearing, aging, or stress.

Dysfunctional couples are often sexually incompatible. One partner may be compulsively sexual, for example, and the other repressed, turning sex into a battleground. A partner may share sexual details with friends, other family members, and children. A child may become the focus of a parent's sensual and sexual expression.

6. **The partners share significant interests.** In a healthy family system, the adult partners have mutual interests and activities. While they do some things apart, they share many interests. They add variety to their lives by going on "dates," taking vacations without the children, and cultivating shared activities. As a result, the children witness a marriage that looks interesting and fulfilling.

Nurturing the marriage relationship is seen as an essential part of positive parenting.

In the unbalanced family, the partners share few activities. Their interests center around work, the children, or activities outside the family. Little effort is made to develop joint projects or to spend time apart from the children. As a result, the children grow up thinking that marriage is no fun and, following the example of their parents, may fail to put energy into their own love relationships.

7. **The partners are confidants.** Partners in a healthy love relationship share their thoughts, feelings, and dreams on a regular basis. They use each other as a sounding board. They maintain an ongoing dialogue about daily life, which strengthens their emotional ties. They freely share their concerns, woes, frustrations, and joys. They plan for the future. This honest, easygoing communication serves as the glue that keeps them together through rough times.

In an enmeshed family, the adults violate the intimacy taboo separating parents from children. They share concerns with their children that don't involve them. They give their children information they're not equipped to handle. They share critical or demeaning remarks about the other parent. This inappropriate sharing burdens the child with adult concerns, impeding the child's emotional growth.

8. **The adults are financial partners.** In a healthy system, the adult partners have a mutually agreeable system for paying bills, making purchases, investing money, and planning for future financial needs. They consult with each other frequently so each is well informed. They have common property. They value each other's contributions to the household, whether the work is inside or outside the home. When money problems arise, they work together to find solutions.

In families that are out of balance, financial matters can become a source of conflict. Quite often, financial resources are distributed unevenly among the children, reflecting parental favoritism. In some families, money may be used as a tool to ensure a child's dependency: "You can have money to go to college if you go to a college close to home." In some families, a child or an in-law may have a strong voice in money matters, intruding into the adult partners' decision-making process.

9. **The adults are each other's primary social partner.** Committed couples attend social functions together, whether it be family re-

unions, weddings, business affairs, church, or school activities. Appearing together at social functions builds common experience and makes a public statement of union and permanence.

In enmeshed households, the husband and wife may avoid adult functions altogether, perhaps relying on the common excuse that there is not adequate child care. When the children are old enough to stay by themselves, this excuse may be replaced by a reluctance to "leave the children alone." Other parents "take turns" going to outside activities, or go together but always include a child. All of these maneuvers may be an attempt to avoid intimacy with the partner.

10. **The adult partners resolve conflicts and work out problems.** In a functional family, the adult partners work together as a team to find solutions to problems. They brainstorm, form strategies, and set goals. This mutual problem-solving develops a sense of shared accomplishment. If the partners have problems within their relationship, they respectfully express their feelings of anger, hurt, fear, or resentment. Each person listens with full attention to the other. Apologies may be necessary, as well as comfort and reassurance.

In a dysfunctional family, problems are either denied or blown out of proportion. Rather than work together to resolve issues, the adult partners may blame each other for the problems. Verbal and physical abuse may be evident. Children are frequently used as scapegoats.

Do you know any marriages that match the first paragraph in each of these ten sections? Does the healthy family model sound too farfetched? As a family therapist, I can assure you that marriages that meet all of these criteria do exist, although they are the exception rather than the rule. When I read a description of a healthy marriage to groups, I can always count on seeing some puzzled expressions and blank stares. One man made this comment: "It sounds to me like you're describing an affair, not a marriage relationship." In a sense he was right, because many people engage in affairs precisely because their marriages don't satisfy some of these needs.

What's important to realize is that when a marriage doesn't live up to this model, *there is the conscious or unconscious wish that it would.* People expect their love relationships to satisfy all their emotional needs, including support, comfort, intimacy, sexual expression, respect, and companionship. If a marriage does not meet these needs, the individuals experience a void in their lives, and the size of the void corresponds to the degree that the relationship diverges from this model. Unless the individuals take steps to improve their relationship or find some other means of adult support, they will be likely candidates for emotional incest.

One fact has been confirmed to me over and over again in my work with families: *people instinctively try to satisfy their emotional needs within the family group.* The family plays a unique role in people's lives. It's an envelope of intimacy that buffers them from the harsh reality of the world. It's a place to be open about their needs and to find love and reassurance. When a marriage partner fails to live up to expectations, many adults automatically and unwittingly turn to a child.

Satisfying the Emotional Needs of the Single Parent

As you read the preceding description of the spousal unit, some of you may have wondered how this information applies to single-parent households. With no partner to turn to for love and support, is it possible to have a healthy family system? Is a single-parent family by definition a dysfunctional one?

It is important to realize that all adults have the same emotional needs, whether they are single or married. They all need intimacy, companionship, some form of sexual expression, intellectual stimulation, and so on. Without a partner to turn to, the single parent must make a conscious effort to satisfy those needs outside the family. If the single parent succeeds in creating a support network of *adult* family members and friends, a perfectly viable family system is created.

Jan is the single parent of three school-age children, two girls and a boy. She has a life that many married people would envy. She thrives on her work as a management consultant, and when she's not working or spending time at home with her children, she can be found kayaking, bike riding, or singing in a choir. To satisfy her need for intimacy and daily companionship, Jan has banded together with two other single mothers. She calls one or the other of them every day just to debrief about the day's happenings, which is the kind of intimate exchange that is usually reserved for marriage relationships. On weekends and holidays, it's not uncommon for all three families to join together under one roof, forming an impromptu extended family. Although Jan is open to the possibility of remarrying, she is in no hurry, because she has managed to satisfy the bulk of her needs as a single parent. (Chapter 13 goes into detail about developing such a support network.)

* * * *

The second family subgroup is the parental unit, which means the father and mother or other nurturing adults. Although the same two individuals may be both partners and parents, the two roles are worlds apart. *Making a clear distinction between them is one of the keys to creating a healthy family.*

I have divided the parenting role into ten separate functions, once again contrasting a model family with a dysfunctional one. As you read the material, think about how well your parents measured up to the healthy model.

✽ The Parental Unit: Roles and Responsibilities of Parents

1. **Functional parents provide food, clothing, shelter, and medical and dental care.** It goes without saying that parents need to provide the basic necessities of life. They are also responsible for enhancing the child's well-being by making sure the food is nutritious, by encouraging the child to get adequate exercise, and by modeling a healthy lifestyle.

In a dysfunctional family, the parents may fail to take care of even the basic needs of the child. This responsibility may be foisted onto the child, making the child overly responsible for his welfare. Many parents further fail in this area by indulging in unhealthy or addictive behaviors, providing poor role models for the children.

2. **Functional parents offer their children adequate protection.** Functional parents protect their children from obvious hazards such as stormy weather, criminals, busy streets, and dangerous animals. They also protect them from more subtle dangers, however, such as information and experiences they are not equipped to handle. To this end, they supervise their children's exposure to the media, they

monitor their children's activities in and away from the home, and they withhold from them any information that might prove damaging.

In an enmeshed family, the adults may be so focused on their own needs that they fail to supervise the children. They expose their children to danger and to information and experiences they are not able to handle. The problem is compounded when the adults share their own worries and concerns with the child.

3. **Functional parents are physically affectionate.** In a healthy family, parents use hugs, pats, and kisses to convey their love just as often as words. They know that touching is vital to the physical and emotional health of the child. Infants who are deprived of physical contact may fail to thrive and may even lose the will to live.

In a dysfunctional family, parents may withhold their affection or, on the other extreme, use their children to satisfy their own unmet needs for physical contact. Some parents go one step further and use a child for sexual stimulation or expression.

4. **Functional parents understand and accept normal stages of child development.** Functional parents have a basic understanding of child development. They know, for example, that a year-old child spills things, cries a lot, and is easily tired. This is age-appropriate behavior, which is freely accepted. Wise parents are also alert to behavior that does *not* fit within normal bounds. If a 10-year-old consistently acts like a 5-year-old, for example, they will not hesitate to seek professional help.

Parents who are enmeshed with a child often fail to ascertain the child's developmental level. They err on one side or the other, expecting either too much or too little. A parent with too-high expectations, for example, might insist that a 3-year-old exhibit a high degree of compassion for others. A parent with too-low expectations might consistently overprotect an older child from the consequences of his or her behavior.

5. **Functional parents take into account each child's age and stage of development when assigning privileges and responsibilities.** Wise parents respect the age differences in the family. This means, for example, that they grant a teenager more privileges and freedom of movement than a grade-school child. A policy of issuing rewards and privileges on an age basis contributes to the well-being of each child. The younger child learns that there are privileges associated

with maturity; the older child feels rewarded for assuming added levels of responsibility. When parents are logical and consistent in the issuing of these privileges, the children are assured of the predictability, order, and fairness of the family system.

When a family system is out of balance, the sibling hierarchy is disrupted. A parent's whims may dictate prestige and privilege rather than the age and capabilities of each child. One child may get extra attention or material rewards, another may be singled out for abuse. When this occurs, children learn to associate rewards not with age or responsibility but with the ability to please or placate a parent.

6. **Functional parents establish clear rules and guidelines.** Limits give children a safe and secure environment in which to grow. The way the limits are determined depends on the circumstances, age, and disposition of the child. For example, wise parents set limits for toddlers by child-proofing the home and distracting them or removing them from dangerous situations. They set limits for older children by offering explanations, presenting clear choices, rewarding good behavior, and devising logical consequences. They set flexible limits for teenagers by invoking the principles of negotiation and compromise.

When a parent and child are "best friends," rules and limits go by the wayside. Many parents of Chosen Children have told me, "I don't set limits because I don't want my child to be mad at me," and, "I make threats, but I don't follow them up." When a child grows up without limits, the child will not have the proper respect for authority and natural hierarchies. She may feel that she's above the law and disobey traffic rules or participate in juvenile crime. She may have difficulty adhering to school rules and regulations. She may have little guilt or remorse associated with these violations, feeling that she can write her own rules. This attitude may carry over to the workplace, making employment difficult except where there is an unusual degree of freedom.

7. **Functional parents validate the child's thoughts and feelings and teach appropriate ways to express them.** Effective parents encourage their children to express their thoughts and feelings. They do this by being attentive, listeners. When necessary, they help their children find appropriate ways to express negative emotions. A good way to do this is by setting a good example, then establishing consistent rules and guidelines. In a functional family, children

learn that they can say what they are thinking and feeling without risking ridicule or undue criticism.

Parents who are enmeshed with their children often negate the child's thoughts and feelings. They reward their children for thinking and feeling the same way they do, or for conforming to an ideal. Through these daily lessons, the child learns to equate intimacy with invasion; they learn that being close to someone invites repression and manipulation.

8. **Functional parents respect and encourage each child's uniqueness.** Ideally, parents make an effort to reinforce the special qualities of each child. To do this, they must be able to see each child as a unique human being, distinct both from themselves and from other children. Then they need to approach the child with a positive, accepting attitude.

When a parent is overinvolved with a child, the parent fails to be objective. The parent may be unaware of key traits in the child, expect the child to mirror his tastes and interests, or insist that the child live up to unrealistically high standards. As a result, the child may experience a great deal of confusion and anger.

9. **In a two-parent household, the parents support each other's authority.** Few parents are in total agreement about how to handle their children. It is important, however, that they publicly support each other. Whenever possible, they negotiate behind the scenes and present a united front to the children. When that is not possible, they support each other's decisions. For example, if one parent issues an edict while the other is away at work, the other parent supports that decision, even if he or she is in disagreement: "I may not have made the same decision as your mother, but I expect you to do what she says."

In a dysfunctional family, the adults may openly disagree about parenting issues. They further complicate matters by involving the children in the conflict. Most children will play the system for all it's worth. They will go to Dad for money, for example, and to Stepmom for permission to stay up late. This maneuvering drives a wedge into the family. In some families, the polarization is extreme. One parent may be overly permissive, the other punishing and restrictive. This degree of dichotomy is devastating to children.

10. **Functional parents encourage their children's independence.** Children start out life totally dependent on their caretakers. By the

time they are old enough to leave the family, they need to be able to make wise decisions, provide for their own safety and well-being, accept responsibility for their actions, and have the social skills to develop a network of supportive friends. Wise parents know that their job is to create a mature young adult who can survive and thrive in a given culture, and they do this by encouraging the child's natural drive toward independence at all stages of development.

Unwittingly, many parents frustrate a child's independence. They do too much for the child, make the child unduly fearful, put too many restrictions on the child's behavior, make the child feel guilty for moving away from the family, or undermine the child's natural abilities. Some children will oblige the parent's efforts to keep them dependent by remaining in close proximity or staying emotionally connected. Others will break away in anger, often in a dramatic fashion. They may move far away and never look back, believing that they have escaped from the enmeshment. But until the basic separation issue is fully resolved, the Chosen Child will bring this unfinished business to other relationships, re-creating the pattern of enmeshment or putting up invisible roadblocks to intimacy.

88 Defining the Crucial Differences Between Parenting and Partnering

Now that you've seen a description of the way adults function in a healthy family system and a dysfunctional one, you may have a better understanding of what went wrong in your family. As you can see, in a healthy family, there is little overlap between the spousal and the parenting roles. In an ideal marriage relationship, the adults nurture and get nurtured, they support and get supported, they confide in each other, they give and seek advice, and they exchange sexual and nonsexual pleasures. It's an intimate, equitable relationship characterized by give and take.

Parenting, by contrast, is largely a selfless task, one that requires a great deal of sacrifice, patience, and self-discipline. The parents offer advice to the child but don't expect any in return. They listen to the child's woes but don't depend upon the child to listen to theirs. They take care of the child's needs but they don't allow the child to feel responsible for their needs. Although there are intrinsic rewards to being a parent, they come on an infrequent basis. When I have a client who professes to "love being a parent," I'm often suspicious. Although loving a child is easy to understand, when someone loves the parenting role itself, I look for clues that the person might be using a child to satisfy unmet emotional needs, which should be met by another adult.

*   *   *   *

Now we come to the third family subgroup, the sibling unit. It may surprise you that in healthy families, brothers and sisters have important roles and functions to perform for each other. As you will see, they operate in a distinct and important sphere.

◷ The Sibling Unit: Roles and Responsibilities of Siblings

1. **Siblings teach each other valuable social skills.** In a healthy family system, brothers and sisters form a social laboratory that teaches them how to get along with peers. They learn about the use and abuse of power, they learn how to make a point, and they learn how to resolve their differences. This is where children learn to give and take. This is where they learn just how far they can go.

When parents treat their children unequally, the system is out of balance. The Left-Out Child may react to the exclusion by being rebellious, by indulging in attention-getting behavior, or by trying too hard to please. The Chosen Child may act superior or saccharine-sweet, capitalizing on the role of the "good child." This exaggerated behavior gets in the way of normal brother-and-sister interactions and intensifies sibling rivalry.

2. **Children form a natural support group.** In a healthy family system, siblings have a support group within the family that is independent of the adults. For example, it is not uncommon for siblings to have information they withhold from their parents. They support each other when confronted by those outside the family. Siblings who get along well identify with each other's successes and go out of their way to pass on valuable skills. When they mature, these positive experiences make it relatively easy for them to participate in group activities and to be team players.

When the sibling unit is disrupted, the children miss out on an important source of support, protection, and information. The children may be antagonistic toward one another and turn ordinary interchanges into competitions. They are deprived of the opportunity to feel "one of a group," and are likely to have difficulty with peer relationships in later years.

3. **Brothers and sisters form a society of near equals.** In the sibling arena, the child has an appropriate frame of reference. The older child gets to feel superior to the younger child, and the younger child has a role model that is not out of reach. This contributes to the child's emerging sense of self.

If a child spends an inordinate amount of time with an adult, the adult becomes the frame of reference. The child will begin to act like an adult and compare himself to adults. This may make the child highly motivated, but it can also contribute to low self-esteem.

4. **Siblings provide a social setting for learning.** The "work" of young children is to develop motor and verbal skills, explore, play, learn, fantasize, create games, and develop a host of other rudimentary skills. A brother or sister relatively close in age can make a good playmate.

When a parent is a child's regular companion, the parent often imposes adult standards. The adult is more likely to be interested in performance, mastery, goal setting, and achievement, which interfere with a child's natural development.

5. **Brothers and sisters help each other develop and refine an accurate personal history.** As siblings grow up, they realize they have a lot in common. They discover that they are united by a common body of experience and by having been raised in the same (or similar) religious, economic, ethnic, and social environment. Talking about the past with a sibling can correct, reinforce, or clarify privately held notions and contribute to a common sense of reality.

Children who are at odds with each other growing up tend to continue the conflict in later years. As adults they will either interact with a lot of hostility or will avoid each other to spare themselves further grief. In either case, they don't have the opportunity to trade notes and share key observations. This can contribute to a sense of isolation and to a one-sided view of the past.

If you were an only child, how did that fact affect your development? Were you deprived of all the benefits that come from having siblings?

It is reassuring to note that many sibling functions can be performed equally well by friends and schoolmates. Children can learn how to share and cooperate with a friend just as with a brother or sister. They can find an appropriate frame of reference at school and in extracurricular activities, not just at home. However, if your parents did not provide you with opportunities to play with friends, or if they frustrated your desire to have friends, you may have missed out on some important opportunities for growth.

✤ Consequences of Living in a Functional versus a Dysfunctional Family

When the three family subgroups—the spousal unit, the parental unit, and the sibling unit—conform to the outline of the healthy family system described in this chapter, every member of the family benefits. When adults have a strong support system, whether from a partner or from friends, they have the energy and emotional stability required to be good parents. Good parents tend to have well-adjusted children who progress along a normal path of development. Such children tend to interact with one another in a more or less positive manner, which means that the parents spend less time intervening in squabbles and have more time to spend with each other—which reinforces the marriage relationship. This in turn makes them better parents. It's an upward spiral that creates a sense of harmony and well-being in adults and children alike.

When the family subgroups break down, on the other hand, every member of the family is adversely affected. When the adults in the family do not have adequate emotional support, they often turn to their children for the satisfaction of their needs. The children suffer in three significant ways: (1) they are deprived of good adult role models, (2) they feel obliged to meet the needs of their parents, and (3) they have to suppress many of their own needs. Children who are burdened in this manner have more trouble relating to their siblings. Some of their anger at their parents is transferred to their brothers and sisters, which can turn minor conflicts into protracted struggles. This discontent in the ranks makes the adults' lives more difficult, adding a source of strain to the marriage relationship that doubles back on the family.

In the first part of this book, you've seen numerous examples of families in crisis. The next chapter, which gives you an overview on healing the wounds of enmeshment, marks a turning point in the book. From then on, I'll be giving you specific advice on how to overcome the emotional problems that result from growing up too close to a parent.

CHECKLIST 2:
Characteristics of the Healthy Family

The following checklist is designed to help you compare your family of origin to the functional and dysfunctional models presented in this chapter. The exercise has three parts. Part A examines your parents' marriage relationship. Part B examines their parenting skills. Part C examines the relationships you had with your siblings. When you are finished with the checklist, you will have a more objective view of the psychological health of your family.

Directions: Circle the number that best describes your family. As in the earlier checklist, you may want to clarify some of your responses. (For example, you may find it helpful to write comments such as, "This was true of my stepmother, not my mother," or "This was true before my father quit drinking.")

Most of the time	Some of the time	Rarely, if ever	Never or does not apply
3	2	1	0

Part A: The Spousal Unit

3	2	1	0	1. My parents had a strong, loving relationship.
3	2	1	0	2. My parents were interested in each other.
3	2	1	0	3. My parents had fun together on a regular basis.
3	2	1	0	4. My parents spent private time together.
3	2	1	0	5. My parents had a healthy sexual relationship.

3	2	1	0	6. My parents treated each other like best friends.
3	2	1	0	7. My parents communicated honestly and directly.
3	2	1	0	8. My parents socialized together.
3	2	1	0	9. My parents resolved conflicts effectively.
3	2	1	0	10. My parents had an effective method of financial planning and action.
3	2	1	0	11. My parents maintained a home in a mutually satisfactory way.
3	2	1	0	12. My parents had mutual interests.
3	2	1	0	13. My parents showed their affection through words, gestures, and deeds.
3	2	1	0	14. My parents seemed willing to compromise.
3	2	1	0	15. My parents were faithful to each other, to the best of my knowledge.

Part B: The Parental Unit

3	2	1	0	1. My parents praised their children.
3	2	1	0	2. My parents respected the uniqueness in each child.
3	2	1	0	3. My parents modeled appropriate behavior for their children.
3	2	1	0	4. My parents gave their children information geared to their age level.
3	2	1	0	5. My parents provided the physical necessities.

3	2	1	0	6. My parents understood and accepted what was normal behavior for children at each age level.
3	2	1	0	7. My parents respected a child's feelings.
3	2	1	0	8. My parents admitted their mistakes and apologized when necessary.
3	2	1	0	9. My parents accepted their children's understandable mistakes.
3	2	1	0	10. My parents expressed their thoughts and feelings in a nonthreatening, nonjudgmental manner.
3	2	1	0	11. My parents set clear rules and limits and reinforced them in a kindly, consistent manner.
3	2	1	0	12. My parents established clear family rules.
3	2	1	0	13. My parents practiced effective, humane forms of discipline.
3	2	1	0	14. My parents spent ample time with the children.

Part C: The Sibling Unit

3	2	1	0	1. The children spent ample time with siblings and/or friends.
3	2	1	0	2. The children had ample time to play and relax.
3	2	1	0	3. The children developed peaceful ways to resolve their conflicts.
3	2	1	0	4. The children had secrets and information not shared with the parents.

3	2	1	0	5. The children turned to one another for support and information.
3	2	1	0	6. The children respected one another.
3	2	1	0	7. The children had their own space where privacy was assured.
3	2	1	0	8. The children tolerated one another's differences.
3	2	1	0	9. The children treated one another kindly a good deal of the time.
3	2	1	0	10. The children could count on one another when they were really needed.

There is no specific number to determine whether you lived in a functional or dysfunctional family, although it's generally true that the higher the score, the healthier the family.

One way to use this questionnaire is to look for major trends. Did the adults in your family function better as partners or as parents? Were you and your siblings on good terms? Was most of the tension between parents and children or between siblings?

You might find it interesting to have a brother or sister take this questionnaire, then compare results.

If you like, take this survey once again, this time using it to gain some clarity on your current family. Are the patterns similar or dissimilar? In which areas has there been some improvement? Which problems (if any) have been carried over to the next generation?

PART TWO

RECOVERY

Defining
the Cure

8

Blazing a Path to Recovery: Follow the Yellow Brick Road

❊❊

In recent years I have counseled more and more people who were raised by Invasive Parents. The majority come to me for help with relationships. Typically, they have in-law problems, marital problems, or parenting problems. Some suffer from anxiety or depression, eating disorders, or problems with drugs or alcohol. Although the reason for the initial appointment may differ from person to person, my clients all share the same goal, which is to relieve their pain. Few are aware of the connection between their current difficulties and their relationship with a parent, and few are thrilled about the prospect of delving into the past. What they want to do is alleviate their symptoms as quickly as possible so that they can get on with life.

Fortunately, my goal in working with people who were enmeshed with parents is precisely the same—to help them overcome their difficulties in the most efficient way possible. But to do this, they need to bring to mind some of the forgotten pain of childhood; there's no way around it. In order to heal the wounds of enmeshment, they need to recall key events from their childhoods and summon up the feelings associated with them. It is in the act of bringing thoughts and feelings to consciousness that growth occurs. To quote author John Gray, "What you feel, you can heal."[1]

A Personal Philosophy of Healing

Before I go into more detail about the recovery program that comprises part 2 of this book, I want to talk for a moment about the psychology of healing, the mechanism by which people repair the emotional damage of childhood. I want to acquaint you with the theoretical underpinnings of the journey upon which you are about to embark.

First, it is my belief (and the belief of many philosophers, theologians, and theoreticians) that human beings are created whole. By this I mean most of us come equipped with fully functioning bodies, exquisitely powerful brains, and a full complement of emotions. There are innate gifts, a genetic endowment perfected over the millennia, which allow us to move toward our greatest potential. But we are also born needy, vulnerable to emotional injury, and 100 percent dependent. In order to survive and thrive, we need consistent nurturing from loving and reliable caretakers. When our parents fail to respond to our needs, or when they misinterpret our needs, we experience psychological wounding.

Tragically, psychological wounding is an inevitable occurrence, because there isn't a parent alive who can adequately respond to all of a child's needs all of the time. And each and every time a need is not satisfied, there is a psychological injury. A child may be lucky and have nurturing, reliable parents, or he may be habitually mistreated and shamed, but to one degree or another, we all go through childhood with unmet needs and struggle most of our adult lives trying to satisfy them.

There were many years when I despaired about this bleak state of affairs. It didn't help that my job as a therapist required me to listen to tales of abuse and neglect day after day. There were times when I drove home from my office consumed with sadness about the fragility of human beings.

One evening, after a stressful series of counseling sessions, I tried to unwind by watching a wildlife documentary on TV. As I watched, I found myself getting irate at the apparent good fortune of other species. The segment of the film that touched off my anger showed a pregnant black bear growling at her 2-year-old cubs and chasing them up a tree. When the cubs were on the uppermost branches, she ambled off into the bushes, never to see them again. Her instincts were telling her it was time to abandon her fat, capable 2-year-olds so that she could devote herself to her unborn cubs. Eventually the cubs clambered down from the tree, grunted for a while, and then went about their business of foraging berries. The narrator assured the viewing audience that despite the mother bear's "inhumane" treatment of her cubs, they were fully able to cope, seemingly inured to the pain of abandonment.

As I watched the interaction between the mother bear and her cubs, I was painfully aware of the marked difference between bears and human beings. A 2-year-old child who is abandoned by a parent won't cry out a few times and then get on with life. He or she is likely to develop a severe neurosis and show up in my office thirty years later wanting help in recovering from a series of failed marriages. Why aren't human beings more resilient? Why are we so frightfully dependent on our caretakers? And why are we dependent for so many years? In my despondent mood, I concluded, that either we should be less vulnerable to emotional injury, or that we should all be assigned perfect parents.

As I look back on that period of my life, I realize that a lot of my anger was about my own suffering. I was railing not only against the human condition but against my own lot in life. I was furious that I had been such a vulnerable little girl and had been raised by such neglectful parents. It wasn't fair. I was tired of dealing with the ramifications of my imperfect childhood day after day, of having a hair trigger around abandonment issues, and of overreacting to everyday events. I was tired of having to be in therapy year after year to mop up the damage that took place so long ago.

In the back of my mind, something else was troubling me as well. I was not only upset by my personal plight but troubled by a vague sense that there must be some positive, counterbalancing force I was overlooking. A part of me refused to believe that we would be created so vulnerable to emotional injury.

Years later, when I stumbled upon the reality of an innate, self-healing capacity, I felt a surge of elation. The world made sense to me once again; the dark forces of evil no longer held sway. I was filled with a new optimism, not only about the state of humanity but about my own journey to recovery.

The revelation came from a helpful source, a book titled *The Theory of Re-Evaluation Counseling*, by Harvey Jackins.[2] What became clear to me after reading this book was that although human beings are born dependent and vulnerable, *they are also born with a spontaneous mechanism for healing*! For every psychological injury, there is an automatic regenerative response.

The reason I had been unaware of this self-healing potential is that it is so easily damaged. By the time most children are 2 or 3 years old, their well-intentioned parents have inadvertently interfered with the process. Without realizing it, they have made their children even more vulnerable to their imperfect parenting.

The Miracle of the Self-Healing Child

So, what is this self-healing process? The best way to find out is to observe very young children. Imagine a 3-year-old boy playing in a sandbox in a crowded park while his father keeps watch nearby. The child is absorbed in play, but every once in a while he glances up to make sure his father is still there. He's old enough to play on his own but young enough to need frequent checking. One time when he looks up, he is startled to discover that his father is nowhere in sight. He scans the area around the sandbox, looking for a familiar face. He doesn't realize that his father is a mere fifty feet away, hidden behind a tree, drinking at a fountain. The little boy starts running around the playground, tears flooding his eyes. Without knowing it, he wanders farther and farther from his father. At one point in his frantic odyssey, he comes face to face with a large dog. He is acutely aware that there is no long-limbed father to scoop him up. He cries out in terror.

By this time the father has discovered his son's disappearance and is frantically searching the playground. He berates himself for leaving his precious little boy unattended for even a few minutes. Fortunately, father and son meet up with each other five minutes later on the opposite side of the park. Greatly relieved, the little boy runs into his father's arms.

This is a common occurrence. It is likely that most children have been separated from a parent for at least five minutes and have come face to face with the terror of abandonment. Now what was underscored for me in Harvey Jackins's book was that whether the little boy will be scarred by the episode or experience only a brief setback depends on what happens in the next few minutes. *If the father allows his son the full and natural expression of his emotions, the boy will quickly recover from his fear. He will go through an automatic, regenerative process.*

First, the boy will be overcome with relief to see his father. More tears may come, brought on by the safety of being in his father's arms. He may sob deeply and cling tightly to his father. Depending on his temperament and verbal ability, he may talk about being lost and the big dog that scared him. He may cry for what seems a long time and be afraid to go back to the sandbox unless his father is willing to play with him.

To the father, the child's reaction is likely to seem excessive. After all, his son was out of his sight for only a few minutes. But a wise father will permit the boy to go through the entire debriefing process. He will hold his son, listen to his expression of fear, acknowledge the reality of his terror, let him cry and talk for as long as he wants to, and comply with his request for extra closeness. He will let his son's instincts determine his response. If the boy is permitted to cycle through this natural progression of emotions— neither stifled nor abetted—he will eventually calm down and go back to the sandbox. The event will pass like a blip on a screen, leaving only a trace of its occurrence.

Now, as simple as it would be to allow the boy full expression of his emotions, few parents would do it. One way or another, they would not allow him to work through his terror of abandonment. He would be negated, blamed, coddled, belittled, or stopped in midstream.

Here are some ways that various types of parents might interfere with the process:

ANGRY, BLAMING PARENT: Why did you wander off like that? You should have stayed put! You are a bad boy for scaring Daddy! Don't ever do that again!

OVERPROTECTIVE PARENT: Poor little baby! I was so worried about you! Did you get hurt? Let's go home where there's a fence to keep out big dogs. I should never have taken you to a park. They're not safe.

DIMINISHING PARENT: Good grief! What are you crying about? I only went to the water fountain. There was no reason to be worried. And why were you so afraid of the dog? He wouldn't hurt you!

DISTRACTING PARENT: Don't cry, honey. I know what will cheer you up! Let's go get a big ice cream cone. Oh, look at the puppy over there. Isn't he cute? Would you like to pet the puppy?

SEXIST PARENT: You look like a girl when you blubber like that. Come on, son, shape up! Big boys don't cry. Make Daddy proud of you! Let's find that dog and show him a thing or two!

One way or another, these parents would invade the boy's emotional space. Because his natural, healing response would be short-circuited, the brief experience in the park would remain a live issue in his psyche.

Just as children have a natural way to work through fear, they have a built-in way to process all their other intense emotions, including anger, apprehension, joy, and sorrow. The anger response, like the fear response, is a frequent target for repression. Imagine a 6-year-old girl who is angry at her 10-year-old brother for teasing her. In response, she might make an angry face, yell at her brother, and strike out at him with her fists. It's an instinctual, energizing reaction designed to protect her from danger. Someone is violating her sense of well-being, and she's afraid that if she doesn't stop the intruder, she'll get hurt.

A wise parent would validate the girl's anger—it's infuriating to be teased—and help her find a verbal rather than a physical way to express it. "You are very mad at your brother for teasing you," says this model parent, "I would be, too. Tell him in words how angry you feel. He needs to know." This way, the girl can protect herself from her brother and purge herself of her anger without having to resort to physical violence. Her self-protective anger remains intact. It has simply been given a more "civilized" form of expression.

Less knowledgeable parents interfere with their children's anger by ridiculing them, ignoring them, isolating them, goading them on to greater violence, punishing them, distracting them, hitting them, or trying to make them laugh ("I see a smile coming on . . ."). When a parent interferes with a child's anger response in these heavy-handed ways, the anger increases and is redirected at the parent: now the parent is the one who's violating the child's sense of well-being by interfering with a natural and necessary outlet of emotion. Most parents stifle this secondary outburst of anger, too, only this time with more force. "Don't make a face at your mother! What a naughty girl. You'll get a licking for that! Shame on you!" Instead of allowing the anger to flow through the child's system the first time it's expressed, the parent unwittingly fans the anger, then dams it up. The anger becomes trapped in the little girl's stomach, muscles, and jaw, and becomes an enduring wound.

If the parent represses the girl's anger not just once but over and over again, a deeper injury occurs: *the girl will eventually dismantle her anger response.* Ultimately, it's safer for her to cut off a part of her being than to battle the person on whom her life depends. When her brother abuses her, she will no longer respond with a surge of anger. She'll find some other route. She might run to her mother for help, or pretend she's not mad, or find a more devious way to get back at him. The clean, instant, automatic response will be gone.

❦ Jim: "Most of my life I've been in neutral."

I have a vivid memory of Jim, an overweight, friendly-looking man who came with his wife to one of my marriage workshops. He, like many others, had lost his capacity to respond normally to pain and fear. When he was asked to write down a list of painful memories from his childhood, he came up with a blank slate. Try as he might, Jim couldn't think of a single instance when he had been afraid or unhappy. His wife was very annoyed with him—not only because he was slow in completing the exercise, but because he rarely showed any reaction to anything. He went through life with a placid grin, seemingly impervious to pain. She felt as if she were living with a zombie. Overcome with frustration, she waved her hand and begged me to come over to help.

I talked with Jim privately for a few minutes and quickly garnered the following facts: (1) His father had died when he was 3 years old. (2) His mother had had a full-time job and would come home from work every evening and drink herself into a stupor. (3) He had been rejected by his two older brothers and rarely allowed to join in their play. (4) His mother had later married a violent man who, among other things, fired a bullet at Jim while he was lying asleep in bed, the bullet hitting the pillow a few inches from his face!

Jim rattled off this information to me as if he were reading numbers from a phone book. "Why didn't you put any of this down on your list of childhood injuries?" I asked in amazement.

"Because those things didn't bother me," he said matter-of-factly. "You said we should write down things that made us angry or scared or sad. I wasn't bothered by those things. They just happened. I didn't feel much one way or another. I wasn't happy. I wasn't sad. I guess I was locked in neutral." At some unknown point in his childhood, Jim had experienced such trauma that he had anesthetized himself to emotional injury. His natural expression of anger, fear, and sorrow had been numbed by a self-administered drug. This "psychic surgery" may have made him invulnerable to pain, but it had also made him a stranger to joy.

✿ Psychotherapy and the Wizard of Oz

As I thought about the fluid emotional responses of a healthy child and how often those feelings are dammed up, I began to have a different view of psychotherapy. Psychotherapy isn't a twentieth-century artifice imposed on nature, but the reinstatement of a natural healing process. My job as a therapist is not to teach my clients new skills or impart sacred knowledge but to reacquaint them with innate tools. I am there to trigger a delayed progression of feelings, to lubricate an emotional processing system that has become rusty from lack of use.

Not long ago I saw the movie The Wizard of Oz for the first time (I'm probably the last adult in America to see it). As I watched the movie, I couldn't help but identify with the man behind the curtain who was pulling the levers and pushing the buttons that created the frightening spectacle of the Wizard. There was no Wizard after all, just an old man putting on a show to dazzle and frighten the believers of Oz. Instead of magically granting his supplicants' requests, all he could do was reach into his black bag and hand them symbolic objects certifying that through their own efforts, they had regained their original wholeness. The Cowardly Lion, for his "conspicuous bravery against wicked witches," was given a medal of honor. The Tin Man, in consideration for his loving treatment of his new friends, was given a symbolic heart. The Scarecrow, for his brilliance in battle, was given an academic diploma and a title, "Doctor of Thinkology."

When the Wizard came to Dorothy, however, he had nothing to hand her. "I don't think there is anything in that black bag for me," she said wisely. She wanted to end the nightmare and journey back home to her original wholeness, but he couldn't help her.

It was Glinda, the Good Witch of the North, who finally told Dorothy what she needed to know. "You've always had the power to go back to Kansas," she told her. "Just click your ruby red slippers three times and say, 'There's no place like home.'"

When Dorothy's friends heard this simple solution, they were understandably irate: "Why didn't you tell Dorothy before?" they demanded to know. Why hadn't Glinda explained the magic property of the shoes when Dorothy was still an innocent in Munchkin Land, before she had to confront the poisoned poppies and the terrifying Wicked Witch of the West and all the unholy creatures that guarded her castle?

"Because she wouldn't have believed me," said Glinda. "She had to learn it for herself."

When the movie came to an end, I thought, "This is the best exposition of the role of therapist I've ever seen." People come to me hoping I'll magically relieve their suffering. They want me to pull the levers and push the buttons that will make them all better. They want me to be the Great and Beneficent Wizard of Oz who can "fix anything."

I do my best to oblige them. Like the Wizard, I tell them I'll be happy to fix what ails them, but first they have to prove themselves worthy by performing "a very small task." The Wizard of Oz asked Dorothy and her friends to journey through the Haunted Forest and bring back the broomstick of the Wicked Witch of the West. I assign my clients an equally daunting task: I ask them to wander through the Haunted Forest of their childhood memories so they can reexperience their repressed fear and anger. I ask them to wend their way back through all the feelings they were not allowed to have as children so they can work them out of their system.

The brave souls who give up their wish for a miracle cure and take on this challenge come to the end of the yellow brick road with an amazing discovery: they were whole all along, they just didn't know it. My modest role in the drama is to give them permission to be who they once were. By helping them work through the stale, unprocessed events of childhood—*this time with me by their side as a supportive, noninterfering "parent"*—my clients are able to reacquaint themselves with their original, healthy responses to the world. They go back to Kansas purged of the past and able once again to think and to cry and be angry and be sad and feel joy, their innate self-healing capacity alive and well, ready to protect them from further injury.

🏵 Repression and the Chosen Child

The great popularity of the movie *The Wizard of Oz* is due partly to the fact that it is an allegory of the repression of human society. We can all identify with Dorothy, the Cowardly Lion, the Tin Man, and the Scarecrow as they search for parts of themselves they feel are missing. The story is of particular significance, however, to those of us who grew up with an Invasive Parent. Because our parents turned to us for their emotional needs, they did not have the objectivity or the self-discipline to allow us to be who we were. We were *habitually* denied the opportunity to respond naturally to life events, and as a result, ordinary circumstances became lasting injuries.

To a large degree, our parents determined which parts of the self we were allowed to keep. Some of us were allowed to have needs, but not to be independent. We were catered to and indulged, but kept immature. Some of us were allowed to have a great deal of freedom, but not to have needs. We were allowed to wander at will around the neighborhood, but were not given enough comfort and reassurance. Some of us were permitted to develop our talents, but were asked to repress our needs and emotions. We grew up to be compulsive achievers to hide an inner sense of inadequacy. To a greater degree than other children, we were not allowed to be whole. In exchange for love and a position of privilege in the family hierarchy, we had to give up a large portion of the self.

🏵 The Two-Stage Recovery Program

As you will see, there are two separate stages to the recovery process outlined in this book. **During the first stage, you will be taking a guided tour back through childhood.** In order to be healed, you need to work through your backlog of unprocessed emotions. You need to cry about the lack of sensitivity with which you were treated; to be angry about the violation of family boundaries; and to summon up the fear of being a young child with no one looking after your needs.

The more you can connect with these feelings, the more you will be in touch with your original nature. You will discover that you haven't lost the capacity to respond naturally to daily events, you've just been denied permission to do it. Once you practice being more emotionally alive in a safe, supportive atmosphere, you will become more true to yourself, more in tune with your wishes and needs, and less willing to tolerate unhealthy situations.

As you will see in chapter 9, one of the best tools for initiating this process is to create an autobiography, either by writing it or by talking with a trusted friend. As you do so, you will recall what it was like to be a child growing up in your family. You will bring to mind significant life events and the feelings associated with them. By recalling those emotions and *expressing them more fully than you were allowed to do in the past,* you will regain parts of your original wholeness.

Some of you have been engaged in a similar healing process for years. Through therapy, self-help books, support groups, or recovery groups you've worked your way through many of your blocked emotions. You may even be a therapist yourself. What this part of the recovery process will do for you is consolidate your gains, put them in a new framework, and help you become more focused in your growth.

If you haven't spent much time in introspection, you will find this a more challenging but also a more productive part of the journey. The exercises in the coming chapters will lead you step-by-step through the healing process, allowing you to proceed at your own rate.

The second stage in the recovery process is to realign your present-day relationships. The problems you experienced in your original family are invariably reflected in your current relationships, whether with spouse, children, friends, or co-workers. Although you can't go back and change the way your parents related to you, you can make some adjustments in the way you relate to others today.

If the thought of altering your relationships with family and friends seems a formidable task, I want to reassure you that the course of action I propose is not "psychic surgery." I won't ask you to wade through your relationships with scalpel in hand, severing connections and suturing new alliances. Instead, I advocate a rather simple, "chiropractic" adjustment of your family. Once I help you determine where your relationships are most out of balance, I will show you how to give a push here and a tweak there, so that the whole system can gradually fall into better alignment. I want to say at the outset that there will be no need for traumatic scenes or dramatic confrontations. You won't be required to bring up past issues with family members or heap blame on them. For the most part, you will subtly alter your behavior so that all your relationships will rest on a more loving, stable foundation.

For many of you, the most important work you will do in this second stage of recovery will be to shore up your adult support system. Just as the human body functions best when the spine is in proper alignment, the family functions best when the adults—the backbone of the family—have a strong system of support. When the adults satisfy their needs with other adults, they automatically reduce their dependence on their children, and the all-important boundary between parents and children remains intact.

Five key chapters in the second half of this book will help you improve your relationships. Chapter 10 will help you make peace with your parents, whether they are living or dead. Chapter 11 will help you resolve any lasting tensions between you and your siblings. Chapter 12 will show you how to create a more intimate, lasting love relationship. Chapter 13 will help you expand your network of friends. Chapter 14 will give you advice on becoming a more effective parent and breaking the cycle of enmeshment.

❀ Second Order Change

As you read about this two-stage recovery process, you may wonder, "How long is this going to take? How rapidly can I expect to see improvement in my life?" Recovering from emotional incest, just like recovering from any childhood problem, is an ongoing and gradual process. It takes time to identify the numerous problems that result from the syndrome, time to integrate all the information you will absorb, and time to recall significant childhood events and bring forth the emotions connected with them. For some of you, just realizing that your childhood wasn't perfect will be an enormous first step. Once that fundamental awareness settles in, there will be many more insights ahead of you.

But wherever you are on the road to recovery, significant

progress likely will take place in the first few weeks after reading this book. Just having a name for what happened to you and realizing how common the problem is can be therapeutic. Then, when you begin to take part in the exercises, you will experience a surge of growth. A graph depicting your rate of progress might look something like this:

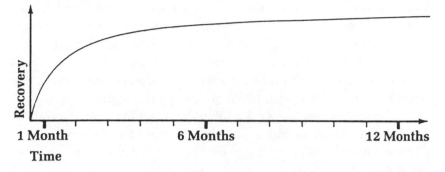

In this diagram, the horizontal line represents time, and the vertical line represents personal growth. As you can see, rapid growth often occurs in the first few weeks. The phenomenon responsible for this initial surge is called "second order change."

Second order change is defined as a sudden shift in perception that results in significant, permanent growth. This is in contrast to "first order change," which is a change that alleviates symptoms only. For example: Suppose you are awakened several nights in a row by a distant, throbbing noise. The noise starts out quietly, grows in volume, then fades away. You aren't sure what is making the noise, but as you lie tossing and turning in bed, you visualize an enormous, smoke-belching machine. Some nearby factory must be turning on a huge piece of equipment.

A week goes by and the noise awakens you every night at around 2:00 A.M. You are irate. To keep from being awakened, you begin to stuff cotton into your ears before going to bed. Occasionally, you manage to sleep through the din, but most nights this "first order change"—a change that addresses symptoms only—is not sufficient, and you are rudely awakened.

You wake up one morning so upset by lack of sleep that you call a neighbor to see if she's been bothered by the noise.

"What noise?" she asks.

"That horrible noise that comes out of nowhere at two o'clock every morning," you reply, wondering how anyone could sleep through the racket.

"Oh! *That* noise," she replies. "That's just the train. The train is on a new schedule and comes through every night about that time."

Instantly, you know she's right. Of course it was a train! How could you have been so blind?

That night you feel less irritable as you go to bed, because the image of a belching factory has been replaced by the image of a freight train, and you've always had a good feeling about trains. Instead of a sweaty foreman throwing the switch on an evil machine, you envision a conductor happily escorting his cargo through town.

At 7:00 the next morning, you awaken and look at the clock. Despite the fact that you forgot to stuff your ears with cotton the night before, you managed to sleep through the night.

The reason you had a good night's rest is that you had a sudden change of perception. You managed to let go of a disturbing, false illusion and replace it with a more positive, accurate one, and this realization filtered down to your unconscious. When the train rumbled through town at 2:00 in the morning, your unconscious mind registered the noise, flashed the benign image of a train, and you were able to sleep through the night.

When your view of a problem is significantly altered, you experience just such a "second order change." Instead of making minor adjustments to cope with the situation, your entire outlook is transformed. As a result, your emotional response is automatically and permanently altered.[3]

88 Sibling Rivalry and Successful Change

Here is an example of how this phenomenon is manifested in relationships. I worked with a young man named Frank, who had been his mother's favorite son. Frank didn't get along well with his younger brother, Steven, who was understandably jealous of all the attention Frank received. When they were younger, Steven used to pick fights with Frank. Now that they were both adults, he criticized Frank and put him down. Frank believed he had only two options: to make himself scarce whenever Steve was around or to put up with the abuse—the price he had to pay for being the Chosen Child. On an unconscious level he felt responsible for the preferential treatment meted out by his mother, so he absorbed whatever punishment Steve wanted to dish out.

Then, by gaining some insight into his childhood, Frank had a significant change of perception. Following my advice, he interviewed his father about his childhood. His father told him that his mother had been preoccupied with him from the moment he was born. "She wouldn't let me touch you," his father told him. "I still remember the monologue she carried on with you on the way home from the hospital. It was like I didn't exist. All I was good for, in her mind, was producing a perfect son. Once you were born, I no longer mattered. I was put out to pasture."

As Frank listened to this sad story, he realized that he wasn't responsible for his mother's attachment to him. Yes, he had been his mother's favorite son. Yes, his brother had gotten the short end of the deal. But no, he, Frank, was not responsible. His mother had transferred her affection to him at the moment of birth. He couldn't be blamed for that!

From that moment on, Frank felt less guilty about the way his mother treated him, and this second order change freed him to forge a new relationship with his brother. Not long after his conversation with his father, the family got together for Easter dinner. At the table, Steven started telling everyone an embarrassing anecdote about Frank, a story calculated to diminish Frank in the eyes of others. This was typical behavior, and ordinarily Frank would have put up with it. But not this time. To his surprise, he heard himself say, "Stop it, Steven. I don't want to hear that again. I've heard that story too many times already!" To Frank's amazement, Steven meekly changed the subject. What was even more startling to him was that Steven was kinder to him during the remainder of the visit than he had been in a long time.

As Frank related the incident to me he said, "My heart was pounding when I told Steven to back off. I was afraid he was going to become even more aggressive, or haul off and slug me. It was such a shock to me that he did nothing. The fact that I have the means to protect myself from him is a revelation. I've let him walk over me all my life. Now I'm not afraid of him anymore. I have a tremendous sense of power."

Frank didn't consciously make up his mind to relate to his brother in a different manner—the change came about automatically because he had destroyed the debilitating myth that he was responsible for being the Chosen Child. Freed from this burden of guilt, he was able to react in a normal, self-protective way. He had undergone a second order change.

33 "JNDs: Just Noticeable Differences"

As you gather data about your family and begin to view your personal history with more objectivity, it is likely that you, too, will experience a marked change of perception. As a result, some of your anxiety, guilt, and confusion is likely to dissipate. Perhaps, as in Frank's case, you will experience a new sense of power.

After a while, you will notice a change not just in your feelings but in your behavior. At first these may be small, barely observable changes. You might find yourself acting more warmly to one of your parents, or, like Frank, less subservient to a brother or sister. You might find yourself spending more time with one particular family member and less time with another. These changes are what some therapists refer to as JNDs—Just Noticeable Differences. Over time, however, these JNDs will add up, and you will gradually replace an old, dysfunctional style of relating with a more loving, productive one.

Note: As you scan the remaining chapters, you will notice a variety of exercises, including surveys, essay questions, and guided fantasies. This is consistent with my "banquet" approach to therapy. From my experience as an educator, I've observed that people respond to exercise material in highly individual ways. Some people like checklists; others find them a waste of time. Some people like to work alone; others work best with a partner. Some people are prolific writers; others like to share their insights verbally. Some people get a lot of insight from visualizations; others draw a complete blank. For this reason, I encourage you to scan each exercise, then choose the ones that address your unique problems and suit your personal style. I don't expect you to complete them all. I suspect that only a few of you will have the time and inclination to select every item from the menu!

9

Making Your
Personal History,
History

88

DOROTHY: *"But how do I start for Emerald City?"*

GLINDA (the Good Witch of the North):
"It's always best to start at the beginning."

This chapter contains several exercises that will take you on a journoy back to childhood. The goal is to picture yourself as a young child growing up in your family, buffeted by all the hidden politics that swirled about you. You will be encouraged to remember the good times, the sad times, the lonely times, the exciting times, and the times when you were angry or afraid. By taking part in these exercises, you will bring to mind the bittersweet reality of being a Chosen Child.

While you are completing these exercises, you may experience some immediate rewards. For example, you may be able to dispel some destructive myths about your childhood. Here's an example: When I was growing up, I was under the illusion that my mother and I were the only members of our extended family who were having a difficult time. I imagined that my grandparents and aunts and uncles led serene and comfortable lives. The reason they didn't give us financial or emotional support, I thought, was that my mother and I weren't worth the trouble; we were the black sheep of the family. As I grew up, I clung to this view and harbored a lot of anger about my relatives. I even went so far as to deny their existence: "They're all dead," I would say.

I went back several years ago and interviewed my aunts, uncles, and cousins about my family history—one of the projects you will be asked to undertake in this chapter. To my surprise, I learned that when I was young, all my relatives had been going through hard times. I was born during World War II, and no one in my family had much money. Many of the men were off fighting the war. An uncle of mine who desperately wanted to go to college had to put aside his dreams and get a job so that he could help with the family income. The reason my mother and I didn't receive any help was that all our relatives were trying to keep their heads above water. When this realization sunk in, I was no longer angry at my family. I had a greater sense of belonging. And for the first time I was able to acknowledge my roots.

❈ Coping with Denial and Resistance

Revisiting the past may also stir up some anxiety. When you are rummaging around in old belief systems, it's inevitable that you will bring up some fear. The beliefs you developed when you were young served a valuable purpose, and rearranging them is bound to make you feel unsettled. A young woman nicknamed Sam, a member of one of my first therapy groups, experienced considerable anxiety as she began to revise her idealized view of her childhood. At the beginning of the group sessions, she had a sugar-coated view of her family. According to her, there had been no violence, alcoholism, divorce, neglect, or abuse. Her parents were still married and seemed to be getting along quite well. In fact, Sam maintained that when she was growing up, they had served as a "model couple" for many of her friends.

During the first few sessions, Sam listened with interest to the life histories of the other group members. She asked them questions, empathized with them, and, in general, did an admirable job of playing co-therapist. The other members of the group looked up to her and sought her advice. When she talked about her own family, it was to serve as a healthy contrast to what she was hearing from everyone else.

The only problem with Sam's view of her past was that it wasn't congruent with the present. Despite what seemed like a storybook upbringing, she had just as many emotional problems as the other members of the group. She was fifty pounds overweight, she was in a destructive relationship, and she suffered from depression and anxiety. It seemed likely that some of her difficulties were rooted in the past.

After the fourth group session—in which several women happened to talk about incidents of sexual abuse—Sam began to have trouble sleeping. One night she was unable to sleep at all and called me in a panic the next morning. She was desperately tired and overwrought and wanted to see me as soon as possible.

When she came into my office a few hours later, she looked exhausted and seemed more vulnerable than I had ever seen her. Sensing an opportunity to break through some of her denial, I led her through a simple Gestalt exercise. "Put your father in the chair," I told her, "and pretend you're two years old. Look up at him and tell him what's on your mind."

Without thinking, Sam blurted out, "Daddy, where are you?" She was startled to hear herself complain about her father's unavailability. She had never before identified any feelings of abandonment.

"Now pretend you're five years old. Talk to your father."

With the same spontaneity, but with a new undertone of anger, she said, "Daddy, I don't need you."

"Now you're thirteen years old. Talk to your father."

"Daddy," she said, her face starting to contort as tears welled in her eyes, "leave me alone!"

"What is that about?" I asked her.

For the rest of the session, Sam was overcome with memories about her father's obsessive interest in her body. Although she couldn't remember a time when he had sexually abused her, he had clearly overstepped the normal father-daughter boundaries. Through her tears, she told me that when she was 12, her father had joked to her about her sexiness and warned her about lecherous men. "He told me that all the boys were going to fall in love with me because of my body and I shouldn't trust them. He would pat my behind even though I would get furious at him for doing it." She recounted the day he had taken pictures of her while she was sunning on the front lawn in a bikini. He enlarged the most provocative pose and hung it in the den. She remembers seeing the poster and feeling ashamed. She took it down, only to be lectured by her father. "You have a lovely body," he told her. "You should be proud of it. You have twice the body of most other girls your age. Your body even puts your mother's to shame!"

Coming to the group sessions and hearing the other women's candid remarks about their families had gradually uprooted these memories, which were in such marked contrast to her idealized view of her family that she had been filled with anxiety. The sleep deprivation crumbled the last of her resistance. Finally, she was open to a flood of memories.

During the next few sessions, Sam began to make numerous connections between her father's behavior and her present-day problems. One of her discoveries was that her excess weight was closely related to her father's inappropriate interest in her body. She realized that she had started putting on weight at age 13, which was about the time her father had begun expressing his interest. By the time she was 16, she was forty pounds overweight. "My father hated to see me fat," she told me. "He took me to a doctor and had me put on a diet. He even talked the doctor into giving me diet pills." Sam lost forty pounds that summer, but put it all back on in a year. "I didn't want to be fat," she told me, "but I think I felt safer that way. I felt more invisible. I think it protected me from my father's obsession."

When Sam was finally able to see the inappropriate nature of her father's behavior, she was greatly relieved. She experienced some anxiety in the process, but she felt that the insights were well worth it. Armed with new self-knowledge, she was able to end a fifteen-year pattern of yo-yo dieting. She was able to lose weight and keep it off, because being thin no longer caused her undue anxiety. At long last, her feelings about her father were out in the open, where they could be analyzed and dealt with. "I only wish I'd done this work earlier," she told me one day. "My life is much less of a puzzle now. I see myself with such clarity."

✿ Removing Guilt as a Barrier to Exploring the Past

For some Chosen Children, guilt, not anxiety, keeps them from gaining a more accurate view of their childhood. This is often true of those who grew up worshiping a parent. How can they go from thinking a parent was the most wonderful mother or father on earth to seeing the parent as the source of their misery? How can they be angry at a parent who sacrificed so much for them? How can a relationship that usually felt so good be classified as bad?

A client struggling with guilt made the following comment to me: "I remember feeling profoundly guilty once for admitting to my father that I didn't like to play tennis—his favorite sport. I couldn't sleep that night for fear I had hurt his feelings. Now I'm supposed to acknowledge all his weaknesses? I'm supposed to see him as the cause of my problems? My anxiety is immense."

If you feel guilty for seeing the negative side of a parent, removing this barrier will hasten your recovery. But how do you do this? It's been my experience that learning more about the complicated psychology of guilt helps reduce its impact. In its simplest form, guilt is a painful but short-lived phenomenon designed to jolt you into awareness that your behavior is not consistent with your beliefs. It's a voice from your conscience advising you to either (1) reexamine your beliefs or (2) alter your behavior so that the two of them line up.

Sometimes it's your behavior that needs to change. For example, if you forget a good friend's birthday, you may feel a pang of guilt. In this instance, your conscience is urging you to be more thoughtful of others. It's unpleasant to feel guilty, so in the future you'll vow to do better. At other times, it's your belief system that needs to be revised. For instance, you may feel guilty for spending two hours Saturday morning reading the newspaper. "This is not a productive way to spend your time," says the Calvinistic voice of your conscience. "You should be mowing the lawn or cleaning the house." But on further analysis, you decide that you don't mind frittering away this time. You work hard all week, and you need this time to recharge your batteries. You diminish your guilt not by changing your behavior but by substituting a new belief: it's important to spend time relaxing.

It's been my observation that much of the guilt of the Chosen Child is best alleviated by changing a faulty belief system. For example, many a Chosen Child feels guilty for receiving preferential treatment from a parent, which made a parent or sibling feel left out. This guilt can be traced to a faulty belief system: "I wanted to be my parent's favorite. I got my wish. Therefore I am responsible for the pain that was caused in others." On some level, the Chosen Child believes that he or she was in control of the family dynamics and must accept responsibility for the fate of other family members.

But, as we have seen, it's the adult who creates the parent-child alliance. A child can't be blamed for wanting preferential treatment from a parent; it's a survival mechanism built into all children: in times of scarcity, being first in line can mean the difference between life and death. A wise parent ignores the child's plea for a place of prominence and keeps all children on the same plane. No child is given preferential treatment or is asked to play the role of surrogate spouse. Ultimately, it's the parent's responsibility to create a balanced family system, not the child's responsibility to suppress a natural and understandable desire to be a Chosen Child.

Ironically, many Chosen Children discover that letting go of this misplaced sense of guilt for what went on in the family makes them feel anxious; it's a Catch-22. Once they place the responsibility where it really belongs—squarely in the lap of the parent—they may experience a surge of anxiety for having "bad thoughts" about the caretaker. Here's the internal logic: "If I was not responsible for being the Chosen Child, then my mother and father were to blame. It makes me feel anxious to see my parents in a negative light, however, because my unconscious mind assumes they are still responsible for my well-being. Even though I am 20 or 40 or even 70 years old and have outlived both my parents, I am still fearful of abandonment. It may be better to accept the guilt for what went wrong in my family than to blame my parents and stir up my anxiety."

For many people, this complicated and erroneous belief system stands in the way of recovery. Understanding the way the unconscious mind operates is a first step to letting go of the unnecessary burden. Here, once again, is the faulty train of logic:

1. When children are young, they feel responsible for the tension in the family because of the false belief that they are in control of the situation.

2. In later years, if they try to change this belief and assign full responsibility to their parents, they feel anxious.

3. The underlying cause of this anxiety is the erroneous belief that they are still dependent on their parents for survival even in their adult years.

If the thought of identifying the mistakes your parents made in raising you makes you feel guilty or anxious, you need to revise your belief system. You were not to blame for what went on in the family, and you have nothing to fear for placing the responsibility where it really belongs. You are now capable of taking care of yourself. And remember that you don't have to confront your parents or disassociate from them to recover from emotional incest. You just need to remove some of the mythology that keeps you from seeing and experiencing the truth.

83 Tapping in to a Well of Pain

People who had especially bleak childhoods may be reluctant to look at the past for yet a different reason. They don't have illusions of family perfection to overcome, and they don't feel guilty for seeing the truth—they just don't want to be swamped with grief. They're afraid that once they open the floodgates, there will be no end to their tears.

I can sympathize with this point of view, because there was a time when I thought there would be no end to the reliving of my pain. I remember an occasion many years ago, shortly after my mother died, when I thought I would never stop crying. My first husband and I had just moved into a new house, and I was in the basement sorting laundry. For some reason, I started thinking about my mother and how much she would have enjoyed seeing our new house. It would have pleased her so much to see how well we were doing. Suddenly, I started to cry. The doorbell rang, and I went upstairs to answer it, confident that I could stifle my tears. I wiped my eyes and opened the door. A man from our church had come to visit, and I invited him into the kitchen for a glass of iced tea. Much to my embarrassment, I burst into tears as soon as he walked into the house. In a matter of seconds I was crying so hard that I couldn't talk. I couldn't even explain to him why I was crying. The poor man let himself out the door, no doubt thinking he had stumbled into a madhouse.

I cried all afternoon, unable to stop. I was crying not only about my mother's death but about the neglect I had experienced as a child. I was crying about having had no one to come home to after school and about waking up to an empty house. I was crying about having had to lie about my mother's neglect. And I was crying about having never really gotten to know my father. I was learning that, on some level, all pain is interconnected, and when you tap in to a portion of it, the rest is right there, waiting to be released. I was afraid I'd cry for days without stopping.

By the time my husband came home that evening, however, I had finally cried myself dry. There was an end to the tears. Since then, I have visited this well of sorrow many times. By now I've gotten so acquainted with my childhood pain that I've lost my fear of it. I know where it comes from; I know what feelings I wasn't able to express as a child; and I know how this repression has interfered with my life. And each time I've visited the well, I've released more of the pain and the reservoir has gotten smaller and smaller. Now, instead of feeling as if I'm plunging into a bottomless well, I feel as if I'm stepping into a puddle on the sidewalk.

These deliberate excursions into the past have transformed my life. Instead of relying on the false sense of confidence imparted to me by my mother, I have a secure, grounded feeling of self-confidence based on reality. My natural emotions are alive and well, helping to protect me from injury and make healthier choices. People who meet me often come to the mistaken conclusion that I must have come from a loving, nurturing family. I take that as a compliment to years of hard work.

My only regret is that no one told me at the beginning of my journey what I'm telling you now: there *will* be an end to your pain. And once you've released all those pent-up emotions, you will experience a lightness and buoyancy you haven't felt since you were a very young child. The past will no longer feel like a lode of radioactive ore contaminating the present, and you will be able to respond appropriately to present-day events. You will feel angry when someone infringes on your territory, but you won't overreact. You will feel sad when something bad happens to you, but you won't sink into despair. You will feel joy when you have a good day, and your happiness won't be clouded with guilt. You, too, will have succeeded in making history, history.

88 Introduction to the Autobiography Exercise

The first exercise in the recovery section of this book requires you to construct an autobiography. There are two ways to approach it: you may either write down an abbreviated version of your life story or share it verbally with a friend. Whichever medium you choose, the success of the exercise will depend on your ability to amplify your feelings. Instead of pushing down any pain, sadness, or anger you may feel, you need to exaggerate it. If you feel a twinge of sadness— cry, sob! If you feel angry, clench your fist and shout, "I am so angry!"

For some of you, tapping in to your emotions to this degree may be an uncomfortable experience, bringing forth feelings of embarrassment, humiliation, or guilt. This is an understandable reaction. Your role in your family was to be there for others; to express your own needs was out of character. When you let down this facade and admit that you have unmet needs, you may feel very vulnerable. Your feelings may seem foreign, even frightening to you. One woman expressed it this way: "I feel like a crab that has just come out of its shell. All the other crabs have a protective shell, but I don't. I feel so fragile. Even admitting this to you makes me feel scared."

Be prepared for this feeling of vulnerability and open yourself up to your flow of emotions, nonetheless. Your feelings are your friends; they are invaluable tools. They are designed to guide you to a healthy life. Each of your primary emotions has a distinct role to play in the maintenance of your well-being. Fear warns you of imminent danger; anxiety keeps you on guard; anger protects you from physical and emotional abuse; jealousy safeguards your turf; sadness steers you away from unnecessary pain. When these emotions are fully acknowledged and expressed in an appropriate manner, you become a joyful, vital, responsive, rational, responsible human being. You regain the original wholeness that is your birthright. *The key to emotional health is to break up your logjam of unprocessed emotions until the river runs free and clear.*

BE PATIENT WITH BLOCKED FEELINGS

If you follow all these suggestions and still have little or no reaction to telling your life story, be patient with yourself. If you've been out of touch with your feelings for a long time, they'll need reassurance that it's safe to come out. I worked with a client named Jacob for two full years before his emotions began to surface. At first they came in the form of a slight flush in his face. Later, I noticed a quiver in his chin. A few months later, his mouth formed a slight pout. It was a real breakthrough the day that tears came to his eyes.

I was surprised by the event that finally triggered his emotional release. His car had broken down and he had decided it would cost too much to repair. As Jacob related this seemingly insignificant news, tears came to his eyes. As we gently explored the feelings behind this incident, he told me that his father had spent countless hours working on cars with his older brother, Tom. Jacob, however, had been a Chosen Child and his mother had not allowed him to play "outside getting dirty." The incident with the car had connected him to the pain and rejection he felt at not being allowed to be close to his father.

A good way to unlock deeply buried emotions is to encourage emotions whenever and wherever they surface. You may be able to tell your whole life story without any reaction, for example, but tear up when you watch a sad movie. You may have no feelings about what happened to you as a child, but you might become irate when you read about child abuse in the newspaper. It doesn't matter what it is that gets you to respond, because in reality, all your feelings are about you. So make it a point to note any emergence of sadness or anger. When you are alone and in a safe place, see if you can amplify those feelings. You will experience some healing, whether or not you can connect the feelings to specific incidents in your life.

RESISTANCE TO THE AUTOBIOGRAPHY EXERCISE

For most people, creating an autobiography is an excellent way to uncover repressed emotions. Your first reaction to the exercise, however, may be that nothing this simple will unearth your childhood wounds. Deep down you believe that it's going to take something drastic like hypnotism or two years with a therapist or a month-long residency program to effect your recovery. An autobiographical exercise seems too simplistic to get to the root of your issues.

It has been my experience that most effective therapy techniques are quite simple. For example, counting to ten is an excellent tool to manage your anger. Counting allows time for the surge of adrenaline to work its way out of your system and puts you in a rational frame of mind. But many people reject this tool because it's too simple; it's become a cliché. But like most clichés, it contains an element of truth.

Some of you may experience a different form of resistance to the exercise: it seems like too much work. You want to read the book and be healed. Spending two or three hours writing your memories or arranging a talk session with a friend seems too arduous.

Whatever the nature of your resistance—"I don't have time," "It's too stupid," "I've done this already," "I'll do it next week"—I urge you to plunge ahead and put the exercise to the test. Do it exactly as directed and then decide whether it has merit. I have seen dramatic breakthroughs happen as a result of this exercise.

EXERCISE 1:
Creating Your Autobiography

Your autobiography can be as personal and unique as you are. You can "begin at the beginning" and develop your own structure, or refer to the outline provided. As you will see, the outline is quite thorough.[1] You may need to consult relatives or family friends to supplement your information. Before you begin, read through it and check the items that seem most pertinent to you. Keep in mind that the purpose of the exercise is to help you recall the feelings you had as a child, so focus on issues that have the potential for evoking the greatest response.

As I mentioned earlier, there are two ways to do this exercise. One way is to write down your memories. Writing is a good method if (1) you like to write, and/or (2) you want to keep your thoughts to yourself. The second way is to share your life story with a friend. This is the preferred method if: (1) you don't like to write, and (2) you look forward to sharing your personal history with a friend, and/or (3) you want to encourage your flow of feelings (many people discover that openly sharing their life story with others brings up the most emotion).

If you choose the verbal method, select a friend who is comfortable with emotions. Ask your friend to be a supportive listener. Listening does not mean taking action, offering suggestions, or giving interpretations. What you want is your friend's time and attention. To structure your verbal autobiography, you can let your thoughts and memories carry you along, or you can refer to the outline on the following pages. If you like, you can listen to your friend's story at a later date, or tell your stories simultaneously.

Remember, whichever medium you choose, the goal is to get in touch with your feelings. It may help to amplify them. Cry. Yell. Shake your fist at the sky! If you experience some puzzling physical symptoms such as a headache, backache, tightness in the chest or throat, sleepiness, even dizziness as you do this exercise, note at which point in your story they begin. See if you can gather any clues to the emotions that might be hiding behind these sensations. Could it be that you're repressing a sob or stifling a yell? Experiment with different emotions to see which ones fit.

A cautionary note: If you have any fear or hunch that there was severe abuse in your family or incidents of terror, I suggest you consult a therapist before participating in this exercise. You may need professional help to guide you on your journey.

✿ Autobiography— General Outline

Read through this outline and check the questions that seem most pertinent. Then write or verbalize your responses. Strive for maximum emotional expression.

I. Infancy

    A. What was the atmosphere of the family into which you were born?
- 1. Were your parents together?
- 2. Were they happy?
- 3. Were you a planned baby?
- 4. Were your parents happy with you?
- 5. Do you know if they were hoping for a boy or a girl?
- 6. Did you have older siblings?
- 7. Who was your primary caretaker?

    B. What kind of a baby were you?
- 1. How was your health?
- 2. What was your personality as an infant?
- 3. What were your favorite pastimes, toys?
- 4. Where did you sleep? What were your sleep habits?

II. Early childhood (ages 1 to 5)

    A. What do early pictures say about you?

    B. What are your earliest memories?

    C. List the most prominent feelings you had as a child (e.g., sadness, happiness, anger, disappointment, hurt, shame, guilt, love, etc.).

    D. What were your favorite pastimes?

E. If you had siblings, describe your relationships with them.
   1. Which one(s) were you closest to?
   2. Which one(s) did you have problems with?

F. Did one of your siblings have a special relationship with a parent?
   1. Describe that relationship.
   2. How did you feel about it?

G. What did you like the most and the least about your early childhood?

III. Later childhood (ages 5 to 11)

A. What was your school experience like?

B. What kind of student were you?

C. How did your caretakers respond to your school performance?

D. Did you have friends?
   1. Who were your friends?
   2. Describe your relationships with them.
   3. How did you spend your time?

E. What was your home like?
   1. How did it look?
   2. How did you feel about where you lived?

F. Did your caretakers respect your feelings?

G. Did they demonstrate a healthy way of dealing with their own feelings?

H. Did you (or could you) express feelings of anger, fear, sadness, guilt, love, affection?

I. Did you feel safe as a child?
   1. With whom did you feel safest?
   2. Did you feel unsafe with anyone?

J. Were you touched and held by your caretakers?
   1. If yes, by whom?
   2. If not, why not?
   3. How did it feel to be touched, or not to be touched?

K. How were you disciplined?
   1. By whom?

    2. Was it fair and humane?

    3. What were you disciplined for?

L. Were you "spoiled" by anyone?

    1. How, in what way?

    2. How did others respond to your being spoiled?

M. Were you anyone's favorite in your immediate or extended family?

    1. How was this favoritism shown?

    2. How did others respond to this favoritism?

N. Were you physically abused by anyone?
(This includes hitting, shaking, slapping, head banging, hair pulling, malicious tickling, etc.)

    1. If so, by whom?

    2. Describe the abuse.

    3. How did you feel about it?

    4. Did anybody try to protect you?

    5. Was there anyone you could tell about the abuse?

O. Were you sexually abused by anyone?

    1. Was there overt abuse? (This includes intercourse, fondling, rape, sexual kissing, sexual touching, pornography, voyeurism, and exhibitionism.)

    2. Was there any covert sexual abuse. (This includes lack of privacy in the bathroom or bedroom, sexual teasing, sexual jokes or innuendoes, being treated as a date by a parent or relative, sexual glances, and being used as a source of sexual stimulation.)

    3. Did anyone try to protect you from the abuse?

    4. Did you seek help? If not, why not?

P. Was your family flexible?

Q. Were the adults clearly in charge?

R. Did the adults have a clear, healthy support system from friends, family, neighbors?

S. Did your family relate to the broader community in a healthy manner?

    1. School

    2. Church

    3. Neighbors

    4. Friends

    5. Work

T. In a word or phrase, how would you describe your life from ages 5 to 11?

    1. What were the high spots?

    2. What were the low spots?

    3. What would you change if you could?

IV. Adolescence (ages 12 to 20)

A. What type of young teenager were you?

B. What were your major feelings as a teenager?

C. Describe your relationship to your caretakers during this time.

D. How did you relate to friends, classmates?

E. How did you feel about your appearance?

F. To whom were you closest?

G. Describe your sexual development.

    1. Did you have any anxieties about it?

    2. How did your caretakers respond to your sexual maturity?

    3. Were you given adequate information?

H. Describe your relationship with friends of the opposite sex.

    1. Did you date?

    2. How did your caretakers respond to your interest in the opposite sex?

    3. Did you experiment with sex?

I. Did you have personal privacy at home?

J. Were your caretakers happy with their lives?

K. In later years, were you given support to leave home and become more independent?

    1. Were you given help and information about career options?

    2. Did you feel any pressure to stay home or to stay close to home?

    3. Did you feel guilt or anxiety about leaving home?

    4. Were you eager to leave home?

    L. What were the hardest times of your adolescence?

    M. What were the highlights?

    N. If you could now change your adolescence, how would you change it?

V. Young adulthood (ages 21 to 30)

    A. List and summarize each of your significant love relationships.

    B. What was your job history?

    C. Describe any additional schooling and how you felt about it.

    D. Describe your physical health.

    E. If you got married during this period, discuss your marriage(s).

    F. If you had children, discuss your relationship with your children.

    G. If you had it to do over, what would you change about young adulthood?

VI. How has your life been since young adulthood?

    A. High points

    B. Low points

    C. Job or career history

    D. Health

    E. Friends

    F. Love relationships

VII. Present day

    A. What feelings do you experience on a regular basis? (E.g., tiredness, anger, sadness, depression, joy, elation, aimlessness, confidence, a feeling of purpose, etc.)

    B. What recurring thoughts and fantasies do you have?

    C. To whom are you closest?

When you are finished writing your autobiography or sharing it with a friend, you may feel exhausted—especially if you brought up a lot of strong feelings. You may feel unusually open and vulnerable. Be kind to yourself and allow yourself time to relax and regroup.

If you find yourself thinking about the past more than usual in the days following the exercise, encourage these thoughts. This is your emotional processing system kicking into gear. Talk about the past with anyone who will listen. My husband has often said to me, "How many times do I have to hear about your early days in Sistersville, West Virginia?" and I've replied quite bluntly, "Until I don't need to talk about it anymore." Fortunately, he has been kind enough to listen to me again and again. With each retelling, my pain diminishes. I urge you to tell your story until the emotional voltage is all but gone—even if you have to risk boring your friends; after all, what are friends for?

EXERCISE 2:
Family Interviews

Once you've completed your autobiography, gain additional insight into your childhood by interviewing family and friends. You will not only clarify your own memories, you will open up new chapters of family history. Learning more about your parents' lives can be especially useful. When you discover how they were treated by their parents, you may have a better sense of why they treated you as they did.

If your parents are living, they may be able to provide much of this information. Since you will be asking them questions about their early history—not about their relationship with you—you may be surprised at how much they are willing to tell you.

You can either make a special date for the interview or weave your questions into an already scheduled visit. You be the judge. Do what feels right to you.

If your parents volunteer few insights, they may be unusually defensive or even denying what happened to them as children. Supplement what you are able to glean from them by talking with other relatives. It could be that others are more forthcoming. (See the suggestions for interviewing relatives and friends on page 151.)

Following is a list of possible questions to ask your parents. Look through them for ones that seem most thought-provoking. Write down other questions that come to mind. Ask yourself: What do I really want to know about my parents?

Questions to Ask Parents:

1. What was it like growing up in your family?
2. Tell me about the house(s) (or apartment) in which you grew up.
3. Did you like where you lived?
4. What kind of child were you? (E.g., happy, outgoing, shy, curious, etc.)
5. What were the spoken and unspoken rules in your family?
6. Did you feel closest to your mother or your father?
7. What were your parents like?
8. Do you think your parents were happy?
9. What did your parents do for fun?
10. Do you think your parents enjoyed being parents?
11. What was the best part of your childhood?
12. What was the toughest part of your childhood?
13. What was the family atmosphere like?
14. Was one of your brothers or sisters especially close to one of your parents? How did that make you feel?
15. Was there any obvious favoritism in your family?
16. Was there one child who always seemed to be left out?
17. Was there one child that a parent was especially hard on?
18. Was there one child who was "spoiled" by a parent?
19. Was there one child who "could do no wrong"?
20. What were you like as a teenager?
21. Did your parents openly reveal their emotions?
22. What did you want to be when you grew up?
23. What attracted you to Mom? (Dad?)
24. What was it like the first years you were married?
25. What were the most difficult years of your marriage?
26. Did you have any traumas as a child?
27. Did you want your first child to be a boy or a girl?
28. How did your parents react to your marriage?
29. How did your parents react to your dating?
30. Do you think a parent relied on you for emotional support?
31. Were either of your parents violent or abusive?
32. How did they discipline you?
33. What was it like living through the Depression? (or World War I or II?)
34. Was money a problem when you were growing up?

For added insight, you might ask your aunts and uncles similar questions about your parents: "What was my mother/father like as a young child?" "What do you remember most about my mother/father?" "How did my mother/father get along with your parents?" "Were you jealous of my parent or was my parent jealous of you?" These discussions can be very revealing.

Childhood friends, cousins, and neighbors can also be good informants. You alone can determine which questions to ask and how to phrase them. You might feel comfortable asking Aunt Frances searching, personal questions, for example, but you'd instinctively steer clear of those areas with Aunt Ruth.

Questions to Ask Friends, Aunts and Uncles, Cousins, and Neighbors:

1. How did you feel when you visited my house?
2. What were some of the major differences between your parents and mine?
3. Did you think either of my parents played favorites?
4. What do you remember about me as a child?
5. Was there anything that seemed odd or strange about my family?
6. What did you like about visiting my house?
7. What didn't you like about visiting my house?
8. How did my parents treat you?
9. How did my parents treat each other?
10. What do you remember about each of my brothers and sisters?

Siblings can be a storehouse of information about your family of origin. They went through many of the same experiences as you did, but with a different point of view. If you get along well with them, you've undoubtedly had many helpful conversations already. But if a difference in age, physical distance, or simple reticence has kept your interaction superficial, take this opportunity to ask more probing questions. (If you have a conflicted relationship with a brother or sister, skip this exercise. Turn to chapter 11 for suggestions on healing sibling relationships.)

Questions to Ask Siblings:

1. What do you remember most about the house(s) (or apartments) in which we grew up?
2. Do you have recurring dreams about the family? If so, what are they?

3. Did you feel closer to Mom or to Dad?
4. Did you think either Mom or Dad played favorites? (This could be a sensitive area.)
5. What were the saddest times for you growing up in the family?
6. What were the happiest times for you?
7. What did you want from Mom and/or Dad that you never got?
8. What did you appreciate most about Mom and/or Dad?
9. If you could change something about our family, what would it be?
10. What do you think were the unspoken rules in our family?
11. Did Mom or Dad (or Stepdad or Stepmom, etc.) influence you the most?
12. Did you pattern yourself after either Mom or Dad?
13. Did you deliberately distance yourself from Mom or Dad?
14. Do you feel that you have traits like Mom or Dad? How do you feel about this?
15. Which of our brothers and/or sisters did you feel closest to?
16. Do you think our caretakers treated us fairly?
17. Do you remember ever being very angry at Mom or Dad?
18. Which event hurt you the most?
19. Which event made you the happiest?

Other areas to explore: relationships with other relatives, specific events such as family moves, or traumatic events such as fires, accidents, divorces, or deaths.

EXERCISE 3:
Family Genogram or Political Map

Making a genogram, or psycho/political map, is a way to express key family relationships in graphic form.[2] This exercise is commonly used by family therapists to highlight recurring family patterns.

There are some limitations to this technique. A genogram is static; a family is ever-changing. A genogram illustrates only the most obvious family dynamics; families are a maze of complex interactions. Nonetheless, you can learn a great deal when you reduce your family dynamics to their simplest form. It's like flying in an airplane at 30,000 feet: suddenly you see all the mountains and valleys instead of just the cracks in the pavement.

I routinely ask my clients to construct genograms, and most of them find it a powerful exercise. When they see their family from afar, they see recurring patterns such as alcoholism, divorce, early pregnancies, poverty, criminality, large families, or parent-child triangles. They begin to see their present lives in a larger context and can pinpoint continuing trends. These insights often spark a greater interest in exploring childhood issues.

✸ Directions for a Family Genogram

In a traditional genogram, female family members are represented by circles, males by squares. Name or initials of each individual, along with his or her age, are placed within each symbol. An X is drawn through the symbols of those who have died and the dates of death are inscribed inside. Marriages are represented by horizontal lines between two individuals, with the date of the marriage written on the line. Common-law marriages, cohabitation, or long affairs are indicated by a dotted line connecting two individuals. Divorces or deaths are represented by a diagonal line through the marriage line, and the word *divorce* or *death* and the appropriate date are written on the line. Subsequent marriages are indicated by drawing a line below the first marriage line to the new marriage partner. Children are indicated by vertical lines descending from the marriage lines. Most commonly, the oldest child is on the left and the youngest child is on the right.

Once you have the basic skeleton sketched in, you are ready to add additional symbols to represent other traits. There are no universally accepted symbols for these concepts. Following are my suggestions. Invent your own symbols to represent areas I haven't covered.

Here is how the Jones family might be depicted in a genogram. Pamela and Ed Jones were married in 1965. They have three children—Maggie, 20; Ed Jr., 17; Suzie, 15. Ed Jones is overly attached to his youngest daughter, Suzie. He has a strained relationship with his wife. There is a lot of tension between Maggie and Suzie.

The Stewart family has a more complicated genogram. Gwen and Robert Stewart were married in 1946. They had two children— Mathew, who is now 40, and Thomas, who is now 38. Robert died in 1957. Gwen married her second husband, Lawrence, in 1959. They had one child, Stephanie, who is now 26.

Genogram Symbols

1. Use a jagged line between individuals to indicate a strained relationship. Example:

2. Draw a capital letter "A" to indicate alcoholism and capital letter "D" to indicate drug addiction. Examples:

3. Indicate depression or mental illness by a black check. Example:

4. Represent sexual abuse by drawing a jagged arrow from the offender to the victim. Example:

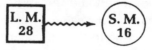

5. Show love affairs with a dashed line. Example:

6. Represent affluence by a dollar sign and poverty by a minus sign. Examples:

$ —

7. Underline the dominant personality in a marriage relationship. Example:

8. Indicate overly close parent-child bonds with a line with arrows running from parent to child. Example:

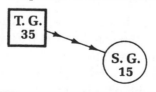

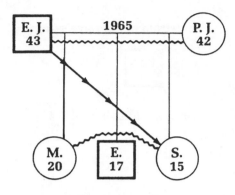

**Genogram of
the Jones Family**

Robert and Gwen never got along very well, partly because of Robert's alcoholism. Seeking companionship, Robert turned to his oldest son, Mathew. When Robert died, Gwen resumed where Robert left off and formed a close alliance with Mathew. Son Thomas is not only a Left-Out Child, he is an alcoholic. Gwen's second husband, Lawrence, is a recovering alcoholic, indicated in this example by a capital "A" with a circle around it. Lawrence is overly close with his daughter, Stephanie, which causes a lot of problems in the remarriage.

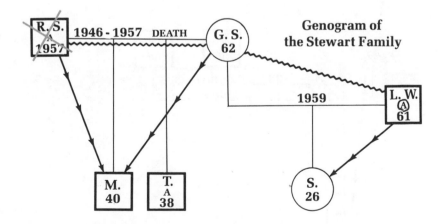

**Genogram of
the Stewart Family**

For added insight, carry your genogram back through as many generations as possible. On the next page is a four-generation genogram of my family. Notice the recurring pattern of alcoholism, divorce, and cross-generational coalitions.

Genogram of Pat Love's Family

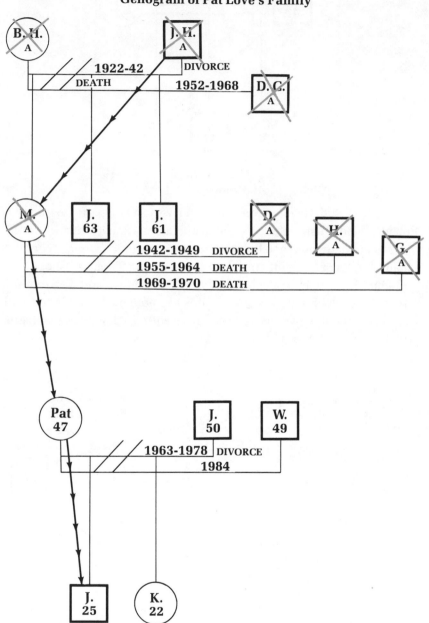

Once you have completed your genogram, ask yourself these questions: What would an impartial observer say about my family? Do the problems in my family seem to be increasing or diminishing over time? To what do I attribute the change? You might find it interesting to do this project with a sibling or have a sibling do the project separately and then compare notes. What similarities do you observe? What differences?

EXERCISE 4:
Summarizing What You've Learned

In this initial phase of recovery, you've had an opportunity to create an autobiography, interview relatives, and construct a genogram.

Which exercise affected you the most deeply?

Have your feelings changed about certain family members? If so, how have they changed?

What feelings have been stimulated by this process?

If you've been in therapy before, the work you've done in this chapter will have helped you crystallize earlier insights about your childhood and, I hope, given you some new ones. No matter how many times I examine the past, I always come up with new discoveries.

If this is your first concerted look at early family relationships, my hope is that you will be motivated to continue this work, either on your own, with a therapist, or in a support group. It takes time and dedicated effort to peel away the layers of myth and misinformation that encrust the past. Each time you journey into the past, you will come back with more and more information, and each discovery will relieve you of another piece of unfinished business.

10

Making Peace
with Your Parents

❀

Once you've begun to explore the past, the next stage of recovery is to evaluate your present-day relationships. Of all your relationships, the one with your parents is the most influential. Whether you live in the same house with your parents or have moved three thousand miles away, whether you continue to be entangled in each other's lives or haven't spoken for twenty years, improving the emotional climate between you will result in significant personal growth. Even if your parents are no longer living, there is work you can do to resolve old parent-child issues.

The reason that your relationship with your parents is so important is that it manifests itself throughout your life. Everyone around you inherits the unfinished business you have with your caretakers—your colleagues, your spouse, your friends, your children. Even if you've banished all conscious thoughts of your parents, they continue to insinuate themselves into your daily life. Without knowing it, you are drawn to people who treat you the same way your parents treated you. You project your feelings about your mother and father onto other people. You may treat your children the same way your parents treated you—even though you are trying to be a very different kind of parent. One way or another, unresolved parent-child issues resonate in your life. If you tackle the problem head-on and focus directly on your relationship with your parents, not on secondary relationships, you will make swifter and surer progress.

❸ Beth: "I could never figure out why Mother was so angry."

Beth was a college student who benefited greatly from realigning her relationship with her mother. She came to me because she was anxious about her grades. An "A" student when she was in high school, she was having problems adjusting to the higher academic standards of the university. Although this was her "presenting issue"—the issue that got her into therapy—I soon learned that there were other things bothering her. She was intimidated by her roommate, for example, and was in a destructive relationship with a young man.

As Beth talked about her family, it became clear to me that she was a Chosen Child. She had "a very special relationship" with her father and a tense relationship with her mother, Marion, a strident, self-centered woman who dominated the household. Her main problems were with Marion. She coped with her mother by being submissive, which allowed her to sidestep her wrath. Her younger brother, Arnold, the family's Scapegoat Child, absorbed most of their mother's abuse.

Although Beth's docility was useful when she was young, it was now a drawback, because she was so passive that even her friends took advantage of her. Her passivity seemed also to be the source of many of her problems at school: she was reluctant to ask questions in class, for example, and struggled with assignments that weren't really clear to her. She wasn't assertive enough to be a top student.

In our work together, Beth was able to see the connection between the way she acted around her mother and the way she acted around other people. To her, all people were potential Marions, and to protect herself she automatically assumed a compliant attitude.

To help Beth become more assertive, I guided her through a series of role-playing exercises. The first week, I asked her to pretend to be a little girl and talk to her mother, represented by an empty chair. I encouraged her to tell Marion how it had felt to grow up in her care, how intimidated and threatened she had felt. This exercise was fairly easy for Beth to do, because she was well acquainted with her fear and anxiety.

The second week, I asked her to turn to the chair and tell her mother how she wanted to be treated. This was more difficult for her. At first she spoke in a whisper. After a half-dozen rehearsals and some role-modeling from me, however, she was finally able to sit up tall in her chair and say in a strong voice, "I want you to get off my back! And get off my brother's back, too!" Having said this, she laughed at herself in amazement. "Who was *that* talking?" she wanted to know.

The third week, I had Beth reverse roles. This time she played her mother, and I played Beth as a little girl. In my guise as Beth I asked her, "Why were you so angry all the time, Mother? What was going on in your life that made you so hard to live with?" Beth thought for a while and was able to come up with some plausible answers, which helped her gain some insight into her mother's point of view as a Left-Out Spouse. In just three sessions, Beth had been able to acknowledge her pain, summon up some of her repressed anger, and begin to understand her mother's motives.

The test came when Beth went home for Thanksgiving vacation. She was relieved to discover that the sense of power she had developed in the role-playing exercises carried over into real life. To her surprise, her mother seemed less commanding to her—even physically smaller. "In my imagination, she's six feet tall," she told me later. "In reality, she's only five foot six. I'm a half-inch taller than she is!" Her work had reduced her mother to realistic proportions. She also discovered that she felt some compassion for the woman. "For the first time, I looked at her and saw a lonely old lady," she said.

In the following months, Beth became more confident in all her activities. She improved her grades, became more assertive with her roommate, and broke off her self-destructive relationship with her boyfriend. "If I can find the nerve to stand up to my mother," she concluded, "I can stand up to anyone." Her success at resolving tensions with her mother created a ripple effect that enhanced her power in all other realms.

88 Becoming More Objective

Just as Beth was able to scale her mother down to size, you need to learn to see your mother and father in human scale. Philip Guerin, noted family therapist, spent some time exploring his feelings about his parents and managed to achieve this objectivity. In a comment in *The Book of Family Therapy*,[1] Guerin wrote, ". . . working on my own family has enabled me to see my parents as real people. At this point I don't believe I over-value or under-value either of them. Although on the one hand I am perhaps more aware of their shortcomings, I believe that each one of them is more knowable to me now and that I am closer to each of them than at any other time in my life. One thing is certain; I don't view them as the malignant cause of my shortcomings."

How do you know if you've attained this balanced view of your caretakers? There are four indicators to look for:

1. **You can interact with your parents (stepparents) without being unduly upset or disappointed.** Your parents may not act the way you would like them to, but at least you are mentally prepared for their behavior. You are rarely caught off guard by their actions.

2. **Your assessment of your parents tends to correspond with others' assessments of them.** This means you neither overrate nor underrate your parents as compared to the judgment of other people. You see them more or less the way others do.

3. **You see positive and negative traits in both caretakers.** Instead of idealizing one parent and diminishing the other, you see positive and negative characteristics in both of them. For the most part, they seem like ordinary people with a standard assortment of strengths and weaknesses.

4. **You no longer blame your parents for all of your difficulties.** Although your parents were responsible for your upbringing, you are able to transcend your tendency to blame them for all of your shortcomings. Over time, you have accepted the fact they did the best they could given their circumstances.

✷ Accepting Your Parents' Negative Traits

A key part of obtaining this objective view of your parents is accepting their faults. Your caretakers, like all caretakers, were not always the wise, warm, and wonderful people you needed them to be. There were times when they failed to satisfy some of your needs and interpreted other needs incorrectly. They had personality traits that made your life difficult.

If your parents are living, you need to accept the fact that they still have negative traits today and will continue to have them in the future. Their personalities are well established; they are who they are. Short of getting them to sign up for intensive therapy, it's not likely that they will change in any significant way. You need to accept their limitations and let go of your wish that they undergo a miraculous transformation.

I know how difficult it is to give up the wish for perfect parents. We cling to an idealized view of our caretakers because on some level we still view life through the eyes of a child and believe we are dependent on our parents for survival. When we see flaws in their characters, we are not merely annoyed—we are terrified. Our very existence seems threatened. A voice inside cries out: "No one is taking care of me!" To ward off this anxiety, we hold on to the dream that our parents' faults will magically disappear: *this* visit, our parents will be sensitive to our needs; *this* reunion will be smooth and uneventful; *this* phone call or *this* letter will repair old wounds and bring us closer together.

Not surprisingly, the character flaws we have the hardest times accepting are the ones that wounded us most during childhood. When our parents act in destructive and familiar ways, our present anguish is magnified by our early pain. Underneath our grown-up dismay is a little child crying out for more love and safety.

At times I have seen my own regressive response to my mother quite clearly. For example, twenty-five years ago my stepfather died, and my husband and I went home for his funeral. On the evening of the burial, we dropped by my mother's house to console her. We knocked on the door, but there was no answer. We walked into the bedroom, and I was startled to see my mother embracing a man I had never met before. I almost fainted from shock. My husband saw how upset I was and hurried me out of the house.

Now, it is understandable that I would be upset by my mother's behavior. To take up with a relative stranger on the night of your husband's funeral is not expected behavior. But my misery went deeper than that. Weeks went by before I could think about that episode without disintegrating into tears.

What I eventually realized is that my mother's behavior tapped into some very old pain. When I was growing up there had been times when she would come home from the tavern with a strange man, and I would be banished to the downstairs while she and the stranger disappeared into the bedroom. Once I was awakened in the middle of the night to see my mother standing beside my bed with a man I had never seen before. At my mother's request, he picked me up out of my bed and carried me downstairs. My mother followed silently behind. As he and my mother turned to walk up the stairs, I cried out, "Mommy, don't leave me! Don't leave me!" But my cries went unheeded. I cried out in terror and panic for what seemed like hours until finally I fell asleep from exhaustion.

Ten years later, when I went home for my stepfather's funeral, my mother's imprudent behavior triggered this memory. It was more than I could handle. For six months, I would neither see her nor answer her letters. On an unconscious level, I was still furious for having been abandoned.

Eventually, my deep need to be connected with my mother overcame my animosity. About a year after the encounter, I had cooled off enough to write her a letter. In the letter I said that although I didn't approve of her behavior, I didn't want that one encounter to come between us. I was willing to let bygones be bygones.

Neither of us brought up the incident ever again. We just picked up where we had left off and went on from there. My mother died rather suddenly, not long after. Now, twenty years later, the passage of time and years of therapy have erased most of my anger at her. I am eternally grateful that I had the sense to reach out to her before coming to a complete resolution. If I had waited for total understanding, it would have been too late.

It is easy to think that "accepting" your parents means liking them or approving of what they do. *To the contrary, accepting them means giving up your fantasy of whom you want them to be.* You don't have to like your parents; you don't have to agree with them on important issues; you don't have to have similar tastes or values. All you need to do is see them and accept them for who they are.

There's a simple but effective exercise that will help you increase your level of acceptance of your caretakers. (I was first introduced to it by my friend and former mentor, Ed Jacobs.) I assigned a variation of it to a 40-year-old woman named Sandra who was having a difficult time coming to terms with her mother. What bothered her most was her mother's negativity. "My mother calls me up just so she can bitch," she told me. "It makes me so angry! When

I hang up the phone, I'm upset for hours. I have to soak in the tub to untie the knots. When my husband hears me talking to her, he automatically starts running the bath water. He knows I'm going to need it."

To help Sandra get some perspective on her strong reaction to her mother, I asked, "In one hundred phone calls from your mother, how many of them would you say are loving and supportive?"

"About two—at most," she said.

"And how many are negative?"

"Ninety-eight!"

"So, overall, would you describe your mother as a positive or negative person?"

"Negative. Negative!"

"Then for you to expect your mother to be positive when she talks to you on the phone is unrealistic about ninety-eight percent of the time. Right?"

Sandra took a deep breath, let it out with a sigh, and nodded in agreement.

I told her that it wasn't likely her mother would change at this late date; she was too set in her ways. But she, Sandra, could change the way she reacted to her mother by getting her expectations in line with reality. If she had a more realistic attitude, her stress level would be greatly reduced.

To help her get a more accurate view of her mother, I asked her to log every phone conversation with her. After each one, she was to mark down whether it had been a negative or a positive encounter. If it had been negative, she was to say to herself, "That was Mother being Mother. That's the way she normally is." If it had been positive, she was to say, "That was unusual. My mother is rarely this positive."

This exercise proved to be the breakthrough Sandra needed to accept her mother's difficult personality. Although she experienced some sadness at letting go of her fantasy of a transformed mother, she also experienced a welcome sense of relief.

If you are chronically disappointed by one or both of your parents, I suggest you try the following exercise.

EXERCISE 1:
Accepting a Parent's Negative Traits

Think about one of your caretakers. Now list the five qualities that bother you the most about this parent.

1.

2.

3.

4.

5.

Next, write five sentences that show your willingness to accept these traits. Here are some examples: "I acknowledge the fact that my father has a low opinion of himself." "I acknowledge the fact that my father is often depressed and negative." "I acknowledge the fact that my mother is often critical of me." You may find it helpful to repeat this exercise just prior to a visit with your parent. If you prepare yourself mentally for what is likely to happen, you will spare yourself some disappointment.

88 Affirming a Parent's Positive Qualities

Just as you may have difficulty accepting a parent's failings, you may be blocking a parent's positive qualities as well; you can be in denial of the good as well as the bad. This may be especially true of a parent from whom you were estranged. Here's an example: I was visiting a friend of mine who had been over-bonded with her father and persecuted by her mother. While I was there, she received a letter from her mother and read it to me. I found her mother's writing witty, humorous, and full of homespun wisdom, and I told her so. She began to read other letters. She spent an hour reading to me from her collection of letters, and I thoroughly enjoyed what I heard.

The next morning my friend told me it had been helpful to get my reaction to the letters. "I never realized that my mother had such a good sense of humor. I've always thought of her as demanding and selfish. I've only seen her dark side. Hearing your laughter helped me appreciate a whole new side to her."

If you think you could be blocking a parent's positive qualities, you might consider going home for a visit and bringing a friend along. Ask your friend (or partner) to be an observer, not a therapist or mediator. Your friend may see some positive qualities you've overlooked.

Another way to broaden your scope is to find out how your brothers and sisters or other relatives view the parent. It may be strikingly different. For example, one of my clients had grown up idolizing her father and diminishing her mother. Following my advice, she initiated a conversation with her older sister about their mother and discovered that her sister had a great deal of respect for her. My client had assumed that everyone in the family felt the same way she did. She admired her sister a great deal, and hearing her viewpoint helped her become more aware of her mother's strengths.

EXERCISE 2:
Becoming More Aware of a Parent's Positive Traits

Think about a caretaker with whom you have (or had) a conflicted relationship. Now list five admirable qualities that best describe this person. If you can't think of that many, talk to a friend or family member to see if you can come up with more.

1.

2.

3.

4.

5.

The next time you visit or talk with this person, see if you can add to this list. What positive traits do you share with this parent?

✿ Setting Limits Around an Invasive Parent

An essential aspect of making peace with your parents is to establish clear boundaries between you. As I explained in chapter 7, a healthy family system has a firm but flexible barrier between parents and children. When the children mature, this barrier is reinforced. The adult child no longer needs to turn to the parents for protection, guidance, day-to-day affection, nurturing, or financial support, because those needs are now taken care of by a partner or adult friends. The two generations stay in touch because of the love between them and because they are genuinely interested in each other, not because they meet each other's fundamental needs or feel a sense of obligation.

The exceptions are worth mentioning. I believe a parent and adult child are obligated to keep each other apprised of their status and whereabouts. A significant illness, a death in the family, a job change, a divorce or a marriage, and a change of address are examples of information that needs to be shared. In addition, I believe that adult children have a responsibility to care for their aging parents in some fashion. Whether that entails home care or institutional care is for each family to decide.

Beyond these minimal obligations, a healthy relationship between a parent and adult child is one characterized by choice. For example, one reason to stay in touch is to give everyone a sense of history. When family members play the game "remember when," everyone has a sense of belonging and a connection to earlier times. Through repetition of these anecdotes, a family identity is passed down from generation to generation.

Sharing celebrations and rituals is another reason why adults and their parents choose to stay together. Celebrations add joy, drama, and meaning to everyday life and provide a public statement of family unity. Celebrations can also promote healing. In most families, people will bury the hatchet when Uncle Buzzy gets married, and feuding brothers and sisters will call a truce long enough to work on Mom and Dad's fiftieth wedding anniversary. These festivities offer the opportunity for transition and reconnection; they provide a time for starting over, an unofficial New Year's Day.

The need for guidance may also connect adult children and their parents. The older generation may have expertise in a special area or have overall wisdom that comes from having lived a few more decades. The tables turn as the parents become limited by poor health or age, and the older generation may turn to the younger generation for advice. In this exchange of insight and information, two ideas are kept in mind: (1) asking for advice is not the same thing as taking it, and (2) unsolicited advice can lead to resentment— especially if the advice is coupled with expectation.

A desire to express affection, history sharing, celebration, and guidance are key components of a healthy parent/adult child relationship. Ideally, these interactions and any beyond this—mutual interests, cooperative ventures, and joint activities, for example— should be a matter of personal choice.

🕱 Marcos: "I could never win in my family."

I worked with a 28-year-old man named Marcos whose interaction with his parents was quite different from the healthy model I just described. His father gave him unsolicited advice, offered gifts of money with strings attached, and either directly or indirectly intervened in his affairs. A lack of boundaries was evident between Marcos and his sisters as well. They, too, felt they had a right to insinuate themselves into his affairs, and any exchange that would normally take place between two family members brought in all the players from the bench.

Marcos described to me an incident that typified this absence of boundaries. Marcos owns a small art gallery outside of Austin, Texas. Although the gallery is gaining in popularity, Marcos has had to struggle to make ends meet and has been in dire need of a car for several years. His father had pressured Marcos to accept money for a car, but he had steadfastly refused. His father had given him money before, and there had been a price to pay. For example, several years ago his father had paid off his graduate-school loan, then felt he had earned the right to criticize Marcos for his choice of profession. "After all I've done to help you get established," his father told him, "you turn around and sink money into an art gallery! How could you do this to me?"

The controversy over the car came to a head when Marcos went home for Easter and two of his sisters independently brought up the subject of the car. One lobbied him to accept their father's offer, because, according to her, one of their father's greatest pleasures in life was giving money to his children. The other sister hammered away about how much a new car would improve the image of his art gallery. Marcos finally relented and went to his mother to tell her he'd decided to talk to his father about a new car. To which his mother responded, "Why would you talk to him about cars? He doesn't know anything about cars."

Instantly Marcos realized that his father hadn't talked to his wife about the gift of a car—he'd made the offer without consulting her. Marcos quickly changed the subject to give himself time to think. Later that day, he went to one of his sisters and asked her to tell their father that he, Marcos, would be willing to accept the offer if his father would talk it over with his mother first. So Sister talked to Father, who talked to Mother, who talked to Daughter, who relayed the message to Brother. The end result was that Marcos eventually accepted the money for a car. "I'm sorry I did, though," he told me later. "Now my father expects me to drive home every weekend. It's a real burden."

This is a classic example of a family with diffuse boundaries.

To help Marcos draw clearer boundaries between himself and his parents and siblings, I asked him to come up with two lists, one showing information he considered his own business, and the other showing information he was willing to share with his family. Here are his lists:

My Business	My Family's Business
My finances	My general health
My sex life	How I can be reached
My love life	Major life changes
How I spend my time	Health of mutual friends
Whom I choose as friends	Death of mutual friends
Whom I choose to marry	Health of family members
Whom I date	Death of family members
What goes on between me and my friends	**Whatever information or activities I choose to share with them**
Maintenance of my home	
My choice of career	
What goes on between me and a relative	

We both agreed that the most important item on these lists was the one in bold. He wanted to feel free to involve his family in his life to any degree he wished, but he wanted it to be his choice, not theirs. Otherwise, it was a perpetuation of the enmeshed family system that had been so damaging to him as a child.

Making this list proved to be quite helpful to Marcos. For the first time he had a clear sense of when his boundaries were being violated and was able to defend his own territory.

88 Examining Your Reasons for Staying Enmeshed

Does Marcos's family sound anything like your family? Do you keep getting tangled up in confusing, emotional transactions with your parents? If so, it may be time to build some fences.

Before you start digging holes for the fenceposts, however, it may help to figure out your role in the continuing boundary violations. You may be playing a more active part than you realize. For example, some people allow their parents to intrude in their lives because of a misplaced sense of guilt. On some level, they think they owe their parents something. They feel they've done something wrong in the past, so they need to make reparations in the present. In effect, they are saying, "Go ahead. Trespass. My earlier behavior denies me the right to my independence."

This kind of thinking is especially common between the Chosen Child and the Left-Out Spouse. On some level, the Chosen Child feels responsible for the fact that the parent was left out in the cold. I counseled a woman who was closely linked with her father and estranged from her stepmother. Following the death of her father, she was roped into becoming her stepmother's confidante. She sat up with her stepmother night after night, listening to the woman's interminable laments. "I felt powerless to draw away," she told me, "I had no will. I would be sitting there hating her, but I couldn't get up and walk out of the room. I was under her power." The reason that she allowed herself to be trapped in this role, she eventually realized, was that she felt guilty for the fact that her father had preferred her. She felt she had to atone for past sins.

Other people put up with a parent's invasive behavior because they feel overly responsible for the parent. This is a common reaction. A child who is trained to take care of a parent's emotional needs will have a hard time letting go of this role in later years—especially if the parent is very demanding. I recall a man who came in for marriage counseling because his mother insisted on interfering in his life. She lived with him and his wife and seemed to be bent on ruining his marriage. Even though she criticized his wife daily, he was afraid to tell her to back off. "I don't want to upset her," he told me. "I'm all she has. What would she do without me?" His exaggerated sense of responsibility for his mother was causing severe difficulties in his marriage. I pointed out to him that his mother was a healthy, physically active, financially independent woman in her mid-sixties. She had a lot of options besides him. His early experience as a Chosen Child had given him the false impression that he was her only resource.

Some Chosen Children stay entwined with their parents for a very different reason: they want to hold on to the advantages of being a child. They turn to a parent for financial support, luxuriate in the security and comfort of living at home, or allow a parent to take care of their daily needs. In exchange for these favors, the Chosen Child is asked to relinquish some of his privileges. Typically, Mom or Dad dictates how he spends their money, demands detailed reports of his personal life, puts inappropriate limits on his behavior, or demands an excessive amount of his time and attention. The Chosen Child will be unable to demand all the privileges of an adult unless he is willing to let go of the advantages of being a child.

If you have murky boundaries between you and a parent, take a moment to pinpoint the reasons you've allowed your rights to be violated. Is it a misplaced sense of guilt? Is it an overly developed sense of responsibility? Is it a fear of making waves? Is it a desire to hold on to the advantages of being a child? Is it fear of a parent's anger? Is it a combination of these reasons?

88 Mastering the Art of the Ten-Second Confrontation

Once you have identified the part you play in allowing a parent to violate your territory, there is a simple technique that will help you reinforce your boundaries. I call it the "Ten-Second Confrontation." A Ten-Second Confrontation is an honest, direct, on-the-spot statement that you make the moment that your boundaries are violated. You don't have to be rude or violate a parent's rights in order to establish your boundaries. You just need to make your point, then get off it.

I can remember the very words that heralded my separation from my mother. I had returned home from college for Easter break. My boyfriend was with me, and we had made plans to drive forty miles south to visit his roommate. When it was time to leave, my mother said to me, "It's stormy outside. I don't want you to go in this weather." My reply was simple: "We're going to go." My mother and I looked at each other for a moment, absorbing this new behavior. I had stated my position calmly but forcefully, and, to her credit, she didn't argue. From that point on, our ways were more divided. I made more and more of my own decisions, and she didn't object.

Here are some examples of how other people redefined their boundaries with a parent. Ellie was a single woman who had been her father's favorite daughter. He came to stay with her for several months shortly after his wife died. One night, Ellie came home late from a date and found her father waiting up for her. As soon as she stepped in the door, he launched into a tirade: "How dare you come home this late! I've been worried sick about you! Don't ever do this to me again!" To which she replied: "Dad, I understand you're upset, but I'm here to tell you, you can't treat me this way. I'm thirty years old, and I'm not going to report to you like a teenager." Her father got the message and never interfered in her social life again.

Martin began having trouble with his mother soon after he married. His mother did not like his wife from day one and made no secret of it. She even tried to band her other children against the newcomer in the family. Martin put a stop to it by saying, "Mother— Mazzie is my wife. I love her and intend to stay married to her. You may think you're driving her away from me, but you're driving *me* away from *you* instead."

If you think a few cautionary remarks might help realign your relationship with a parent, read through these comments for more inspiration:

"Mother, I don't want you to call me after ten o'clock at night. I like to spend quiet time with my husband at that time."

"I am not willing to talk with you on the phone if you criticize me over and over. Call me when you have something pleasant to say."

"I'd rather you not call me at work. Call me at home instead."

"Dad, I really don't want you to talk to me about Mom. Let's talk about something else."

"Mother, I'd be glad to take you shopping once a month, but not every week."

"Mother, even though you live in the same house with us and can't help but hear the arguments Dan and I have, what happens between us is our business. If I want to talk about it with you, I'll bring it up."

"Dad, I don't want you to brag about me in front of my sister. It makes me feel bad to hear you go on so much about me."

When you make a statement like one of the above, you may need to reassure your mother or father that you are simply eliminating one undesirable form of interaction, not cutting off contact altogether. For example, you might say to your mother, "I have no room in my life for you as a critic, but I have a lot of room for you as a mother." Or you might say to a father, "I appreciate your concern for me. I've always counted on your support. I don't want to hurt your feelings. It's just that Robert and I are doing our own financial planning from now on."

If you're planning to limit the amount of time you spend with a parent, it may help to give some advance warning: "I'm planning to go to my friend Erma's house for Thanksgiving, so I won't be coming home in November as usual." Or, "In four weeks, I'm going to cancel my membership in the club. I guess you'll have to find a new tennis partner. How about Betsy?"

Once you've stated your intentions, *strive to keep the rest of your interactions as normal as possible.* This is very important. Continue to call on the phone, to joke, to act friendly and relaxed, to get together for holidays—whatever you used to do and can continue to do without violating your boundaries. You don't have to disown your parents just because you've decided to make some positive and long-overdue changes!

Coping with Guilt and Anxiety

For some of you, the idea of a Ten-Second Confrontation with a parent may seem intolerable. There's no way you would feel comfortable limiting a parent's or stepparent's behavior. The very idea sends chills up your spine.

If so, you may find it helpful to build up your courage by rehearsing a Ten-Second Confrontation with a trusted friend. Have your friend pretend to be your mother, father, or stepparent, and rehearse what you would like to say. Or you may want to do this exercise mentally, visualizing your parent hearing your message and respecting your wishes. Imagine being just as powerful as your parent. The more times you go through these drills, the easier the new behavior will be.

Then, the next time you are with your parent, look for opportunities to speak your mind. If you don't feel up to a Ten-Second Confrontation, say the words silently and look for smaller ways to assert yourself. Don't try swimming the Amazon River if you're terrified of backyard pools. Allow your confidence to build gradually. Just identifying the behavior that you don't like and telling yourself how you would like your parent to act may be a significant improvement.

If guilt is preventing you from establishing clear boundaries, remind yourself that the goal of this exercise is not to hurt your parent or to destroy the bond between you. The goal is to realign the relationship so that there is room for both of you to grow and function in the fullest possible manner. Ultimately, you will be creating a stronger, longer-lasting, and more resilient relationship.

Some of you may go through a grieving period when you begin to limit the excessive contact you have with a parent. You may find yourself feeling depressed, despondent, perhaps longing for the old relationship. You may be surprised to discover how much of you wants to hold on to the overly close ties. If you continue to maintain clear boundaries and allow for the passage of time, the intensity of these emotions will diminish. Meanwhile, redirect some of your energy into creating ties with other family members and friends.

88 How to Free Yourself from an Extremely Invasive Parent

If gaining more distance from a parent is exceedingly difficult for you, I suggest you enlist the aid of a therapist. You may need additional support to establish appropriate limits. A cautionary remark here and there is not going to work: family therapy is required.

One of my clients, an 18-year-old woman, had great difficulty separating herself from her possessive father. He was so dependent on her for emotional support, he insisted that she spend just as many hours with him as she did with her boyfriends. She was required to keep actual records. Whenever she began to get close to a young man, she felt guilty or disloyal and began to find something wrong with him. For months we explored her relationship with her father, but she was unable to separate from him until I invited him to a therapy session.

My role in the separation process was to ask the father the tough questions my client had been too afraid to ask: "Are you going to commit suicide if your daughter finds someone she loves?" "Can you take care of yourself?" "Will you be okay without her to take care of you?" "Are you willing to release your daughter from responsibility for your well-being?" Once he assured his daughter that he was not planning to take his life and could manage without her, she was able to take the first small steps away from him. She needed continual reassurance, however, to make the transition.

If you have a lot of difficulty separating from a parent, by all means seek professional help. A therapist will help you come up with new options and cope with your guilt and anxiety. It's a sign of wisdom—not weakness—to get help when you need it.

✿ Creating a More Positive Relationship with a Parent

In addition to clarifying your boundaries with a parent, you may feel the need to create a more positive relationship between you. Years of conflict may have created a tense, unpleasant atmosphere. If this is true for you, there are several ways to come closer together. With some parents, the old saying, "the least said, the best mended," is good advice. You may not need to bring up the past to get resolution, just make a small, friendly overture and go from there. This is an effective course of action with an uncommunicative parent or one who is invested in saving face.

To carry out this approach, just send a nice note, extend a lunch invitation, give a heartfelt compliment, or show a sincere interest in a parent's activities—anything that demonstrates your intention to be on better terms. I had a client who managed to bridge the gulf between her and her mother by writing her a special Mother's Day poem. Her mother was deeply touched by the gesture, and their relationship began a gradual warming trend that has continued to this day.

Reaching out to a parent in a small, positive way is one of those simple suggestions that is easy to dismiss: "That wouldn't work with my mother (or father), our problems are too complex." My advice is to try it before you reject it. It may provide the breakthrough you've been looking for.

✿ Fake It 'Til You Make It

There's a variation of this technique that I find quite useful—which is to imagine a better parent-child relationship, then play-act your part of it. "Fake it 'til you make it," as they say. I helped a client named Mave develop a more positive attitude before going home to spend the holidays with her mother and stepfather. Despite her anxiety at being around her hypercritical mother, she forced herself to appear happy, calm, and cooperative. She chatted about her activities as if her mother really wanted to hear about them. It was impossible to insult Mave or get her to take part in the usual games. At one point, her mother aimed a heat-seeking missile in her direction, and Mave simply ducked. This strategy worked amazingly well. Mave had the best time she had had with her mother in years, and a precedent was established for all subsequent reunions.

It's possible that if you perfect this technique, you will not only find it easier to be around your parents, you may even see some changes in *their* behavior. It's hard to mouth the same old lines when someone else is reading from a revised script. A lasting transformation requires patience and a significant investment of energy, however. People cling tenaciously to old habits—especially family members who have settled into well-worn grooves. But your parents may eventually respond to a sincere and persistent effort to let bygones be bygones. Meanwhile—start defining your boundaries.

✇ Do the Unexpected

In some instances, casting yourself in an unexpected role can dramatically improve your relationship with a parent. Instead of making subtle behavioral changes, do something dramatically different. If you dare to disrupt the unspoken family rules, remarkable changes can occur. The following example involves an exchange between a woman and her husband's grandmother, although the principle applies equally well to parent-child relationships.

Katie, a participant in one of my seminars, told me of a momentous encounter she had with her grandmother-in-law, a commanding, intimidating woman known to everyone as "Baba." Katie's husband was Baba's favorite grandchild. This fact was well known and resented by other family members. Baba gave her Chosen Grandchild more expensive gifts at holidays, always remembered his birthday, took his side in family feuds, and invited him to visit more often than she invited any of the others. Baba took an immediate dislike to Katie, no doubt sensing stiff competition for her grandson's affection.

At first, Katie modeled her behavior after that of other family members and treated the matriarch with respectful reserve. But when she saw that this was getting her nowhere, she did an about-face. One particular exchange proved pivotal to their relationship. Out of the blue, Katie asked Baba if she wanted to stay with them the following summer. Baba, a practiced martyr, responded in typical fashion: "That's a nice thought, but the way I've been feeling lately, it's doubtful I'll live through the winter." Katie refused to play Baba's game. Instead of offering the expected reassurance, she blurted, "Well, if you die, I'd just as soon you not come. I don't want any dead people hanging around my house!" Baba was aghast. No one talked to her that way! She said nothing for a few moments, then to everyone's surprise she gave a dry laugh. Then another. She continued to cackle for several minutes. Katie's irreverent remark had broken through her crusty reserve. Baba lived for many years thereafter (despite her complaints, she was in excellent health), and the two women became friends. Because Katie had risked doing something radically different, she had ducked beneath Baba's formidable defenses.

If you are trapped in a negative, stagnant relationship with your mother or father, consider doing the unexpected. If you've been subservient, be outrageously bold. If you've avoided a parent for years, start sending gifts. If you always go home for Christmas—and hate it—fly to Hawaii instead. The point is—*do something different!* So many times clients have said to me, "When I walk into my parents' house, I become twelve year old." Well, don't walk into their house! Meet them in Santa Fe instead! Shake up the system! If what you've been doing hasn't been working, dare to be different! One man who hadn't been on speaking terms with his father since he was 20 years old invited his aging father to raft with him down the Colorado River. It was a momentous trip, and they've been much closer ever since. Throw a curve ball into *your* family relationships and see what happens.

88 The Formal Reconciliation Meeting

In some families, a more direct approach is called for. Instead of changing your attitude and style of behavior, discuss the conflict directly. This method works best when both you and your parent feel comfortable expressing your feelings, and when your parent has some degree of self-awareness. Don't try it with a mother or father who habitually denies all responsibility for past behavior—you'll be wasting your time.

There's another prerequisite, which is that you must have a realistic, positive attitude. You should go into this reconciliation meeting with two intentions: (1) to improve the relationship, and (2) to set the record straight. If you have a hidden desire to break off the relationship or punish your parent, go talk to a therapist, not to your parent.

Once you are clear about your intentions, you might want to take the edge off your feelings by writing them down or sharing them with a trustworthy person. This rehearsal will help you feel more calm and rational. The meeting isn't intended to be cathartic; it's an announcement of your desire to improve the relationship.

It may also help to gird yourself for your parent's likely response. If there has been a great deal of conflict between you, be prepared for more of the same. For example, if your father has been critical of you in the past, he is likely to be critical in the meeting. Just because you've changed doesn't mean he's ready to jump on the bandwagon—at least at first. It may be wise for you to prepare yourself for a defensive response despite the fact that you will be careful not to blame or judge.

Finally, be open to your parent's perspective, which could be quite different from yours and just may contain an element of truth. It's not likely that your point of view is the only valid one. Cultivate an open mind. Ask yourself, "What can I learn about myself from this meeting? How have I been blind?"

Once you've done this homework, you're ready for the actual meeting. Following is a suggested outline of the discussion.

DIRECTIONS FOR A RECONCILIATION MEETING WITH A PARENT

1. **Statement of purpose**. In clear and simple language, state the reason that you arranged the meeting. Strive for a relaxed, confident tone of voice. Practice beforehand if necessary.

Examples:

"I would like our relationship to be better. I'm willing to work toward that, and I hope you are, too."

"I would like to talk with you about our relationship. It's been troubling me, and I'd like to make it better."

"I've been thinking about what happened between us for a long time. I'd like to see if we can work toward a reconciliation."

2. **Ownership of your role in the difficulty.** This is your chance to describe how you contributed to the conflict in the relationship. Keep to an objective description of your own behavior.

Examples of comments to an estranged parent:

"I know it must have been hard on you to have me be so angry all the time. You must have had a hard time knowing how to handle me. I wasn't the easiest child to raise."

"I was mean to you when you married Dad. I didn't give you the respect you deserved. I must have been really hard to live with."

Examples of comments to a parent with whom you were overly bonded:

"I took on too much responsibility for you in the past. I'm going to get that in better balance."

"I feel like I shut Mother out when I was younger. I wish I had been more appreciative of her. I think I added to the tension between you."

"I had mixed feelings about being so connected to you when I was younger. I liked feeling special to you, but I also felt uncomfortable sometimes. You must have felt my ambivalence."

3. **Statement of how you would like your relationship to be in the future.** This is a positive description of the changes you'd like to see happen. Again, no blaming or accusations.

Examples:

"I'd like us to feel more comfortable around each other."

"We've never really talked. I'd like to hear from you what it was like all those years when there was so much trouble in the family."

"I'd like us to bury the hatchet and start over again. What happened to us was really beyond our control. We were both trying to get our needs met."

"I'd like to spend time with you and with Mother individually. Just because I spend time with her, it doesn't mean I'm abandoning you. I still care about you. But I care about Mother, too."

"I'd like us to start celebrating the holidays together. I always feel lonely not being together at Thanksgiving. Maybe that would be a good place for us to start."

Note: If you believe that a reconciliation meeting would be helpful for you and a relative but doubt your ability to do it effectively, you might want to seek the help of a therapist. You can contract for a couple of short sessions or one long one; You don't have to sign up for life. Just make your intentions clear and be sure that the therapist believes in your goals. If you shop around, you should be able to find a therapist who will respond to your request. If possible, select a therapist who works with families, not just individuals.

✿ Resolving Your Feelings About a Deceased Parent

I have helped many clients resolve their feelings about a deceased parent. A technique that seems universally helpful is to write a letter to the parent as if he or she were still alive, expressing all your pent-up feelings. If you think this approach would help you, here is a suggested model.[2]

MODEL FOR A LETTER TO A DECEASED PARENT

1. **State the facts about what happened.** This is your chance to set the record straight. Be specific and thorough. For example, you might begin with a statement like this: *"You relied on me too heavily when I was a child. I felt responsible for your happiness. I could never leave home without feeling guilty. You led me to believe I couldn't make it on my own. . . ."* Get it all out. Don't hold back.

2. **Acknowledge your feelings.** Let your feelings flow. Express any anger, shame, fear, sadness, guilt, or resentment that comes up as a result of this experience. Full expression is your goal. Exaggerate your feelings if that feels right. Writing this portion of the letter will free up a lot of stored feelings. It is important to know that you can feel the feelings without acting on them.

　　Examples:

　　"I am so angry that you never noticed me. I needed help so badly and you acted as if I weren't there."

　　"It angers me that you treated Mother so rudely. She really cared about you."

　　"I feel so ashamed that I treated you so meanly when you were sick. I didn't know how bad you were feeling."

3. **Explore what might have been.** Let your parent know about your unfulfilled wishes.

Examples:

"If we had been closer, I could have learned so much from you."

"I feel cheated because you died when I was so young. I hardly remember a thing about you. I know more from pictures than I do from memory."

"I keep thinking about how my life would have been different if you had stood between me and Mother. I was so vulnerable. I was so scared. If you had been more protective of me, I think I would have a lot fewer emotional scars."

"If you had put more limits on my behavior, I wouldn't have gotten into so much trouble later in life. You gave me the feeling that I could do anything I wanted to do. I wish you had been more of a parent and less of a friend."

"I wish I had grown up knowing what it was like to be loved and cherished by you. I bet I'd feel a lot more secure."

"I wish you had treated my brothers and sisters more fairly. They wouldn't have resented me so much if they had gotten some of your attention."

"I wonder what it would have been like growing up feeling free, not like everything I said or did was the subject of scrutiny."

4. **Be honest and expressive about everything you miss about this person.** Once again, full expression is important.

Examples:

"I really miss sharing my life with you."

"I miss your sense of humor."

"I miss the long talks we used to have."

"I miss seeing you standing in the kitchen cooking breakfast."

"I miss you at Christmas. No one ever gave presents that touched my heart the way yours did."

"I wish you could have known my children. Especially Carl, he looks so much like you."

5. **Bring your parent up to date.** This is a way to reintroduce yourself to your parent. Tell him or her how you've changed. Share your dreams and aspirations. Share parts of you that you concealed as you were growing up. Also, let your parent know how your thoughts of him or her have changed in recent years.

Examples:

"You'd hardly know me now. I'm no longer so insecure. Since my second marriage, I'm a lot more centered."

"My feelings have really changed about Mom. I'm much closer to her now. In a way, your death brought the two of us closer together. We both had so much to grieve about."

"My new plans are to go back to school. A bachelor's degree isn't worth much anymore."

"When I was little, I didn't tell you how lonely I felt. You didn't ask, so I didn't tell."

"Most of my time is devoted to my job. I don't have enough time with Marge and the kids, but I suppose you'd understand that. It's hard supporting such a large family."

"I wish you could see how successful I've become. I'm highly respected in my field and making a lot of money. You always said I'd do well, and I am."

"I used to think you were perfect. Now I know that you had some real self-centered moments. This has helped me gain more perspective about myself as well. I share some of those same traits. Sometimes I even hear your words coming out of my mouth."

When you have exhausted your thoughts, put the letter away. In a few months or years, you might want to reread the letter and add additional thoughts. You'll likely be surprised at how healing this simple exercise can be.

✽ Making Peace with Your In-laws

If your spouse is a Chosen Child and continues to be enmeshed with a parent, you undoubtedly have some in-law problems you would like to address. (I realize this may be an understatement.) What I've said about parents holds doubly true for in-laws: your relationship should be voluntary and based on compatibility and mutual interests. But there are some special considerations that apply only to in-laws.

A book that gave me some insight into the unique nature of in-law problems is *The Evaluation and Treatment of Marital Conflict*.[3] One comment in particular stuck in my mind: "an in-law child is rarely accepted to the same kind of membership in the family as that of the biological child." This rang true to me. The truth is, your partner is going to be closer to your in-laws than you will ever be, appearances to the contrary. Blood is indeed thicker than water.

Two other comments from the book also proved helpful to me. "Each spouse takes responsibility for the relationship with his or her own biological family and works toward a functional connection with them." And, "neither spouse cuts off his or her own family and joins the other family." What I got from these remarks is that if you have interfering in-laws, it's important to figure out who owns the problem. If your mother-in-law is violating your rights, then you have reason to discuss it with her. However, if your mother-in-law is violating your husband's rights, then it's up to your husband to set the record straight. It's not your problem—it's his. You'll have to discipline yourself to stay out of matters that don't directly concern you.

For example, you may be very upset at the way your mother-in-law smothers your husband. You may be thinking, "Look at how she treats him! She expects him to meet all her needs! Why can't she leave him alone?" What you need to ask yourself is, "Is my mother-in-law's behavior a problem to my husband?" It could be that her behavior is more troubling to you than to him; he may have resigned himself to her treatment long ago. In any case, it's up to him to resolve the matter. All you can do is make your sentiments known to your husband and let him take it from there. What you can do is focus on issues that crop up in *your* relationship. It is very likely that there are some similar dynamics in operation.

On the other hand, what appears to be an in-law problem can in reality be an undiagnosed marital problem. For example, if you approach your wife with a suggestion that you go skiing over spring vacation and she says, "No, I feel obligated to spend time with my parents," then you have a complaint with your wife, not your in-laws. She is allowing her parents to be more influential to her than you are. In a healthy family system, the husband and wife view each other as a priority and allow both sets of parents to recede into the background. Since your wife is not doing this, the two of you have a legitimate issue.

Margarita, a woman I interviewed, told me about how she realigned her relationship with her mother-in-law. When she and her husband, Pietro, were first married, Stella, her mother-in-law, frequently took her aside and gave her marital advice. Stella acted as if she and she alone understood her son and had insights that held the key to the success of their marriage. Margarita found this demeaning both to her and to her husband. Further, she sensed that her mother-in-law was just looking for a way to continue her excessive involvement with her son. His two earlier marriages had ended in disaster, in part because of Stella's meddling.

One day Margarita had had enough of Stella's unsolicited advice and said to her in a kind but firm voice: "You are more than welcome to be a guest in our home, but while you are here, I'd rather not talk about our marriage. That's between Pietro and me. Let's talk about something else." That's all it took to realign their relationship. On some level, Stella wanted to be confronted. Pietro, by the way, was amazed at how decisively Margarita handled the situation. His two previous wives had given in to his mother, and he had been exhausted by the whole ordeal. He was happy to have Margarita's support in maintaining a strong boundary between the two generations.

✵ A Success Story

A client named Nathan told me an encouraging story about how he made peace with his mother. Nathan grew up in a small mining town in Colorado where everyone knew everyone else. He'd been his mother's helpmate and guardian for as long as he could remember. She had numerous health problems, which made him afraid to venture out of the house, because she seemed to have a relapse whenever he was gone for any length of time. Out of a misplaced sense of responsibility, Nathan chose not to participate in after-school activities and severely limited his friendships.

When Nathan graduated from high school, there were few jobs in town, so, like other young people, he entertained the notion of leaving town to seek work. His mother was deeply threatened by the idea, which made Nathan feel guilty and anxious, but his need to find work and his growing sense of independence made him throw caution to the winds. To his mother's dismay, he moved to Houston and began to work with his uncle in the oil fields.

For years his mother wouldn't talk to him. When he returned home for visits, she made him feel like an intruder. For comfort she turned to her other children, all of whom had obliged her by settling down within a fifty-mile radius of the homestead.

Meanwhile, Nathan married, had two children, and began to earn a good salary. Seventeen years after leaving home, he decided to get out of the oil business and open a restaurant in his native Colorado. He bought a business twenty-three miles from his hometown in a promising tourist area.

For several months his mother gave her wayward son the silent treatment. She extended her anger to his wife and children, giving them little more than a curt "hello" and "goodbye." Nathan was able to weather his mother's histrionics, however, because he had prepared himself for a rocky reentry into the family. It was actually harder on his wife than on him, because she was so hurt by the way he was treated. But she managed to stay out of the way and let him do the work.

One part of his homecoming that Nathan *wasn't* prepared for was being rejected by his middle brother, Jerome. During the years he was away, he had kept in close contact with Jerome. They had visited back and forth, and their children had become quite close. When Nathan left home, Jerome had become his mother's favorite. Prior to that time, Jerome had been the proverbial middle child with no claim to fame. Now he was enjoying being the favorite child, despite the high cost. With Nathan around once again, his position was threatened. His anxiety increased as his mother's resentment toward Nathan gradually thawed. Acting out of his insecurity, Jerome began to find fault with Nathan's children and refused to patronize Nathan's restaurant. Through all of this, Nathan somehow was able to keep a balanced perspective.

Over time, the family relationships stabilized. Nathan's mother once again accepted her oldest son into the family. She never accorded him his earlier status, however, because he was unwilling to relinquish his independence. Nathan's refusal to slip back into the role of Chosen Child made brother Jerome relax, and the tension between them gradually diminished.

Today, Nathan is happy to be living in Colorado, and he enjoys spending time with his parents and siblings. At the end of my conversation with Nathan, he said he wanted to pass on these words of wisdom: "You can go home again, but you've got to be sure to take yourself with you."

11

Making Peace with Your Siblings

❧

My years as a family therapist have convinced me that resolving problems with your brothers and sisters is almost as important as resolving problems with your parents. Just as with parents, if you ignore problems between you and your siblings, you will project that conflict onto others; what you resist, persists. You will look at your daughter and see what you dislike in your sister; you will treat your spouse the same way you were treated by your brother; you will attribute motivations to others that rightfully belong to a sibling. Sibling relationships make a deep impression, and negative feelings can persist for decades.

For example, I know of a wealthy Kentucky family where sibling rivalry has permeated three generations. The problem originated at the turn of the century, when the mother and father of four children each chose favorites. The father favored the youngest daughter; the mother favored the oldest son. Just before the father died, he drew up a secret will leaving his stable of horses to his favorite daughter. The will was not legally binding, however, so his intentions were never carried out. Some years later, his widow sold the horses at auction. The daughter never forgave her mother for depriving her of what she considered her rightful inheritance. When the widow died, she left the bulk of her money to her favorite son, further angering the daughter. The daughter took out her anger on her brother, igniting a feud that was carried on by their children and their grandchildren. To this day there continues to be ill will between the two branches of the family, even though few are aware of the origins of the problem.

Sibling rivalry can cause great pain, but people are often reluctant to address it. I have found this to be true even among mental health professionals. During a workshop I was conducting for therapists, I stated that, as a rule, sibling relationships are given short shrift in counseling sessions. Problems with parents are explored in great detail, but adult brother and sister relationships are often ignored. I suggested that to bring more balance to the process, therapists ought to examine their relationships with their own brothers and sisters. Maybe they would gain some insight into why they often slighted this key area of family life. As soon as I said this, a woman sitting in the front row waved her hand and said in a loud voice, "No way!" Several people laughed at the truth of her outburst. They, too, were reluctant to examine sibling issues. It was easier to focus on their parents, a more familiar—and therefore safer—area of inquiry.

�֎ Seeing the Larger Picture

If there is some unresolved tension between you and a sibling, it's important that you take a closer look at it, despite any resistance. One way to ease into the forbidden zone is to ask yourself whether your conflict can be traced to roles you played as children. This wider view may help diminish your current frustrations by placing them in perspective. Was there a marked difference between the way you were treated by a parent? Was your sibling a Left-Out Child or the Chosen Child of another parent? Did one of you usurp the other's place in the family? Here are a couple of simple (and nonthreatening) exercises to help you begin your inquiry.

EXERCISE 1:
Candid Camera

Imagine that you are at a family reunion. Someone sneaks up and takes a candid snapshot of you, your parents, and your siblings that tells the whole truth about family relationships.

What would each person be doing? How much space would there be between individuals? Would anyone be left out of the picture? How would you caption the photo?

Describe the picture to a friend or write your response on a sheet of paper.

A friend of mine who was reviewing this manuscript completed the exercise and came up with some interesting results. In her imaginary snapshot, her mother and father were at opposite ends of the photo, each with an arm around a child. Her mother was clinging to her oldest brother. Her father had his arm around her. Her youngest sister was in the middle of the picture, clearly liked by her siblings, but not close to either parent. Her older sister was not in the picture, because the distance she needed to maintain between herself and the family was too great to fit within the camera's field of vision. For the first time, my friend realized that her older sister was a Left-Out Child.

EXERCISE 2:
Fantasy Island

Imagine that you and all your brothers and sisters are living on a small island. You are the only inhabitants. Visualize the island and place your house where you would feel most comfortable. Now add a house for each sibling. Who would live closest to you? Who would live farthest away? Pretend that there are several well-worn paths on the island. Which homes do they connect? Suppose a storm demolished several of the houses and someone had to move in with you. Which brother or sister would you choose? Imagine that a boat is your only contact with the mainland. Which of your siblings would you trust to supervise the use of the boat? Suppose your parents visited. With whom would they stay? Would anyone be jealous? Would anyone be relieved?

✿ Second Order Change

A client named Carla spent some time reflecting on her relationship with her siblings and realized for the first time that her brother's antisocial and criminal behavior could be explained to a large degree by the fact that he was the Left-Out Child in the family. She had been favored by her father; her youngest brother had been favored by her mother. John, the middle child, had been largely ignored. The more she thought about it, the more his troubled life seemed a direct result of an unbalanced family system. "There was nobody for him," she realized, "and he's still crying out for attention." This insight gave her more compassion for him. She called him up for the first time in eight years and invited him for Thanksgiving dinner. They've been in touch ever since.

Margaret realized how much her older sister had affected her when she went to a marriage workshop and was asked to identify the negative influences of her childhood. She listed the problems she'd had with her parents and was frustrated because the picture seemed incomplete. The difficulties she'd had with them didn't account for all her emotional problems. When Margaret factored in the abuse of her older sister, however, her family history made more sense. "In many ways, I think I was more harmed by my relationship with my older sister than by the relationship with my parents. She could be vicious and mean." When Margaret read a book describing sibling dynamics, she gained further insight. She realized her sister wasn't evil, she was just intensely jealous of the favored treatment Margaret had received from both their mother and father. Margaret, too, was able to reach out to a sibling with more understanding.

A client named Tia figured out that her brother Randall was still resenting her for favoritism that had ended decades ago. When she was young, she had received more money and privileges than Randall. He was still livid about it more than twenty years later. When Tia went home to visit, which happened about once a year, Randall was rude to her and quizzed both her and her parents about whether any money or gifts had changed hands. Tia put up with his unpleasant behavior because she felt guilty about what had taken place in the past.

When she got a more objective look at what was going on, however, she was able to release some of her guilt. She realized that she had not lived near her parents for fourteen years and had been financially independent from them since completing nurse's training at age 21. Randall, meanwhile, had continued to live in the same town as their parents and had received much in the way of monetary and material support. Tia saw that she was being persecuted for something that had ended years ago.

When these facts became clear to her, she went to Randall and confronted him firmly but respectfully. "I no longer want to be accused of getting more than my share," she told him. "That ended long ago. You're getting more from the folks than I am." Randall denied any jealousy on his part and acted if he didn't know what she was talking about. But a few months after the exchange, he and his wife made a trip to the East Coast to see her—the first time they had ever gone out of their way to visit. Tia is convinced that he would not have gone to this effort if she hadn't stood up for herself and given him a dose of reality.

In essence, Tia had initiated a Ten-Second Confrontation. She had stated her objections and redefined her boundaries. Her message was simple: "I'm no longer willing to be a target of your anger. I don't deserve it. Let me be." Because Randall could see the truth in her statement, he backed away from his jealous position and was able to view her with more respect. A more harmonious brother-sister relationship was the result.

Here are some examples of other Ten-Second Confrontations between siblings:

"Pamela, I'm not willing to do that favor for you. I'm too busy."

"Jerome, I know you know that we've been doing well financially. But I'm not interested in a business deal. We've got other plans for our money."

"Mark, I'm upset that you talked to our sister Maggie about what you and I talked about. I'd rather she hear that directly from me."

"Jane, you need to get someone else to help organize Dad's birthday party. I'm taking a break from that this year."

"John, I'm uncomfortable talking about our sister Jane's problems. I think we should talk to her directly."

"Ruth, I know you feel that Dad gave me a better deal on the property than he gave you, but that's not the case. I'd be glad to discuss the details with you to clear up the matter."

In general, the process outlined in chapter 10 for reconciling with parents holds true for siblings as well. (You may wish to review the exercises in that chapter, substituting the word *sibling* for *parent*.) Here's a summary of that overall process: in order to improve sibling relationships you need to (1) accept the negative and positive traits of a sibling; (2) examine and clarify your boundaries; (3) focus on how *you* can change the relationship, not on how your sibling is going to change; and (4) make a conciliatory gesture to demonstrate your desire to improve the relationship.

I have found that a reconciliation meeting between brothers and sisters can be a particularly useful tool. Here's how such a session might be constructed.

❀ Directions for a Reconciliation Meeting with a Sibling

1. **Statement of purpose**. In clear and simple language, state the reason why you arranged for the meeting. Strive for a relaxed, confident tone of voice. Practice beforehand if necessary.

Examples:

"I would like our relationship to be better. I'm willing to work toward that, and I hope you are, too."

"I would like to talk with you about our relationship. It's been troubling me, and I'd like to make it better."

"I've been thinking about what happened between us for a long time. I'd like to see if we can work toward a reconciliation."

2. **Ownership of your role in the difficulty.** This is your chance to describe how you contributed to the conflicted relationship. Keep to an objective description of your behavior.

Examples:

"I was jealous of you growing up because you got to play by your own rules but I couldn't."

"When we were kids, I was mean to you. I took advantage of the fact that you were a rebel. Sometimes I acted like a saint just to make you look bad. You must have hated it."

"I wish I could go back and live our childhood a different way. I would get to know you and appreciate you more. I would be kinder and less self-serving. I feel bad about the way I treated you."

"There were many times when I was given privileges and you weren't. It must have been really hard on you to see how unfairly Mom treated us. And I know I took advantage of those privileges. No wonder you hated me."

"When we were young, Dad turned to me for advice a lot. He even wanted my help in dealing with you. It was wrong of me to play that role. You must have resented my comments."

You may want to expand on this and talk about ways in which you may be contributing to current tensions.

Examples:

"I'm not at my best when we're together. I'm often distant and guarded. I want to be more at ease."

"I haven't done much to stay connected with you. I've been out of touch."

> *"Instead of talking to you directly, I talk about you to Jane. I feel bad about that."*
>
> *"I still treat you like I did fifteen years ago. I haven't adjusted for the fact that you've changed."*

3. **Statement of how you would like your relationship to be in the future.** This is a positive description of the changes you'd like to see happen. Again, no blaming or accusations.

Examples:

> *"I'd like us to feel more comfortable around each other."*
>
> *"We've never really talked. I'd like to hear from you what it was like growing up in the family."*
>
> *"I'd like us to let bygones be bygones and start over again. The fact that Dad favored one of us and not the other was really out of our hands."*
>
> *"I'd like to be closer to you. I think if we talked about the past, there'd be less tension between us. We'd want to do more things together if there were less hidden anger."*
>
> *"When we were young, we weren't very close. I wasn't allowed to have problems or express any feeling other than happiness. I'd like to be more honest with you. I'd like to share more of my feelings with you."*
>
> *"I think the way Mom and Dad treated us really came between us. I'd like us to put all that behind us and start over again. We really do have a lot in common, especially now that we both have kids."*

Keep in mind that your sibling may not accept any responsibility for the conflict and may even deny that it exists. That's okay. It won't negate the effectiveness of your meeting. Your job is to focus on you—your behavior, your wishes, your perceptions, your apologies.

Your sibling may be more responsive when you state how you want the relationship to be. A brother may not be willing to talk much about the past. This is his right. But he may be willing to work to build a better relationship in the future. When the meeting is over, give your brother or sister some time to absorb your message, and make sure that your future actions are congruent with your stated purpose. It may take a year or two for real change to occur, but it will be worth the wait.

If your sibling chooses to ignore your honest, respectful overtures, you'll have to lower your expectations, knowing you've done what you can to reconcile. Your relationship may never be the way you want it to be. Maybe all you can hope for at this stage of the game is to agree to disagree and to pledge to be more cordial at family gatherings. But even this might be a welcome change. And you can take some solace in the fact that you are no longer responsible for keeping the conflict alive.

88 The Singular Nature of Sibling Dynamics

Much of what I've discussed so far in this chapter could apply to any family relationship. But there are some dynamics that are peculiar to siblings. First, it may behoove you to examine how your birth order influences your behavior. Just because you were the youngest child doesn't mean that Thanksgiving can never be at your house; the few years between you and older siblings make little difference now that you're adults. Similarly, just because you're the oldest child and the only one in the family with a dining-room table that seats twelve doesn't mean you have to be in charge of all family functions—even if you've done so for the past twenty-five years. Nor do you as the oldest child have to handle all the crises, orchestrate all the family functions, and provide all the emotional and financial support. Your younger brothers and sisters can help out, too. If your role as oldest child is placing an undue burden on you, it might be keeping others from developing a sense of responsibility. *Everyone* may benefit from a change. There's no need to stay locked in a position that is detrimental to you and to others.

Second, if you have strained relationships with your siblings, your instinct may be to cut yourself off from them. You may have the desire to move across the continent and drastically limit your contact. But because you and your siblings are contemporaries, there is the strong possibility that you will have to deal with one another in the future. You may need to cooperate in the care of an aging parent, for example, or work out details surrounding a family death. Your children may want access to their aunts and uncles, and you may want to play a positive role in the lives of your nieces and nephews. You may even come to depend on a sibling in your old age. Having the courage to initiate a reconciliation now will eliminate conflict further down the road.

Third, brothers and sisters tend to get embroiled in protracted battles about "who is right." This could be a carryover from the early days when fairness and equal treatment from Mom and Dad were so important and determining who was right and wrong seemed a matter of life and death. Now that you're adults, you have to decide which is more important: being right or being close. Many a brother has said, "I want my sister to see my point of view. I know I'm right, but she won't admit it!" The point to remember is that you can be "right" without having a sibling agree with you; each of you has a unique and valid point of view. If you accept this fact and make family harmony contingent on mutual respect, not identical values, everyone will gain. For example, one of my best friends has a brother with drastically different political views. If she required him to agree with her in order to be in her good graces, she would fracture the family. Instead, she's decided that being close to him is more important to her than whom he votes for in the next election. It's a decision that has paid daily dividends.

Take a look at the issues that divide your family. Are they worth fighting over? Are they a matter of pride and saving face? Did they have their roots in a previous generation? Are they due to the way your parents treated you, a matter over which you had little control? Could it be time for you to pretend that you're all grown up and let bygones be bygones?

12

Strengthening Your Marriage Relationship

❀

If you grew up too close to a parent, you *will* have problems with love relationships; it's practically guaranteed. Although the exact nature of your difficulties will depend on your upbringing, chances are you have at least one of the following problems:

- A history of picking partners who are interested in their needs at the expense of yours

- A history of picking partners who are unavailable (for example, already married, attached to a parent or child, or geographically or emotionally distant)

- Conflict because you have a strong alliance with a parent or child

- A fear of abandonment, resulting in anxiety, jealousy, nagging, a compulsive desire to please, or co-dependency

- A fear of engulfment, resulting in isolation, hostility, silence, withdrawal, being a loner, needing a great deal of personal space

- A history of affairs or a partner who has a history of affairs

- Difficulty in finding a suitable mate

- A lack of romantic attraction to your partner

A moment's reflection reveals that there is a common theme running through this list, which is a lack of commitment to the primary love relationship. One or both of you are withholding your energy and diverting it to parents, children, outside activities, or other partners.

A review of your history will give you some insight into this lack of commitment. If you are the one who is withholding your energy, it could be because your parents failed to provide you with a working model of married life. You didn't learn that marriage can be fun, sustaining, and mutually rewarding. You didn't learn that marriage partners can be lovers, confidants, and best friends. What your parents demonstrated instead was that love and companionship were to be found in a relationship with a child, in a job, or in an addiction. This pattern was imprinted on your unconscious and became a potent influence in later years. People know only what they've been taught, and you were taught to seek pleasure and intimacy outside of marriage.

If you have chosen a partner who is unavailable to you much of the time, or who is slow to respond to your needs, once again your history will help you understand why. When you were young, your job was to satisfy your parent's needs. Your own needs were set aside, so you could cater to a parent or struggle to live up to a parent's unrealistic expectations. Over the years, this way of relating became second nature to you, and you were unwittingly attracted to people who allowed you to perpetuate this role. It felt familiar and natural to take care of someone who didn't pay attention to your needs; it's what you were trained to do.

✸ Marriage and Second Order Change

The work described in the previous chapters, especially the work of resolving problems with your parents, will help remove these barriers to intimacy—even if you do no direct work on your marriage. When you realign your relationship with your parents, you resolve core relationship issues. All your other relationships—and in particular your marriage—will benefit from your efforts.

I recall a session with Mandy, a woman in her mid-thirties who had been closely tied to an adoring father. We spent the entire fifty minutes talking about the passionate nature of that relationship. For the first time she realized the degree to which it had been inappropriate. Her love for her father had been an overpowering attraction. It had been more intense than all her other relationships, except for a brief affair with an older, married man.

During this particular session, neither of us talked about her marriage, a lackluster relationship that was the reason why she had sought counseling; all the talk focused on her father. Yet, when Mandy was driving home from the session, she felt compelled to see her husband. She turned around and drove straight to his office. When she walked into his office, she felt more emotionally and sexually attracted to him than she had in years. This welcome rekindling of romance lasted for days.

We talked about this sudden turnaround—a second order change—during the following session. Mandy realized that facing the truth about her exaggerated bond with her father had had an unexpected consequence: it had helped her see her husband in a more favorable light. She realized that unconsciously she had been searching for a superhuman mate, someone who would rival her father. At long last she had become aware of that goal and seen its futility. No man would ever seem as magnificent to her as her father had when she was 10 years old. Accepting that truth, she was suddenly more aware of her husband's legitimate strengths. No, he wasn't a mythical mate, but he was a kind, reliable, loving husband. She began to think about what a good father he was. She began to think about how patiently he had put up with her dissatisfaction with their marriage. Freed from an unconscious block, she felt attracted to him on a number of levels all at once. A wall of resistance that had been an invisible barrier to intimacy was dismantled.

In addition to a change in perception such as the one Mandy experienced, there are more direct ways to deepen the level of trust and intimacy in your marriage. In my extensive work with couples, I've acquired a series of techniques that will help bring you closer together, whether it's you, your partner, or both of you who have been withholding love.[1] As you will see, making a few strategic changes, combined with new insight, can dramatically improve your relationship.

✿ Creating a Positive Vision

A logical way to begin working on your marriage is to see whether you believe a good marriage is possible between you and your partner. Unless you have some hope for your marriage, you will have little reason to work on it. Let's start with some basic questions. Do you have a clear image of what a good marriage relationship looks like? Can you imagine yourself living in harmony with your partner? Can you imagine being there for each other, meeting each other's needs, growing and learning together?

Many of us who grew up in enmeshed families have a difficult time answering "yes" to these questions. We simply don't have an adequate frame of reference for a healthy love relationship, and we don't have much optimism about our ability to create one. I see this problem over and over again in my practice. A few years ago I worked with a couple, Leita and Sol, who were both therapists. Despite the fact that they had acquired a lot of relationship skills, they weren't able to apply them to their own marriage. They'd been married only nine months, but they were already immersed in a power struggle.

They had a significant breakthrough during one of their sessions. It began when they managed to resolve a stressful issue that had been bothering them for some time. They savored the victory for a moment, then Sol shook his head, looked at Leita, and said, "I can't believe we're sitting here solving these problems we've been fighting about for months. It just seems unreal. I'm amazed we could reach an agreement. I'm waiting for the other shoe to drop."

As I looked at Leita and Sol, I had a sudden insight. They didn't believe it was possible for them to have a good marriage. I said, "You know, the two of you are capable of having a high-quality, loving relationship. You deserve it. You've earned it. You are experiencing it right at this moment. You really can have the relationship you want."

Neither of them spoke for a moment. Both Sol and Leita had tears in their eyes, and I had goose bumps all over my arms. A hidden problem had been brought out into the open: Sol and Leita were just going through the motions of working on their relationship. Deep down, they had already admitted defeat. They were willing to spend thousands of dollars on therapy and do everything I required of them, but neither one believed that what they wanted was possible. Their history of failed relationships and their painful memories of growing up in dysfunctional families had quashed their dreams. My comment had given them the first ray of hope that they could actually have a good marriage.

I suggest you take this opportunity to examine your own unspoken assumptions about marriage. Do you see yourself being a part of a long-lasting, healthy love relationship? Do you believe you can be happy with your present partner? Does your partner have even the remotest chance of pleasing you?

If you have difficulty imagining being happy together, you need to construct a more positive vision. You need to reprogram your brain so that there is a real possibility of success.

One way to do this is through a technique called affirmation. Many of you are familiar with this powerful tool. When you have a quiet moment, sit down and write a list of positive statements about your marriage. Have your partner do the same. Here are some statements you might want to include:

MARRIAGE AFFIRMATIONS

I am loved by my partner.
I am physically attracted to my partner.
I notice my partner's positive traits.
I love my partner.
I feel safe with my partner.
We delight in our time together.
I respect and admire my partner.
We are good at resolving our problems.
We have a mutually satisfying sexual relationship.
We have freedom and space within our relationship.
We love each other but allow each other freedom.
We trust each other.
We are building a lifelong relationship.

Keep your statements positive. Write: "We willingly help each other with the household chores," rather than, "We don't fight over housework." Your partner's list does not have to be identical to yours. What's important is that the items on your list directly relate to your own self-defeating notions, the voice in you that says, "I'll never respect that man," or, "She'll never be a good sexual partner for me." Search out your areas of doubt and despair and work on eradicating them with affirmations.

If you repeat your affirmations over and over, you will gradually experience a new hopefulness in your marriage. You may even see some changes in your behavior. This technique isn't magic or make-believe. It's simply an effective way to erase one tape and replace it with another. It's a way to remove a hidden obstacle that has been sabotaging your sincere desire for a more loving relationship.

83 The Universal Homework Assignment

Once you have a positive feeling about your relationship, your subsequent efforts will bear more fruit. The next task I recommend is the reinforcement of your marriage boundaries, the invisible line that separates the two of you from your parents and children. As you know from earlier chapters, having this demarcation is crucial to the health of the family system.

An influential family therapist named Maria Selvini Palazzoli has developed an exercise that is so effective at setting the marriage relationship apart from other relationships that many therapists refer to it as the "Universal Homework Assignment." This exercise is tailor-made for marriage partners with a history of emotional incest. Simply stated, the assignment is to spend several hours each week doing something you and your partner both enjoy *without explaining the nature of your activities to other family members*, whether parents or children; this is private time reserved for the two of you. All you need to say to your family is something like this: "We're going off to have fun together. We'll be back at eleven o'clock." Or, "We may go to the movies or go for a walk. We're not sure." When you return home, keep your comments equally vague. You don't need to act secretive or play games with the rest of the family, just avoid going into detail about how you spent that time. (Babysitters, of course, will need to be given more precise information.)

This exercise is designed to give you much-needed time together, but it has an additional purpose, which is to separate you psychologically from the rest of the family. The weekly date says to the family, "We like each other. We value our time together so much that we are going to make sure we spend several hours together each week. What we do with that time need not concern you. It is part of a very special and sometimes private relationship." Children, parents, and friends are being told in a polite and gentle way that there is a sacred boundary around your marriage.

I guarantee that if you do no other exercise but this one, you will notice an improvement in your marriage relationship. Family therapists as well as clients marvel at how well this simple technique works.

器 Resistance

One indication of the effectiveness of the Universal Homework Assignment is that you are likely to see some resistance from family members. For example, if you have children, they might try to play on your guilt by asking, "Why do you get to go and I don't?" or, "Are you going out again? You're always going out together. You never spend time with me!" Be honest and firm in your response. Explain that this is adult time. You might point out to a young child that you and your spouse don't tag along when your child goes out to play with a young friend. Another response you might use, tempered with gentleness and kindness, is, "You're not invited." Children need to learn that there are times when they are not included. This is part of learning to be mature and realistic.

If your child succeeds in making you feel guilty for your weekly date, remind yourself that *one of the chief responsibilities of being a good parent is to model healthy adult behavior.* This means demonstrating a healthy love relationship and showing your child that membership in the adult community "has its privileges." Your child will be more eager to grow up and cope with the inevitable hardships of adulthood if he or she realizes that there's fun to be had in the deal. Continue your homework assignment despite your child's attempts to thwart you.

If it's been a while since you've actively worked on your relationship, you may have some resistance of your own to contend with. You may have to do this exercise *despite your feelings* for each other. You may be angry or bored with each other. You may wonder if your relationship is worth the effort. But if you wait until you are overcome with love to reach out to each other, you may wait too long. Just go ahead and pretend that you love each other. Act *as if* your marriage is worth it. You will discover what behavioral scientists have been telling us for years: an excellent way to *feel* more loving is to *act* more loving.

If you still feel the urge to skip this exercise, it is likely that you have spent a number of years in an unfulfilling relationship. Your wounds may be deep and well protected. The deeper the hurt, the stronger your resistance to opening up to your partner. There may not be enough safety in your relationship to make you want to spend additional time together. Your instincts may be to keep up your barriers or even flee the relationship. If so, go against your resistance and do this exercise anyway! It will prove especially beneficial for you, as it will force you to launch a frontal assault on your defense system and thus set the stage for greater intimacy. Go on a date with your partner this week, and while you are away from the house, sit down with a calendar and plan your future appointments together.

As you work against your resistance, be on the lookout for unconscious attempts to sabotage the exercise, such as: not being able to find "acceptable" child care; delaying the search for a babysitter until it's too late in the day; being too busy to go out on a date; not having enough money to spend on entertainment; not wanting to leave older children alone; signing up for activities that conflict with your weekly date; being too tired to go out; thinking that if you've done the exercise two or three times, you've done it "enough."

Making this degree of commitment to your marriage may not be easy for you, but I never promised you that recovery would be easy. You will need to do some work, and my definition of work is "doing what you're not inclined to do." You must make a significant investment in your relationship in order for it to improve, and the first investment is time.

88 Deepening Intimacy

Lack of intimacy is a common problem in love relationships, especially when one of the partners was a Chosen Child. The tendency is to look outside the marriage for support and companionship. Turning this around requires both insight and effort.

What exactly is intimacy? And how do you get it? A lot of confusion would be eliminated if people realized that intimacy is talking and listening, nothing more, nothing less. The more personal and forthright the conversation, the more profound the intimacy. Intimacy that continues over a period of time gradually leads to a greater level of trust, understanding, and commitment.

First, let's talk about talking. We all talk to our partners. Throughout the course of the relationship, we exchange millions of words. But all too often we don't share our innermost thoughts and feelings. We keep them to ourselves or share highly edited versions. Because our parents were either intrusive, disinterested, or overly critical, we've learned to keep our thoughts and feelings to ourselves.

But when we don't share what we're thinking and feeling, we block intimacy. This happens whether the information we're withholding is negative or positive. For example, if I've been disappointed by your actions over and over again but don't share this with you, I will grow more distant from you as time passes; I will store up my resentment until my love for you is all but buried. Similarly, if I have feelings of love for you that I don't share, I am choosing to keep you in the dark about my feelings. I am building a private reality that excludes you.

Below are some examples of intimate communication. Read through them and ask yourself how often you've experienced similar thoughts or feelings without sharing them with your partner.

"I like it when you call me during the day."
"It's hard for me to see you doing so well in your career when mine seems to be falling apart."
"I don't like it when you tell your friends about our private life, especially information about me."
"I'm really looking forward to a quiet weekend with you."
"It's really hard for me to feel sexual toward you when we haven't been getting along very well."
"At times I feel so much love for you I'm afraid I'll lose you."
"There's a part of me that feels stupid and I'm afraid someone will find out."
"I know I'm hard on you and overreact sometimes. It's not all your fault, but it's difficult to explain what goes on inside me."
"When you look at me like that, I feel so loved, so safe."
"Some of my happiest times have been with you."
"I'm glad that you're in my life."

"I know I've been hard to get along with lately. Thanks for hanging in there."

Talking openly about intimate thoughts and feelings can be especially difficult for the Chosen Child. If a parent consistently told you how you felt or trained you to behave in a certain manner or rewarded you for having certain tastes and values, you may not be sure *what* you think or feel. How can you share what's going through your mind when what's going through your mind is so vague, jumbled, or contradictory?

The only child of a domineering, critical mother shared a dream with me that gave her insight into her inability to communicate with her husband. In her dream, she wanted to prune some roses but couldn't find the pruning shears. She thought her mother might know where they were, but she was afraid to ask her. In her dream she asked herself two preliminary questions: "Do I have to ask my mother? Can't I find them on my own?" Since she had searched for the shears for a long time and had been unable to find them, she concluded that asking her mother was inevitable.

Her next move in her dream was to gird herself for her mother's most likely response. She thought of a lot of possibilities: (1) Her mother might say, "How should I know where the shears are? I always put things back. You never put things back." (2) She might say, "You just can't do anything on your own, can you? You're never going to be able to take care of yourself. You'll always need me." She proceeded to run through several other possible responses and came up with a suitable reply for each one. Then she gathered up the courage to ask her mother about the shears.

"You know what?" she told me. "In my dream, my mother gave a response that I was totally unprepared for—she attacked me for wanting the shears! She said, 'Pruning shears? Why do you want the pruning shears? You shouldn't be pruning this time of year!'" She had anticipated every possible response but that one. Not surprisingly, my client had a lot of mental blocks when it came to intimate conversation. If her unconscious mind was telling her that something as simple as asking for pruning shears was likely to bring the roof down on her head, her reluctance to broach more sensitive topics was understandable.

I too have had trouble communicating my thoughts that can be traced to my relationship with my mother. I wasn't afraid that my mother would criticize me, however; I was afraid of causing her problems. I had to screen everything I said to make sure it wouldn't put pressure on her. Years later, after I'd been in therapy for a while, I struggled to be more forthright with people. As I did so, I ran into feelings of humiliation and shame, which made it almost impossible for me to talk. Tears would fill my eyes, and my throat would tighten up. It felt so awkward to speak openly. Eventually, I learned to keep on talking through my tears. This effort to deepen my level of sharing has helped forge closer connections with my husband and friends.

If you would like to become more intimate with your partner, you too may need to practice being more expressive. This doesn't mean divulging each and every thought or telling your partner everything you've done in your entire life. It means expressing what is going on within you right now that has relevance to the relationship.

If you're confused about what you're thinking or feeling, or if you have a hard time expressing yourself, be honest about that, too! People are often too hard on themselves. Start where you are, and if you don't know where you are, start by saying, "I don't know where to start."

I recently worked with a man named Phillip who was recovering from a serious accident. During his stay in the hospital, he was able to see how much distance there was between him and his wife. He told me he desperately needed her help in getting back his equilibrium, but he was unable to ask for it. I suggested that he tell his wife the very words he had just told me: "I desperately need your help, but I don't know how to ask for it. I feel we're not very close and I don't know how to get any closer." He later reported to me that this honest expression of confusion and frustration elicited a warm response from his wife.

Here are some more clear expressions of confusion:

"I don't know what I want."

"I'm totally confused on this issue."

"I want to be closer to you, but I don't have the foggiest idea how to go about it."

"I feel sad, but I don't know why."

"I feel angry, but I don't know why."

"Something you said just now hurt me, but I don't know why."

"I'm feeling closer to you these days, but I can't explain it."

Once you get the ball rolling, it will be easier for you to tap in to your buried thoughts and feelings. The following exercise will provide additional help.

EXERCISE 2:
Complete This Sentence

Get together with your partner and take turns completing the following sentences. The list begins with simple statements and progresses to more intimate topics. One of you talks while the other listens attentively.

Complete the following sentences:

My favorite time of the year is _____
I feel most relaxed when _____
If I could have any job I wanted, I would _____
The thing I worry about most is _____
My closest friend in childhood was _____
My favorite toy as a child was _____
If I could take any trip, I would _____
The question I would most like to have answered is _____
One thing nobody seems to understand about me is _____
I regret _____
Money is _____
I waste time by _____
My thoughts about children are _____
The most stressful part of my life is _____
I still don't understand why I _____
If I had one wish it would be _____
The worst thing that ever happened to me was _____
I would really like you to know that _____
The thing that concerns me most about our relationship is __
The best thing that ever happened to me is _____
What I fear most is _____
What I've never told anyone is _____

When you've finished this list, make up your own. Continue practicing this process until honest sharing becomes a comfortable and spontaneous part of your relationship. As you develop your skill, you and your partner will come to know each other better. This knowledge will deepen the bond between you and reinforce the boundary around your relationship.

❁ Are You Listening to Me?

It doesn't do much good to be forthright when your partner isn't paying attention to what you're saying. As I mentioned earlier, intimacy involves talking and *listening*. But all too often, when one partner is talking, the other partner is (1) thinking his own thoughts, (2) impatiently waiting for a chance to break in to the conversation, or (3) silently crafting a rebuttal. When two people talk but nobody listens, both individuals feel lonely and misunderstood.

Following is a simple communication exercise that will train you to be a better listener. If used properly, it will improve your level of communication—and therefore your level of intimacy—in a very short time.

In order to derive maximum benefit from the exercise, do it exactly as described. If you step out of the harness of the structure, you are liable to revert to techniques that haven't worked well in the past. Following the rules will feel awkward at first, but it is the only way to guarantee success.

The goal of this exercise is deceptively simple—to receive a message exactly as your partner sends it. This does not mean that you have to agree with the message—just hear it and understand it the way your partner intends you to. Practice this exercise until it becomes second nature, and then use it whenever you feel tension rising between you. You don't need to use it when you just want to ask your partner to pass the salt, but if you start to argue about whose turn it is to wash the dishes, shift gears and use this technique.

EXERCISE 3:
Clarifying Listening Exercise

To begin the exercise, think of a sentence that expresses a thought or feeling you want your partner to understand. Have your partner do the same thing. Choose one person to be the sender and follow steps 1 through 7. Then reverse roles and repeat the process.

Step 1. SENDER: Make a short statement you have strong feelings about and want the Receiver to hear.

Step 2. RECEIVER: Paraphrase or restate the Sender's statement without interpreting and without adding to or subtracting from the content.

Step 3. SENDER: Confirm or reject the paraphrase. If you reject it, go back to step 1. If you confirm it, go on to step 4.

Step 4. RECEIVER: Once your paraphrase has been confirmed, ask questions beginning with the words, "Do you mean . . . ?" until you get three "yes" answers.

Step 5. SENDER: Answer "yes" or "no" to the Receiver's questions. (You will have a chance to elaborate at the end of the exercise.)

Step 6. RECEIVER: Once you've received three "yes" responses, summarize what you've learned about your partner's message, or keep going as long as there's interest.

Step 7. SENDER: Acknowledge the summary and clarify previous answers if desired.

Step 8. Reverse roles and start over again with step 1.

Here's a fleshed-out example of the exercise:

SENDER	RECEIVER
1. "I'd like you to help out around the house more."	2. "You would like it if I did more of the house-work."
3. "Yes."	4. "Do you mean that I don't help at all?"
5. "No."	6. "Do you mean you'd like me to do some things I don't do?"
7. "Yes."	8. "Do you mean you'd like me to do most of the housework?"
9. "No."	10. "Do you mean that you would like me to do the things I know I'm sup-posed to do without be-ing nagged?"

11. "Yes."

12. *Summary:* "So what you mean is that you would like me to do things that I know I should do around the house without being reminded and that you will not nag me so much if I do."

13. "That's correct."

This exercise has a way of getting to the heart of the matter, especially if you're dealing with a touchy subject. For best results, stay calm and rational. Once you have all the information, then you can work on solving the problem. Most attempts at problem-solving break down because information and feelings have not been accurately shared.

I have a story connected with this exercise. A young couple, Lucille and Brewster, came to one of my workshops in west Texas and quickly mastered this involved but highly effective method of sending and receiving messages. They invited me out to breakfast a few months later to tell me how much the workshop had helped their relationship. They gave a lot of credit to the communication exercise. Lucille told me about a humorous incident that had taken place a few weeks earlier. She and Brewster had been visiting her mother and an issue had come up between them that needed to be resolved immediately. As Lucille's mother looked on, they automatically went into the "Clarifying Listening Exercise." When they were through, the woman's jaw dropped open and she said, "Do ya'll talk like that all the time?"

Lucille replied, "Yes, whenever we have an issue to resolve."

Her mother quickly responded, "But how do ya'll know who wins?"

We often think of communication as "winning." We assume that to listen to our partners means we have to agree with them or give ground. We're afraid that if we try to figure out what our partners are saying, we'll have to sacrifice our own points of view. What effective communication entails is giving our partners our respectful attention, reflecting back to them what we've heard, and then having the courtesy to ask whether we've heard them correctly. Listen. Paraphrase. Verify. When we follow this simple, 1-2-3 procedure, we automatically deepen our level of trust and intimacy—which makes *everyone* a winner.

❁ Additional Communication Tips

In addition to the above exercise, I have a few miscellaneous tips to improve your style of communication. First, pay attention to your *tone of voice*. If you speak in a harsh, cutting tone, your partner will either withdraw from you or pick a fight. If you speak in a calm tone, your partner is more likely to listen to you and respond in a civil manner. Remember the tone of voice your mother or father used when you were in trouble? (My children always knew they were in for it if I said "James Edward" instead of "Jimmy" or "Kathleen Ann" instead of "Kathleen.") Children respond to this tone of voice by becoming "mother-deaf" or "father-deaf." Adults do the same. When your partner speaks to you in a critical or accusing tone, you turn off your receiver. If you want to be heard, make your voice gentle and matter-of-fact. You will be pleasantly surprised by the results.

The *length* of what you say is also important. The longer you talk, the more you turn people off. Short sentences, direct and to the point, make the most impact. Here are some examples of good, punchy statements:

"I don't like it when you're late for dinner. I'd like you to come home when you say you will or call me if you're going to be more than fifteen minutes late."

"I'd like to know how you're feeling about our holiday plans."

"I'm concerned about our financial situation. I'd like to set aside some time to discuss it with you."

"I feel we're not as close as we used to be."

Listen to yourself speak and find out if you use unnecessary words. If so, editing your remarks will result in a more attentive audience.

The *do something different* axiom applies to communication, too. Many times people fall into ruts and say the same things over and over. When you say predictable things, you get predictable responses. Here are some worn-out phrases to avoid:

"When are you ever going to . . ."

"How many times do I have to tell you . . ."

"I'll do it later."

"Don't get so excited."
"You overreact to everything."
"All you ever want to do is . . ."
"You never listen . . ."

When these ragged phrases drop out of your mouth, your partner goes on automatic pilot. A rebuttal is ready at hand. The two of you might just as well read from a script. If you want to get closer, you'll have to say something different.

Body language can also block communication. If you have been living together for a number of years, you may have fallen into some bad habits. When your partner speaks to you, do you continue to read the paper? Do you look up with a glazed expression? Do you put your hands on your hips and tap your foot? Do you roll your eyes when you're in disagreement? Do you keep your eyes glued to the TV?

The next time your partner speaks to you, give the gift of your complete attention. Drop what you're doing. Look up with a pleasant, interested expression. Turn and face your partner directly. If necessary, pretend you're listening to a very attractive stranger. An improved emotional climate will be your reward.

Offering unsolicited advice is an effective way to sabotage the flow of conversation. When your partner shares a personal problem, your first instinct may be to try to solve the problem. If you can't come up with a quick solution, you may feel guilty or helpless. This is a common reaction for those of us who grew up in enmeshed families and were rewarded for taking responsibility for others.

The next time your partner comes to you with a problem, remind yourself that this is your partner's problem, not yours. You don't have to solve it. Besides, your partner is looking for sympathy and understanding, not a quick fix. Take a deep breath and suppress the urge to give advice. Listen attentively. Paraphrase your partner's remarks and make supportive statements such as, "It must be hard to . . ." or, "What a lousy thing to have happened to you," or, "I really understand your dilemma," or, "It's easy to see why you've been so worried. I would feel that way, too." Being heard and understood is therapeutic; you don't need to complicate matters by offering advice.

Humor can dissolve a long-drawn-out stalemate into a moment of shared laughter. Not long ago my husband was suffering from a chest cold and refused to take any medication. He felt rotten and was cranky and ill-tempered. Finally, one afternoon he wandered into the kitchen and said to me, "Do you know where the handgun is?" "Yes," I replied, somewhat alarmed. "Well, could you get it and hold it to my head and make me take this medicine." I cracked up. That one line of self-deprecating humor defused a week's worth of frustration.

There are some of you—and you'll know immediately if this applies to you—*who need to learn when to keep your mouth shut!* It may be the most helpful thing you can do to increase your level of intimacy. I've rarely met a person who complained about a nontalkative partner who didn't unwittingly dominate the conversation. The next time you're together, practice the art of silence. Wait. Be patient. Give your partner a chance to say something. Wait to make sure he or she has finished the thought. Do something different—nothing!

Finally, pay attention to your partner's rate of reception. People, like computers, should be given "baud ratings" to indicate the speed at which they process information. Some people respond almost instantly; they speak as they think (or, claim their disgruntled spouses, *before* they think). Others mull over a thought for what seems like years. More often than not, a fast communicator marries a slow communicator, which is frustrating for both parties. The speed demon has to wait an eternity for a response, and the slowpoke feels gunned down by the partner's machine-gun delivery.

The way around this difficulty is first to identify that this mismatch exists and that it is fundamental; it has to do with the nature of your brains. It is not an unconscious attempt to frustrate each other. Second, be respectful of your partner's unique way of processing information. If you're a fast talker, slow down your data transmission and refrain from hopscotching from topic to topic. Train yourself to be silent long enough for your partner to respond. If you're a slow talker, it may be wise to let your partner know when you're silently mulling over an idea. Otherwise, he or she may feel ignored or may have the impression that you're drifting off to sleep. You might say, "I'm thinking that over. Give me a minute."

In the beginning, it will take a conscious effort to incorporate these various suggestions. Some of your attempts will feel contrived and awkward. At times, you will be tempted to seek harbor in familiar routines. But hang in there! It has been my observation that poor communication lies at the heart of most marriage problems. If you make a concerted effort to improve your flow of communication, you'll be tackling one of the most vexing marriage problems of all.

Resolving Cross-Generational Alliances

Cross-generational alliances are a common feature of relationships where one of the individuals is a Chosen Child. The Chosen Child either remains bonded to the parent, fueling in-law problems, or he or she bonds with a child, replicating the early pattern of enmeshment.

Needless to say, the spouse will resent these alliances. It's hard to be married to someone who is overly attached to someone else. Unfortunately, the way the spouse responds to these extramarital alliances further complicates matters. For example, if you are a woman who is overly bonded with a child, your husband may try to find comfort by having an affair with another woman. Or, if you are a man who maintains excessive contact with your mother, your wife may try to soothe her hurt feelings by turning to alcohol or becoming involved with another man.

At first it may be difficult for you as the Chosen Child to see the relationship between your behavior and your spouse's behavior—especially if your spouse is acting in socially unacceptable ways. You wonder: What does your husband's illicit affair have to do with your attachment to your son? What does your wife's alcoholism have to do with your devotion to your ailing mother? At first glance, the behaviors seem totally unrelated.

If the tables were turned, however, it might be easier for you to see the parallels. Imagine that your partner's first priority and concern is a child or parent. Although this is never openly acknowledged, you know this on some level and deeply resent it. Your birthday gets ignored or is given short shrift, while your daughter gets diamond earrings. Your husband consults your daughter about vacation plans; your advice is ignored. This situation goes on for years unaddressed. You busy yourself establishing a home, pursuing a career, or raising children, pretending that the marriage is meeting your needs. But if you stay with your partner long enough, the void will make itself known. You will become depressed or irritable. You will drink too much, have an affair, get physically ill, or spend more and more time away from home. Because your partner is connected to someone else, you will feel left out and alone, and loneliness and low self-esteem are at the core of most dysfunctional behavior.

A marriage relationship is a system; neither one of you acts in a vacuum. If you siphon off your energy to a child or parent, your partner will search for and find a substitute form of gratification. This will anger you and cause you to withdraw your love even more. This makes your partner even more determined to look for happiness outside the marriage. Before long, your problems escalate out of control.

In order to break this chain of resentment, you need to view your behavior with more understanding. In the beginning, neither of you went outside the marriage with the intention of hurting each other; you were simply trying to satisfy unmet needs. You were trying to find love and freedom from pain, given the fact that you had a less than ideal marriage. Lacking good information and adequate role models, it's not surprising that your search led you astray.

As you cultivate this more compassionate attitude, take steps to defuse any lingering resentments you may have about the past. How you do this depends to some degree on your previous behavior. If you've voiced your grievances over and over again, for example, you may decide that enough is enough. Call it even. Declare a moratorium on dredging up the past and start over again with a clean slate.

On the other hand, if you've kept quiet about your resentments, you may need to speak up. You can do this with just the two of you, or you can enlist the help of a third party, perhaps a counselor. The goal is to voice your resentments in an assertive manner and reveal all the feelings that go along with them.

When you share your grievances, follow these simple guidelines: (1) express your feelings honestly and respectfully; (2) be willing to give them up; (3) be willing to do something different. When you fail at number 2 and find yourself dredging up the past, apologize. Here are some ways to say you're sorry (just in case you're a little rusty):

> "I realize I criticized you when you came in the door this evening. I'm sorry. I was just rehearsing an old tape from the past."

> "If I had it to do over, I'd have been nicer to you when you came in this evening. I'm going to do better."

> "I've really been in a bad mood these last few days. I'm sorry. I didn't need to bring up old garbage."

✿ Learning the Art of Compromise

To keep new problems from cropping up and fueling new resentment, you need some good problem-solving tools. One of those tools is the art of compromise. Compromise means that neither of you gets your first choice. You decide that building a lasting marriage is more important than always getting your way.

As a Chosen Child, you may have a hard time with the concept of compromise. I would not be surprised to find you on one extreme or the other, either having a tendency to give, give, give to your partner—perpetuating your early role as a parent pleaser—or to take, take, take from your partner—operating from a historic sense of entitlement.

It is also likely that you have more than the usual difficulty in acknowledging your wishes and desires. Because your needs were deemed less important than a parent's needs, you may have trouble defining them. If you identify with either of these problems, take heart—the following exercise will be doubly productive for you.

When you first practice the art of compromise, it may seem like a game where everyone loses, because neither of you gets exactly what you want. But before long you will see the rewards. For one thing, you will begin to feel more competent and resourceful: "Hey, we can resolve our differences without getting into an argument!" This leads to greater optimism about the future. No matter how sticky the problem, you know you'll be able to find a solution. For another, you'll discover that sometimes you'll be happier with the compromise decision than you were with your own first choice. Joint decisions demand greater creativity and have to take into account two people's judgment and experience, not just one person's. A shared decision is often a better decision.

The following exercise provides a model for conflict resolution. It has five preconditions for success:

- Sufficient time and adequate privacy must be assured.

- The problem must be well defined.

- Both parties must want to resolve the conflict.

- Both parties must maintain a calm, "adult" attitude.

• Both parties must agree to stay with the process until a decision is reached.

EXERCISE 4:
The Art of Compromise

1. One partner begins by briefly stating a preference. Example: "My first choice in this situation is . . ."

2. The other partner restates the first partner's position for clarification, then states his or her own position. Example: "What I understand you to say is . . . And hearing that, my first choice is . . ."

3. The first partner restates the second partner's first choice and then offers a compromise. Example: "Your first choice is . . . I could live with . . ."

4. The second partner restates the last suggestion and either agrees with it or offers another alternative, moving in the direction of compromise.

5. This process continues until an agreement is reached and specifics are agreed upon.

If you do not come to a resolution within a reasonable amount of time, both of you should check for the following:

• Am I more committed to winning than to resolving?

• Do I have a hidden agenda to hurt or punish my partner?

• Is there more of a need to be heard or understood than to reach an agreement?

• Is this a nonnegotiable issue?

• Can I live with this issue if it's left unresolved?

Once you run through this drill enough times, you can depart from the rigid structure. Aim for: (1) a clear expression of your own wishes; (2) an accurate reflection of your partner's wishes; and (3) a willingness to keep on offering alternatives until you both agree on a course of action.

🎴 Turning off the Projector

When a person grows up in an enmeshed family, it's often difficult to tell where one person begins and the other leaves off. When Dad is sad, Daughter is sad. When Mom is angry, Son feels guilty. When Stepmother is depressed, Daughter feels worthless. Many a Chosen Child feels connected at the mind with a parent. Years later, this mental fusion gets transferred to the husband or wife and causes a host of difficulties.

For example, my husband is a runner, and I used to project onto him my anger at my lack of physical fitness. I made up that his running took time away from our relationship; I made up that running was more important to him than spending time with me; I made up that whenever he was lacing up his running shoes, he was looking for a way to get away from me. None of this was true. He just liked to run and stay in shape. The source of my biased interpretation was the fact that I was angry at myself for being so sedentary, so I projected my anger onto him. I crafted a silent movie in my head—with me playing the role of the neglected heroine—and used him as a movie screen. Fortunately, I finally figured out what I was doing. Now I exercise regularly and no longer resent the time he spends jogging.

Here are some common projections collected from my work with couples. Do any of them seem familiar?

Projection: "You never want sex."

Translation: "I feel insecure about our relationship and I need sex to give me reassurance."

Projection: "You are not in this relationship."

Translation: "I am only partially committed to you. The rest of me belongs to Daddy/Mother/children/work."

Projection: "You never listen to me."

Translation: "I don't listen to you. I only want to hear what I want to hear."

Projection: "You are rude to me."

Translation: "I have my own brand of rudeness. I may not interrupt you when you are talking, but I will make plans without consulting you."

Projection: "You are in denial."

Translation: "I am better at seeing your problems than my own."

Projection: "You need therapy."

Translation: "I need help, but I'm afraid to get it."

Every time you criticize your partner in this manner, check it out for possible projections. If you are about to accuse your partner of being irresponsible, for example, ask yourself first, "How have *I* been irresponsible?" If you believe your partner has been withholding love, ask yourself, "How have *I* been neglecting my partner?" Sometimes you may have to "massage" the answer a little. You may accuse your partner of being insensitive to your friends, knowing full well that this is not one of your faults; you happen to be quite sensitive to your friends. But, outside your awareness, you may be very insensitive to someone else—namely, your partner. *One of the most effective ways to further your personal growth is to turn all your criticisms around and direct them back at yourself.* Ask yourself, "How does this criticism apply to me? What don't I like about myself? What am I missing in my life at this very moment? What negative thought or feeling am I trying to banish by projecting it onto my partner?"

Another common form of projection is to second-guess your partner. Instead of asking for your partner's wishes or opinions, you formulate your own conclusion. I used to do this a lot. For example, if a painting happened to catch my eye at an art gallery, I'd ask myself if my husband would like it. Nine times out of ten, I'd decide that he wouldn't. I'd make up that he didn't like the style or objected to the price. I'd pass the painting by, secretly angry at him for his negativity. All of this would have taken place with no communication from him whatsoever.

I've been guilty of projecting a negative response onto my husband more times than I can count. Some of you may find this behavior totally foreign; others will know exactly what I'm talking about. But whether or not you share this particular malady with me, you can be sure that a high proportion of your negative thoughts and feelings about your partner have more to do with you than the person you're married to. The sooner you realize this, the better your relationship will be. Projections do a great deal of harm to relationships. They create distance when you desire closeness. They block progress by masking the real issues. They make it difficult to sort out the true nature of your problems. Begin now to search for ways in which you may be blurring the boundaries between you and your partner. The more thoughts and feelings you are able to claim as your own, the healthier your relationship will be.

Polarization

Typically, the Chosen Child grows up in a polarized household. Mother thinks Sister is selfish and spoiled; Dad thinks she's an angel. Wife thinks Mother-in-law is a witch; Husband thinks she's a virtuous mother. Mom is a strict disciplinarian; Dad is a pushover. Unwittingly, the Chosen Child may transport this black-and-white thinking into marriage. If he says "black," she says "white." If she says "yes," he says "no." If she is critical of a neighbor, he is supportive. If he is stern, she compensates by being overly permissive.

The process of polarization is not just a marriage problem, it's a universal human tendency. If we sense that someone is seeing only one side of the picture, we have a natural inclination to balance it out. We automatically supply the opposite view. Imagine for a moment that we are friends, and I want you to meet another friend of mine. I begin by saying, "Oh, I just can't wait for you to meet Georgette. She is so beautiful. She is extremely intelligent and has a great sense of humor. Her house is immaculate, and she has gorgeous, happy, well-behaved children. I just love being with her and I know you will, too." As you listen to me, you think, "This person sounds unreal. She must have weak spots. I wonder what they are." You know that no one could be all good or all bad, so you search for the missing pieces of the puzzle. It's an instinctual way to get a more complete picture.

But this tendency to balance out each other's point of view can quickly degenerate into a destructive polarization. You and your partner become entrenched in opposite points of view, never meeting in the middle. A wedge is driven between you that defeats all attempts at intimacy.

There's a deceptively simple way to remove the wedge, and that is to switch sides. If you've been locked in the negative side of an argument, switch to the positive. Search for the other side of the problem and voice it. You don't have to lie or be dishonest, because your partner invariably has a legitimate point of view—you've just been blind to it. You need to open your eyes and look for the merit in your partner's position.

One family that I worked with, a stepfamily, had polarized around a financial issue—the cost of a son's college education. The stepfather complained ad nauseam about the financial strain, while the mother steadfastly defended the expense. Although she secretly felt the financial pressure, too, she was afraid to voice her anxiety for fear of tipping the argument in her husband's favor.

At my advice, the mother began to be more honest about her financial worries. One night she confessed to her husband, "Yes, Daniel's tuition is putting a squeeze on the budget. It's hard to keep our heads above water with that annual tuition payment. I'm not sure what to do." As soon as he heard this candid admission, her husband began to lighten up on his complaints. He was relieved to know that his wife understood his anxiety. Because his concern was finally recognized, he was able to dig his way out of his hole. He told his wife that he didn't want Daniel to go to a less expensive school—he was proud to have his stepson in a top-notch institution. He had just been wanting some acknowledgment for the considerable sacrifice he was making.

✽ Celebrate!

As the two of you spend more enjoyable time together, practice better communication skills, find positive ways to resolve conflict, and clarify the boundary around your marriage, you will notice a marked improvement in your emotional climate. At some point, you may decide to celebrate your renewed commitment to marriage. There are many ways to do this. Consider having:

- A special dinner for the two of you

- A religious ceremony

- A renewal of wedding vows

- An exchange of commemorative gifts

- A pilgrimage to a place that's important to both of you

- A second honeymoon

Find *some* way to acknowledge all the difficulties you've overcome. It's not easy to create a lasting love relationship under the best of circumstances, and your history of being the Chosen Child makes it doubly difficult. Reward yourself for the progress you've made:

You deserve it!

❁ What If Your Partner Doesn't Want to Work on the Marriage?

As you read this chapter, you may have found yourself thinking, "This looks interesting to me, but I bet my partner won't do the exercises." This is a common lament. Dozens of people have come into my office complaining, "I'm willing to work on our relationship but my partner is not." In every marriage seminar I've conducted, most couples tend to split themselves up into a "dragger" and a "draggee." One person is eager to come to the seminar and do the work, and the other is looking for a way to sneak out the back door. This can indeed be a serious stumbling block. Unless both partners are willing to work on the marriage, it's hard to make any progress. Both people need to be committed to the process of growth.

If this is your problem, I want to give you the same advice I give my clients: explore the possibility that *your* attitude may be part of the problem. It could be that your partner has come to believe that "working on the relationship" means satisfying all of *your* needs; your partner may shy away from marriage therapy for fear of being presented with a laundry list of "I wants." What I have learned from years of experience is that *most people will work on their marriages if they have reason to believe that they, too, will reap some rewards.* Ask yourself: "Do I always talk about my own needs and show little interest in my partner's needs? Have I demonstrated a willingness to grow and change to meet my *partner's* needs? Does my partner feel that he or she has anything to gain by working on our relationship?"

If this seems not to address your problem, your partner may lack motivation for an entirely different reason—you've failed to convey the depth of your concerns. Many clients have come to me in an uproar about their marriages, yet they haven't bothered to share their unhappiness with their spouses! They explain their reticence this way: "I don't want to upset her," or, "He wouldn't care anyway."

This is a clear example of how the past affects the present. Because their parents didn't meet their needs when they were young, my clients assumed that their partners wouldn't meet their needs in the present. Early years of conditioning trained them to expect very little from others. To see if this may be part of your problem, ask yourself: "Have I been explicit about the problems I see in our relationship? Have I shared my dissatisfaction? Have I let my partner know that the relationship is not meeting my needs? Do I share my marital grievances with a friend, not my partner?"

If you've thoughtfully explored these two possibilities and still are unable to make any headway, you may need additional support. I suggest you enlist the aid of a marriage or family therapist to help your partner overcome his or her resistance to growth and change.

13

Shoring Up Your Support Network

☙

For the adult Chosen Child, having a healthy support network is one of the keys to recovery. Bolstered by your friends, you lead a rich life. If you are married, your partner is freed from the obligation to satisfy all your emotional needs, and you diminish any tendency to rely on a child. If you are single, friends are doubly important because they are your primary source of support. But maintaining friendships can be a problem for people who grew up in enmeshed families. Because of the lack of boundaries in their family of origin, they tend to shut people out or let inappropriate people in.

My problem was the first one, keeping people at arm's length. My method of avoiding intimacy was quite subtle: I had a lot of acquaintances, but I made sure I was a better friend to them than they were to me; I made sure I was always on the giving side of the equation. Not surprisingly, people found it hard to get close to me. "You're a hard friend to love," a friend once told me, and he was right.

The reason that I kept friends at a distance is a common one. I was so cut off from my wants, needs, and feelings that I couldn't let friends get close to me; I didn't want them to know what *I* didn't know. This meant I had constantly to patrol my borders. I couldn't be intimate with anyone, and loneliness was a constant companion. I remember at one low point saying to myself, "No one knows me and no one wants to know me." I had a lot of acquaintances and a lot of activities, but they were merely an attempt to hide my pain from myself and others.

It's possible to grow up in an enmeshed family and have the opposite problem, which is to rush headlong into intimacy. Unconsciously, you want your friendships to be just as absorbing as the relationship you had with a parent, and you unwittingly cross over the boundaries that normally separate individuals. Your tendency is to have one or two all-encompassing friendships or to expect every friendship to be intense and personal. Twenty minutes after meeting someone, you bring up intimate topics of conversation. Whether this person expresses any interest or not, you go into detail about your health problems, love life, and job frustrations. They know all about you in the first meeting.

People with loose boundaries also tend to expect more from their friends than the normal friendship role encompasses. For example, they may try to resolve deep-seated emotional problems with a friend. This rarely works out, because friends are rarely willing to bond with you to the degree necessary for conflict resolution. That role is best handled by a spouse or a therapist. To expect a friend to get deeply involved in your struggles is to set yourself up for disappointment.

Another consequence of loose boundaries is that they make people vulnerable to what I call "emotional rape." People who crave intimacy are sitting ducks for emotional violation. Karleen, a 30-year-old homemaker, was especially vulnerable to smooth-talking men. Any man who came on to her was allowed into her life. A stranger at a bus stop, a plumber working on a stopped-up sink, a participant in a weekend seminar—any man who had a desire to get close to her was granted the opportunity. Some of these instant "friendships" ended in a sexual encounter; some did not. But they all began as a result of her lack of boundaries. She had an open-door policy of intimacy.

Identifying the Nature of Your Boundary Problems

Recognizing that you have overly rigid or diffuse boundaries is the first step to correcting them. The following exercise may give you some insights. Read the twelve brief scenarios and see which ones describe you. (If you've changed in recent years, you may find it helpful to note which statements used to apply to you but are no longer valid.)

1. You've had a really good day and share your feelings with a friend. Your friend is in a bad mood and gives you a lukewarm or negative response. *Poof!* Your good mood goes out the window.

2. You're having a bad day and a longtime friend calls you on the phone. You keep the conversation impersonal and refrain from sharing your concerns.

3. You went to a movie with friends. You liked the movie, but they hated it. As you listen to your friends pan the movie, you begin to question your own judgment.

4. You go to a movie you really like. Your friends hated the movie, and you automatically turn off their criticisms. While they chatter on, you privately relish your own opinions.

5. A friend asks to borrow your car. You don't want to, but you say "yes" anyway. You end up resenting your friend for asking.

6. Friends rarely ask to borrow anything of yours. As a rule, you don't lend out your possessions.

7. You are dating someone and find out that this person is dating someone else. You are angry and hurt, but you continue to be involved.

8. If you are dating someone and that person is dating someone else, you'd rather not know about it. That's his or her business. You like a separation between your personal lives.

9. All a friend has to do is mention a problem and you try to solve it. You often feel that you know what's best for people, or feel obligated to resolve their difficulties.

10. You rarely give or seek advice from friends. On the whole, you consider your affairs and their affairs private matters.

11. You have a hard time keeping a secret. If you know something that concerns one of your friends, you usually tell. It's just a matter of finding the right time and opportunity.

12. You are quite good about keeping secrets. You may have information that directly concerns a friend, for example, but keep it to yourself. Some people claim it's hard to pry information loose from you.

Look back over your responses. If you have loose boundaries, it is likely that you identified with more of the odd-numbered statements. If you have rigid boundaries, the even-numbered statements probably rang more true. If you checked the same number of odd and even statements, you may have rigid boundaries in some areas of your life and loose ones in others.

器 Firming Up Your Boundaries

People who have loose boundaries may find it difficult to establish an appropriate degree of distance between themselves and others— even total strangers. A client told me the following story: One day, she stopped for gas at a roadside station in a rural area. She went into the station to pay for the gas and buy a pair of sunglasses. As she walked by the counter, the attendant, a tall man with an overhanging belly, started asking her personal questions. "Where are you going?" "What will you be doing there?" In an obliging manner, she answered him and joined in a conversation. When she was about to leave, the man reached for her hand and asked if he could read her palm. Despite feelings of discomfort, she allowed him to do it. In a matter of minutes, they were discussing her marriage, her career choice, her sex life, and her prospects for future happiness. Finally, she was able to extract her hand from his grasp and go about her business of looking for sunglasses.

While she was trying on sunglasses, an attractive young woman came into the station. The attendant immediately launched into the same overly familiar routine with her. In response to his question about her destination, the woman replied, "I'm on vacation." Her tone was pleasant but uninviting. She proceeded to buy a candy bar and walk out the door.

"Why can't I act like that woman?" my client asked me after recounting this episode.

"You can," I replied. "It just won't feel comfortable at first. You'll feel like you're cutting the other person off. But that's just what you have to do with some people to maintain your boundaries."

I suggested that the next time someone tried to be overly familiar, she should say strong words to herself such as: "This is an emotional violation," and immediately impose limits on the situation. If she did this often enough, it would begin to feel natural to erect barriers. It would feel like a violation to lay herself open to whoever came along.

To help instill this new behavior, I walked her back through the encounter with the gas station attendant, slowing down the interchange so that she could decide how she would have liked to respond at each juncture. We both agreed that if she had walked into the station with an assertive, impersonal air about her, the invasion would not have taken place. But just for drill, we play-acted each part of it, from the original hello to the point where he reached for her hand.

Role-playing in this manner, either in your imagination or with a friend, is a good way to program new behavior. If you rehearse having firm boundaries, an assertive response will come more easily to you when you need it.

88 Lowering Your Emotional Barriers

Some of you who grew up with an Invasive Parent have the opposite problem to overcome. Instead of needing to find ways to keep people out of your life, you need to let more people in. Your well-maintained boundaries are keeping you from making friends and creating a functional support system.

A good place to start making changes is to be more open with people you already know and trust. For example, if you're feeling low and a friend calls and asks how you're doing, resist the temptation to parry with an automatic: "Fine. How are you?" Instead, volunteer a more honest reply. Here are some examples of intimate responses:

> "I'm feeling a little down this morning. I don't know why. I just woke up in a bad mood. I almost wish it weren't so sunny out. It's such a contrast to my mood. Do you ever feel that way?"
> "I'm really hassled. It seems I can't get anything done today. All I'm trying to do is clean the house, but I've had a dozen interruptions. I yelled at the kids this morning. I've been a real ogre."

"I'm feeling kind of blue. Ruth's home from her business trip, but we don't seem to be connecting with each other. I worry sometimes that we're drifting apart."
"I've been feeling lonely. It's hard to stay home alone since the divorce. The house feels so empty. I really need to get out more."

Often these revelations will be followed by your friend's revelations; intimacy invites intimacy. As you become more comfortable exploring this personal terrain, your friendships will grow in depth.

If you feel uneasy about sharing your thoughts and feelings to this degree, a less threatening way to deepen a friendship is to spend some time together doing something out of the ordinary. Instead of the usual activities, sign up for a riverboat cruise. Go on a hot-air balloon ride. Go horseback riding. Make candles. Paint a room. Play hooky from work and go for a hike. Sign up for a class together. Drive to a distant town to attend a concert. Play music together. These shared adventures will help create a lasting bond between you.

Some of you will feel some resistance to these suggestions. "I don't have time." "I don't have the money." "It doesn't sound interesting." "There's no one to invite." In order to overcome your resistance, you will have to double your efforts to reach out to others. You will have to extend invitations when your inner voice is telling you to withdraw. You will have to risk being intimate.

After many years of struggle and growth, I've finally been able to lower my barriers with friends. When I'm feeling blue, I own up to it. I freely admit to being needy. When I first began showing my vulnerability, I was surprised to find out that my friends liked me better that way. I had assumed that if I talked about my problems, they would run in the opposite direction. But my friends liked knowing that I had my good days and bad days, just as they did; they liked having me scaled down to size; they liked having the opportunity to help *me* for a change.

EXERCISE 1:
Examining the Strength of Your Support Network

The following exercise will help give you an objective view of your support network. Get a pencil and a blank piece of paper. In the middle of the paper, draw a symbol to represent you. Use a circle if you're a woman and a square if you're a man. Put your initials in the middle of the symbol. (See p. 230 for a completed example.)

Next, draw a symbol for all the important people in your life, including friends, co-workers, and relatives. Use boxes for males and circles for females. Draw large symbols for people who affect your strongly (either negatively or positively), and small symbols for people who affect you less strongly.

Where you place each symbol on your chart indicates how frequently you see the individual. Place a symbol close to the center of the page if you see the person often, toward the edge if you see the person less often. Write each person's initials inside the appropriate symbol.

Now, connect each symbol to the center with a pair of lines. One line indicates the energy you send out toward that individual. The other indicates the energy you receive from that person. If the interaction is positive, use a straight line. If it's neutral, use a dotted line. If it's predominantly negative, use a jagged line. (The line going in and the line going out may be different.)

If you wish, add additional symbols to your graph to represent other aspects of your life, such as family, pets, hobbies, money, or personal interests—anything that's important to your well-being. Once again, the size of these symbols and their location on the chart will indicate their relative importance to you. When you are finished drawing these additional symbols, connect them to the center with lines as described above.

Now go back and check your diagram to make sure that the size of your circles and squares illustrates how important each individual is to you. If you have a very good female friend you see once in three years, she should be represented by a large circle placed on the outer fringes. If you have a minor friendship with a male co-worker you see every day, he should be represented by a small square placed relatively close to you.

When you are through, your diagram should look something like the diagram on the following page.

What can you learn by examining your diagram? A quick count of the number of circles and boxes will give you some indication of the overall health of your network. If you have six or fewer symbols on your chart, you may need more emotional support than your few friends can provide—especially if you are single. On the other hand, if you have dozens of names on your chart, it could be that your friends are demanding more from you than you are able to give. Maintaining a lot of friendships takes time and energy and may be a significant strain in your life. A crowded diagram could also indicate some underlying problems. Are you using sheer numbers to avoid

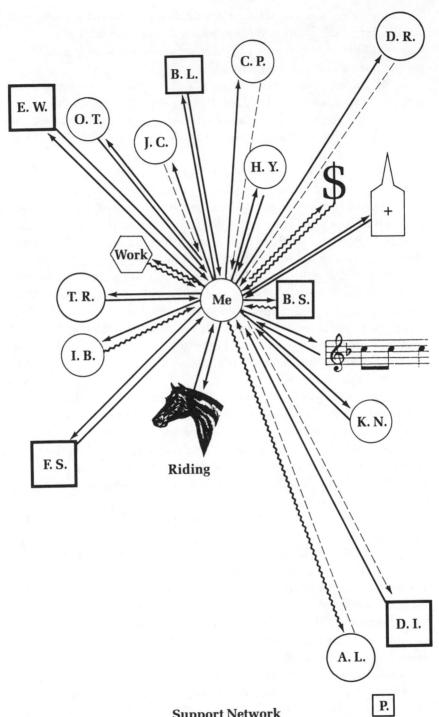

Support Network

intimacy? Are you preventing yourself from resolving marriage problems by distracting yourself with a lot of social events? If so, scaling back your network may be in order.

Next look for the number of jagged lines in your diagram. Do you have many conflicted relationships? Are any of your jagged lines connected to people who have a lot of influence on you? Common sense suggests that you may want to resolve those conflicts or change your routine so you see these people less frequently.

Now look at your chart and note the location of your most significant, positive friendships. Do you have some in the outer circles? What can you do to nourish these friendships? Maybe you could write some letters, make a few phone calls, or plan a reunion to revitalize these important connections.

Here are some additional questions to ask yourself:

1. Which key person did I inadvertently leave off my chart?
2. Am I sending out more positive energy than I'm receiving?
3. Am I getting more positive energy from males or from females?
4. Are my friends more supportive than my family?
5. Is there a lot of negative energy coming from a parent or in-law?

✲ Suggestions for Making New Friends

If this exercise has helped you see that you would benefit from expanding your network of friends, I have some advice. My first suggestion is simple: *Get out of the house!* You can't make friends sitting at home reading a book or watching TV. Go to church. Sign up for classes. Go to neighborhood meetings. Go to PTA meetings. Go to a dog show. Say "yes" to any and all invitations. Go with Jane to a fashion show even if you don't care much for Jane or for fashion. Jane might have an interesting roommate. Go anywhere that gets you out the front door and into the mainstream! The moral is, you may have to kiss a lot of frogs before you make a good friend.

Be alert to the possibilities for friendship in your daily routine. My husband and I went to the opera about a year ago and struck up a conversation with the couple sitting to our left. We chatted before the opera and during the intermission. As we were leaving, my husband initiated an exchange of phone numbers. Later that month we had an open house and invited the couple over. They were happy to come, and since then we've developed a wonderful friendship. If we had been shy about exchanging phone numbers or hadn't thought to invite them to our party, we would never have gotten to know them.

If you meet someone you would like to know better, strike up a conversation. If you like what you hear, introduce yourself. Ask for the person's name and *remember it*. Ask questions and listen carefully to the answers. People are interested in people who are interested in them. If a rapport develops, suggest that you meet for tea or coffee. You may need to take most, if not all, of the initiative— especially if the person has a lot of friends. One woman had to ask me out for coffee three times before I was free to join her. Thanks to her persistence, we're now the best of friends. One note of caution: even though you will have to make the first moves, make sure that after a reasonable amount of time your interest is returned; you don't want the relationship to be one-sided.

Making friends takes time and energy. To build up your support network you may have to take time away from work, your family, or household projects. You may have to invest some money in long-distance calls or travel. But if you need more emotional support, the time and money will be well spent. Ask yourself if you would rather invest in forming new friendships or in medical and psychological services. Being with friends is good preventive medicine.

When you are in the process of making friends, you may experience some rejection. Some people may not be interested in you, and others may be interested but too busy to welcome a new friendship. But don't let one rejection thwart you. Years ago, when I was single, I wanted someone to go to the movies with me. I got on the phone and started calling friends. I got one rejection after another. My friends were either not home, busy, or didn't want to go to the movies. Just as I was about to resign myself to my fate, I thought of one more person to call and dialed her number. She was delighted to go with me, and we had a memorable night on the town. If I had stopped at call number two or five or even seven, I would have spent the evening alone.

While you're making new friends, spend some time cultivating the old ones. Long-term friends play a special role in your life. I have a friend, Tom, whom I have known since we both were 7 years old. Tom and I grew up in the same small town and were often in the same classroom at school. He moved to Arizona the summer before our junior year in high school, and for years our communication was limited mostly to letters. He came to my wedding when we were both 20 years old, but I didn't see him again for years. He went off to the Peace Corps, and I got involved in raising a family. Then one day he called me out of the blue. I hadn't heard his voice for ten years, but I recognized it immediately. He was able to visit me a few months later. His visit reunited me with a part of myself that I had long forgotten. One thing he said to me was, "Where is your sense of humor? You're not as crazy as you used to be." He helped me see how serious I had become. His visit helped me come out of a fog. I realized that I had ventured a long way from the lighthearted person I had once been. I felt a strong determination to reclaim that part of me, a determination that was eventually rewarded. Thank you again, Tom.

Do you have an old college friend or grade-school friend who has drifted away? Do you have close friends who have moved out of town? Are there good friends you write to only during the holidays? You might want to draw them back into your inner circle. If you've lost contact, it could take some sleuthing. Don't give up.

When you begin to realign your boundaries and balance your life, don't be alarmed if you lose some friends. You may decide that some of your friends aren't giving you enough support or are unpleasant to be around. As you get healthier, you'll automatically want to be around healthier people. Also, there may be some people who don't want to spend time with you anymore. When Byron, a man who had worked for a public utility company for thirteen years, started getting his life together, he decided he was no longer willing to lend money to his friends. As a result, a friend who had used him as his personal banker stopped seeing him. Corina, an interior designer, had a similar experience when she reevaluated her friendships. During therapy for being sexually abused as a child, she realized that her role in virtually all her friendships was to listen and give advice; there was no one who supported her. She began testing her friends to see if any of them were interested in a more equitable relationship. Those who weren't able to handle an equal mixture of give-and-take dropped by the wayside and eventually were replaced by new, supportive friends.

🏵 Maintaining Appropriate Boundaries at Work

The workplace offers numerous opportunities for friendship. Because you see your co-workers on a daily basis, you have the opportunity to get to know them before you make any personal overtures. Those of you with loose boundaries should proceed with caution, however: your history makes you an ideal candidate for enmeshed work relationships. A typical example is trying to create a "special relationship" with a boss or supervisor. It doesn't take much imagination to see the parallel between an overly close relationship with an employer and an overly close relationship with a parent.

A woman named Vicki fell headlong into this trap. One of four female supervisors who reported directly to her boss, Vicki worked long and hard to be his star employee. Her efforts were rewarded when he asked her to accompany him on a weekend training seminar. That weekend, Vicki asked her boss probing questions about his personal life. He was receptive to her overtures, and they spent several hours swapping life stories. An intimate friendship developed that deepened in the following weeks. Soon Vicki and her boss were sitting side by side at staff meetings, eating lunch together, and staying late to set strategies for work.

For Vicki, the friendship became an obsession. When her boss took a day off, she took a day off. When he went to lunch early, so did she. She even sneaked into his office to look at his appointment book so that she could arrange her schedule to match his. Although it was widely suspected that they were having an affair, this was not the case. Vicki wasn't attracted to his body, she was attracted to his mind. He was one of the brightest men she had ever met, and she found him mesmerizing.

Vicki's interest in her employer continued unabated until the office Christmas party, when he stunned her with a surprise announcement: he was being promoted to a higher position at a branch office. Vicki was devastated. "I felt like the bottom had dropped out from underneath me. I was furious he hadn't told me first. I felt betrayed."

Vicki quit work a week before her boss was scheduled to leave and sunk into a long depression. It was this depression that brought her in for counseling. Over time she was able to see the many similarities between her relationship with her boss and her relationship with her father. They were both very bright men. They were both drawn to women outside their marriage relationships. She was amused to realize that they also shared a lot of physical characteristics: both men were stocky, had dark hair and brown eyes, and wore glasses. They even had the same pattern of baldness.

Once her eyes were open, Vicki began to see how the politics at work had replicated the politics in her family. As a young child she had successfully competed with three older sisters for her father's attention. At work, she had triumphed over three female co-workers. "I was still trying to be Daddy's favorite," she told me. "I was used to that special status. I've never known how to be on an equal footing with others. I need to be set apart from the rest. It seemed natural and inevitable that my boss would favor me. I would have been crushed if he hadn't." Having these insights made it much less likely that Vicki would repeat this pattern in her next job. "I know all the warning signs," she said, "and I'll be watching for them. I don't want to go through that again. It was too draining."

The workplace, like the family, operates best when inherent boundaries are respected. Be wary of making friends outside your hierarchical level. If you make friends with someone higher or lower on the corporate ladder, keep your friendship after-hours and adhere to company policy while at work. Watch out for these danger signs: getting promoted because of your friendship; granting special privileges to your friend; circumventing the normal chain of command; lowering your standards for your friend; and taking extra time off work because of preferential status.

Also, beware of making friends out of your business partners and business partners out of your friends. Your history of enmeshment increases the possibility that these relationships will get out of hand. Give it a lot of thought before you take action. Get outside opinions. Many a friendship has gone sour over business ventures.

14

Parenting: How to End the Cycle of Enmeshment

❀

Not long ago I interviewed a man in his early fifties named Peter. "My childhood was a classic case of emotional incest," he said. "You're not going to find a better example." He was right. We talked for two hours, and his story was so representative that I could have used it to illustrate most of the points in this book. His father was a quiet, passive man (another Shadow Man) and a heavy drinker. His mother, the dominant member of the duo, directed her energy to Peter, her firstborn son. Peter was a very bright child, and she had elaborate fantasies of his becoming a Nobel prize–winning physicist. With every straight-A report card, her self-esteem puffed up a little higher. Her preoccupation with him was so pronounced that Peter had the eerie feeling she could read his mind. When he was a teenager and had thoughts he didn't want his mother to know about, he would go into his room and play loud music, hoping the sound would block out his brain waves.

Despite the intensity of his mother's involvement, Peter, like many victims of emotional incest, grew up with the illusion that his childhood was normal. His parents hadn't divorced. There was no physical violence. In many ways, they appeared to be a model family. A major midlife crisis taught him otherwise. At age 48, for no apparent reason, he suddenly found himself unable to function. He couldn't cope with job pressures, he lost all interest in physics, and for the first time in twenty-seven years of marriage, he questioned whether he wanted to stay with his wife. Nothing in his life seemed right anymore. The crisis deepened until he had to be hospitalized for depression.

Following his hospitalization, he continued therapy for two years and ended up with a substantially revised view of his childhood. He realized that his mother's excessive involvement with him, coupled with his father's passivity, was the source of his numerous emotional problems.

At the end of our interview, Peter turned to me and asked a question I could feel was coming. "I'm doing fine now," he said. "I've made a lot of changes, and I feel on top of things. I feel more . . ." he paused to search for a word, "more harmonious than I've ever felt. But what I'm worried about is that I'm afraid I might pass on what happened to me to my son and daughter. If I was so blind to what my mother was doing to me, how can I be sure I'm not too involved with my own children?"

Peter's concern was palpable.

"How old are your children?" I asked.

"Five and thirteen," he said.

"Well, one thing to watch out for," I told him, "is that you might want to draw them closer to you as they grow older and start to move away from the family. You might want to keep them dependent on you longer than necessary. You might feel a sense of loss as they go on to create new worlds of their own."

"Boy," he sighed, "I'm doing that already. I keep wanting my older daughter to spend more time with me, to come with us on all our family outings, but she'd rather be with her friends. I'm glad you pointed this out to me, because I think I was about to head down the wrong road."

At some point in their therapy, just about all of my clients who have children become sidetracked from their exploration of their childhoods to dwell on the mistakes they've made as *parents*. Many of them have come to the painful realization that they've unwittingly become overinvolved with a son or daughter. The guilt and anxiety can be overwhelming: "How could I have repeated the very same mistakes? Why couldn't I see what was happening? How could I, of all people, get tangled up with a child?"

Some of you may have had a similar reaction as you read this book. As you scrutinize your current family, you recognize two of the telltale signs of emotional incest: (1) the lack of a supportive, nurturing marriage relationship, and (2) a tendency to turn to one or more of your children for emotional comfort or support. You fear that to one degree or another, you're recreating the same twisted dynamics that were so harmful to you as a child.

It is a distressing but well-documented fact that people tend to pass on the destructive elements of their upbringing. Like dominant genes, dysfunctional behaviors show up in generation after generation, replicating themselves seemingly at will. Children of alcoholics develop drinking or drug problems. Abused children grow up to abuse their own sons and daughters. Children from unstable families wind up with a distressingly high rate of divorce. The tendency is either to duplicate the behaviors we've observed in our families or to run blindly in the opposite direction, creating a whole new set of problems.

How can you keep from repeating the mistakes of the past? And—if you've already made some errors—how can you restore a healthy balance to your family?

The most important thing you can do is to strengthen your support network. This recommendation is both cure and preventive medicine: a strong support network will help those of you who are just starting a family establish a healthy pattern of interaction, and it will help those of you with older children correct any ongoing enmeshment. A strong marriage relationship and/or caring friends will give you the support you need to be an objective and nurturing parent.

But no matter how strong and resilient your support system, you will still have a greater tendency than other parents to step over the hidden boundaries between parent and child. Especially in times of stress, you will be tempted to turn to your children for support—it's a familiar and comforting pattern. To guard against this tendency, you need to be especially clear about the differences between parenting and partnering. I've explored these differences throughout the book, but a summary here might be helpful. If you adhere to the following ten points, you will maintain a healthy separation between you and your children.

✸ Ten Rules for Healthy Parenting

1. **Share personal information with your child only when it's in your child's best interest**. There are some valid reasons to share personal information with a child. First, children need to have their sense of reality confirmed. If you've been distant or irritable, for example, an acknowledgment of your state of mind and a brief explanation is in order: "Yes, I've been snapping at you today. I didn't sleep well and I have a headache. I'll try to be more patient." Children need to know that their perceptions are accurate, and they need to know that they're not to blame. By sharing information, you're offering them a reality check and releasing them from responsibility.

Another reason to share personal information with children 10 years or older is to help give them a realistic view of adulthood. It would be helpful for them to know, for example, that all marriages have their difficulties, that supporting a family is not easy, and that growing old has its drawbacks. This information should be doled out sparingly, however, and you should make it abundantly clear that you are in command of the situation; you know how to cope. You don't want to worry your children needlessly or make them feel obliged to help out. Supporting you is not their role in the family.

Finally, sharing some of your problems with your children lets them see that no one's perfect. Everyone has moments of difficulty, and your candor shows them that there is no reason to be ashamed of this fact.

But it's important to keep all personal sharing to a minimum. If you feel better after having talked to your child, but your child feels worse or feels obliged to offer you suggestions or moral support, then you have crossed over the line. You are asking for the kind of support that should come from another adult.

2. **Keep the details of your marital problems between you and your partner.** This is a subset of the previous rule, but it deserves special attention. If you have problems with your partner, *take it up with your partner!* Leave your children out of it. Children who become involved in their parents' marital problems absorb some of the tension and feel obligated to be a source of emotional support for one or both adults. This perpetuates the cycle of abuse. The only reason to share marital discord with a child is to affirm the child's sense of

reality and to provide reassurance: "Yes, your mother and I were fighting last night. We had a serious disagreement. But we talked long enough to work it out. I'm sorry you had to overhear us."

3. **Turn to adults for your emotional needs.** If you're feeling lonely or sad or angry, don't turn to a child for comfort. Call a friend, confide in your partner, join a support group, sign up for counseling, talk to your parents, call a brother or sister, have coffee with a neighbor, write in a journal, meditate, pray—*do anything but turn to your child.* It is a violation of your role as a parent to seek reassurance from a son or daughter. The only exception to this rule is if you are advanced in years and your son or daughter is an independent, mature adult. Then it may be appropriate for the parent-child role to be reversed.

4. **Reinforce your child's unique qualities.** There is a natural tendency to reward your children for mirroring your thoughts, beliefs, and preferences. It makes you feel supported and less alone. But when you praise your children for resembling you, they suppress key parts of their personalities; they sacrifice parts of themselves to win your approval.

To overcome this tendency, train yourself to make positive comments about the ways your children differ from you. Here are some examples: "I have always liked nonfiction books, but you choose novels. You have a good sense of what appeals to you." "When I saw you skiing down that hill, I realized that you have a lot less fear than I do. We are quite different that way. Even as a child, I was always afraid of getting hurt. I admire your courage." "I felt elated after seeing that movie, but you seemed let down. Isn't it interesting that two people can have such different responses to the same movie?" "I'm a night person, but you wake up singing. It must be nice to feel so energetic in the morning."

5. **Respect and encourage your child's drive toward independence**. A child shows a desire to be self-sufficient at an early age, and this tendency grows stronger with each passing year. If you don't interfere with this drive, there is little likelihood that you will become enmeshed. Your children will instinctively be carried along a path toward greater and greater self-reliance.

What you need to guard against is *unwittingly* frustrating your child's sense of independence. You may think you are simply protecting your child from danger or setting reasonable limits, but in reality you may be fostering your child's dependence. How do you know if you're doing this? The following questions may give you some perspective. Do you put a great many more restrictions on your child's comings and goings than other caring parents? Do you seem more concerned about your child's physical or emotional well-being than most other parents? Are you deeply involved in your child's activities? Does your child complain about your restrictiveness? Do you limit your child's friendships? Have other people implied that you might be an overly protective parent? Does the thought of your children growing up and leaving home make you feel markedly depressed or anxious?

If you answered "yes" to many of these questions, you would be wise to look for opportunities to encourage your child's independence. Gradually loosen your controls so that your child has more freedom to explore outside activities and relationships.

6. **Encourage your child's friendships with other children.** Your child needs a support network, just as you do. (This is especially true for only children.) Get in the habit of saying "Yes" when your child wants to spend a night with a friend or have a friend over to play. Go out of your way to make your child's friends feel comfortable at your house. Be a willing chauffeur. Encourage your child to join youth organizations and to take part in activities that enlarge his or her circle of friends. For the most part, stay out of these activities unless you are needed to play a facilitating role or there is a recital or event your child wants you to attend. Children need to have a private sphere in which to operate.

7. **Give your child the safety and security of limits.** Because of your history, you may have a tendency to be a friend to your child rather than a parent. Since friends don't discipline each other, your child may be lacking the safety and structure of limits. You are the executive in the family and need to set the guidelines. Be prepared for the fact that your child may be angry at some of your restrictions and may try to get you to back down by pushing the limits or saying, "I don't like you!" It is your job to enforce the rules, nonetheless. Underneath your child's protestations, he or she will be grateful for the firm and consistent guidelines.

8. **Search for the positive qualities in each child.** Many parents find themselves drawn to one child more than another. This is especially likely if you were a Chosen Child. On an unconscious level, forming

an alliance with one child may seem natural to you. To block this tendency, look for and reward desirable traits in each of your children. Although it may require some effort to find admirable qualities in a difficult or less appealing child, each of your children needs to be assured of your love and support. In some instances, family therapy may be required to bring this about.

9. **Make your adult relationships a priority.** Set aside time each week to be alone with your spouse and/or adult friends. You are not detracting from your job as a parent when you spend time with other adults—you are getting the support you need to be a good parent. In addition, you are providing your children with a healthy model of adult life. Go on weekend getaways. Go out to dinner without the children. Have a weekly date. Have a weekly lunch date with a friend. Go on a weekend vacation with a friend. Write letters to your friends and call them on the phone. Let your children see that you have a viable network of support.

10. **Assure your children of your well-being.** Demonstrate to your children that you can take care of yourself. When you are having problems, reassure them that you are taking the necessary steps to remedy the situation. If you are feeling good, express it openly: "I'm really enjoying my work." "I've been very healthy lately." "I have so many things I want to do with my life, there are not enough hours in the day." "On days like today, I'm really happy to be alive!" "How did I get so lucky?"

❀ Freeing a Child from Enmeshment

One of my biggest regrets is that I didn't have information like this when my children were young. Without being aware of it, I became too involved with my children and often used them as a target for my anger. This was especially true for my firstborn. I vented anger at him instead of at my husband. In recent years I have owned up to these mistakes and made the appropriate apologies. It felt beneficial both to me and to my children to talk about the past and redefine our relationships.

If you have unwittingly violated some parental guidelines, you too may feel the need for remedial steps. It may not be enough to increase your support network and reinforce the boundaries between you and your child—you may need to make some amends.

If your child is 12 or older, consider having a "Realignment Session," a brief, to-the-point meeting where you explain what has happened, apologize for your actions, and sketch out the changes you are going to make. If you think your child will have difficulty listening to you, write your thoughts in a letter. (Have a trusted friend read the letter and give you feedback before you send it.) Another approach is to conduct the Realignment Session with a third person acting as mediator.

As you plan the session, arrange for sufficient privacy and make sure you won't be interrupted. Tell your child ahead of time that there is something you wish to discuss. Be calm, and don't make it sound like bad news. When you begin the meeting, ask your child to listen without interrupting. Your goal is to deliver a message, not to ask the child for forgiveness or to hear the child's point of view.

Keep to the point. Do not cloud the meeting with other issues. This is not the time to talk about allowances or infractions of household rules. This is a short event that allows you to apologize for past actions and explain any new behavior you'll be exhibiting. The shorter and simpler you keep the session, the more likely you are to accomplish your goal.

Realignment Session with a Chosen Child

1. **Assure your child of your love.** The session begins and ends with a statement of love and commitment. Your child needs to be assured of your continued affection and support. Here are some possible ways to express this:

> *"First and foremost, I want you to know that I love you. You mean so much to me. Your happiness and your well-being are very important to me."*
>
> *"I want you to know that I love you and that I will always be here for you. I will always be your Dad (or Mom)."*
>
> *"Our relationship is very important to me. It's important to me to be a good parent. I love you and respect you and am very happy that you are my daughter (son)."*

2. **State the facts.** Briefly describe your past actions in simple language. Be specific and stick to the subject. You might use words like:

> *"I relied on you too heavily. I turned to you when I should have*

turned to your mother/father or a friend."

"I was lonely and expected you to comfort me."

"I expected you to be like me, to like the same things I did."

"I was thinking of my needs, not yours. I was so wrapped up in myself that I ignored what you needed."

"In many ways, I've been more like a friend than a parent. There've been many times when I didn't set limits because I didn't want to upset you."

"When your father and I divorced, I turned to you for companionship. I expected you to take his place in my life. I encouraged you to stay at home because I didn't want to be by myself."

"I burdened you with information that had nothing to do with you."

"I gave you information that was beyond your years."

"I rewarded you with praise and special attention for being what I wanted you to be."

"I only saw what I wanted to see in you."

"In many ways, I lived my life through you."

"I resented your friends because I was jealous."

"I set up our relationship backwards. I used you for support and depended on you when all along I should have been there for you."

"I rewarded you for not being a problem to me."

"I should have said 'no' more often."

"I taught you that my needs were more important than yours."

"I played favorites. I was easier on you than I was on your brother."

"I invaded your privacy. I gave you mixed sexual messages."

"I gave you too much information about my private sex life."

"I kept you tied to me through money, guilt, and a false sense of responsibility."

"When you became interested in friends your own age, I felt betrayed. I was angry and punished you by withdrawing my love."

"When you left for college, I felt rejected. I was hurt and angry. I punished you by (1) ignoring you; (2) getting sick; (3) trying to make you feel guilty; (4) turning to your brother/sister."

"I made you overly responsible before your time."

"After the divorce, you became my partner. Then, when I married again, I left you out in the cold. That must have been *really hard on you. No wonder you were so angry at your stepfather."*

"I bad-mouthed your father in front of you. I had no right to do that. I took out my frustration on you as well as him."

3. **Share your feelings.** Let your child know how you feel about what you did. If tears come up, let them. Your child may try to protect you (or him- or herself) from your feelings, but don't be deterred. Keep talking through your shame, guilt, remorse, or anger. Reassure your child that he or she is not to blame; you accept full responsibility for your actions.

"I feel so ashamed that I hurt you. I wish things had been different."

"It's really hard for me to say this. It's hard for me to admit my mistakes. But I know that what I did was wrong. I'm terribly, terribly sorry."

"I feel so guilty that I wasn't there all those years when you needed me. It was almost as if you didn't have a parent. I am so sorry I failed you."

"It makes me so sad that you've had to suffer because of my mistakes. It's not fair. It wasn't your fault."

"I'm embarrassed that I treated you so badly when you left home. I had no right to behave that way. When I think about what I've done, I feel horrible."

"I am angry that I didn't know any better. If only I had known more about being a parent, I wouldn't have made so many mistakes."

4. **Share key information.** You had reasons for what you did, and if your child is mature enough, hearing your explanation might answer some questions. Don't give out information that is none of their concern, however, and don't let yourself off the hook. This is your time to take some licks and be accountable.

Here are some examples of explanations that provide important information but do not violate the purpose of the session or transgress the parent-child boundary:

"Before you were born, your mother and I had a lot of tension between us. We didn't know how to resolve it. Even though we loved each other, we didn't know enough to make the marriage work. When you came along, I found it much easier to love you than to love your mother. You made so few demands. And you thought I was wonderful. It was such a contrast to what was

going on between me and your mother. I now know that it was wrong for you to be my friend. It put a heavy burden on you. I taught you to take care of me instead of my taking care of you."

"When your father and I divorced, I went through a very rough time. I felt hurt and rejected, and I didn't know where to turn. I felt like a failure for not keeping the family together, so I tried to make it up to you by spending a lot of time with you and trying to make you happy. I came to rely on your company. I didn't realize how unfair this was to you. When you began to make a life of your own, I got scared. I didn't have many friends—which was my fault. I didn't make the effort to reach out to people. I just stayed at home. I was stuck, and you paid the price."

"When your father died, I was overcome with grief. I should have gotten some help, but I didn't. Instead I turned to you. That was wrong. I interfered with your marriage. I wanted you to be here for me, even though you were married and had a family of your own. I made unreasonable demands. I was not kind to your husband. He must have really resented me. But you were willing to help me, because I had trained you to meet my needs when you were young. You were always thinking about me and trying to be helpful. That was wrong. I should have been taking care of you."

5. **Absolve your child of guilt.** Your child should be absolved of any and all guilt for the enmeshment. If you will recall from earlier chapters, a Chosen Child might feel guilty for a number of illogical reasons, including: winning out over the other parent; being preferred over other siblings; having special privileges; being the cause of your unhappiness; failing to meet your needs; resenting your demands; or choosing to live a more independent life. Let your child know that he or she has no reason to feel guilty.

"It was not wrong of you to move away from home. That was a natural and positive thing for you to do. I was wrong for making you think it was wrong."

"You were not to blame for the way your stepfather treated you. The way I preferred you to him, the two of you were bound to be enemies. It was our fault."

"You were not to blame for the problems between me and your father. We had problems long before you were born."

"You were not to blame for your sister's resentment. I treated

you better than her, which was unfair to both of you."

"It's not your fault that your mother left. Our problems had nothing to do with you."

"You were not a bad child, even though your father told you you were. His anger had to do with us, not you."

"It's not your fault I never remarried. I didn't have enough confidence to date. I was much more comfortable staying home."

6. **Assure your child that you no longer require his or her emotional support.** It's important that you tell your child that he or she is no longer responsible for you or your feelings. Even though you think children know this, it doesn't hurt to say it again.

"I want you to know that I'm an adult. I can take care of myself. I'm making new friends. I'm seeing a therapist. I have a new and interesting job. My life feels exciting and whole."

"You are free to live your life without worrying about me. I want to be a part of your life. I want to see you regularly. But I accept you as a separate individual with a life of your own. I'm responsible for me. You're responsible for you."

7. **Apologize.** Part of the healing process is saying you're sorry. A sincere apology lets your child know that you're not perfect, that you can make mistakes. It also lets your child know that he or she deserves better and that you are planning to change.

"I am truly sorry for what I've done. I wish things had been different."

"I regret that you got hurt in the process."

"I'm sorry that I didn't protect you when your mother was so hard on you."

"If I had it to do over, I'd do it differently."

"I wish I'd been there for you. You deserved it."

"I wish I hadn't been so hard on you. I really am sorry."

"I apologize."

"I regret what I did. It was wrong. It wasn't good for you or for me."

"I'm sorry."

8. **Commit to a healthy relationship.** Before the session, think long and hard about the changes you are willing to make. Be realistic. You may want to write them down. Share these intentions at the end of the session.

"In the future, I will be here as your mother, but not as your partner or best friend. We will be close, but I won't expect you to listen to my problems or be responsible for my feelings. I will be spending more time with people my own age, but that doesn't mean I won't have time for you. I want us to stay in close contact, but not be so dependent on each other."

"I'm not going to be talking with you about my problems with your father. That's between him and me. You've listened to me talk about him enough. From now on, I'll take my gripes to him. That's where they belong."

"I'm not going to be so involved with your music career from now on. I think it would be better for you to be taught by somebody else so you can get some fresh ideas. And I've changed my mind and decided to give you permission to join the youth symphony. I think it would be a good idea. Before, I told you I thought it would take up too much of your time, but, in reality, I think I was afraid of having you move away from me. That was wrong. You need to spend more time with friends."

9. **End with reassurance.** The session begins and ends with reassurance. Your child needs to know that you aren't abandoning him or her and that the changes will be for the better.

"I'm not saying that I don't want to be your parent. I will always be here for you when you need me."

"I love you and am committed to making our relationship the best it can be."

"I am so glad you are my daughter. I look forward to our years together."

"I love you very much and want to put our relationship on better terms."

"When I make these changes, it's going to be even better between us. You won't be worrying about me or feeling you have to come home every weekend. And I won't be feeling guilty for begging you to come home. I think we'll both enjoy our time together more."

10. **Practice what you preach.** The follow-through is vital to the transition process. You need to do what you said you were going to do in step 8. Each time you interact with your child, get in the habit of asking yourself, "Is this for my child's well-being, or for mine?

Could I get this need met from my partner or friend?" If you backslide, admit it. Apologize. Then commit to doing better.

It is likely that some of the changes you make will be welcomed by your child. For example, if you redirect your marital frustration away from your child and back toward your partner, your child is going to breathe a sigh of relief; it's no fun being in the hot seat. But if you stop being a friend and start being a parent, you may be in for a period of rebellion. It's not easy to hear "no" from a person who used to be your best friend. You will need to be decisive without being punitive and without giving ground. And you may have to endure the child's rejection for a while. If you need some help weathering the transition, a weekly parenting group could be an invaluable aid.

If you've spent a long time being a friend to your child, you may be tempted to go overboard on your parenting. Make sure you are parenting at the right developmental level. For example, most older teens don't need a lot of supervision or structure. Your role in this case is quite limited. Once again, a parenting group could be an ideal forum in which to gain some perspective.

88 Making Amends with a Left-Out Child

If you've been overly close with one of your children, it's possible that you've been estranged from another. As you make steps to realign your family, it's important to make amends with the Left-Out Child as well.

If your relationship with the child has been negative for a long time, I advise you to seek professional help; in many instances, it takes a therapist to turn things around. But if the estrangement is mild, you can make significant progress on your own. A Realignment Session along the lines of the one just described for the Chosen Child can be very helpful.

Prior to this session, I suggest you do some homework. Your feelings about the child may be quite complicated, and sorting them out will prove helpful. One way to do this is to be clear about what you dislike in the child. Write it down in concrete terms. Feel free to exaggerate, because this accounting is not meant to be shared with anyone.

Examples:
"I don't like the way he looks."

"I don't like the way she talks. She whines and is insolent."
"He's lazy and inconsiderate."
"He only thinks of himself."
"She reminds me of my father."
"She reminds me of her father."
"She has all my worst faults."
"She's overly dramatic, just like her father."
"I don't like the way he treats me."
"I don't like his attitude."
"I don't like her arrogance."
"I don't like the way he sulks when he doesn't get his way."
"He never helps out around the house. He's a slob."
"She's mean and vindictive. Everything has to go her way."
"She's such a loser. No matter how I try to help, she refuses to make any changes."
"When I look at him, I feel like a failure as a parent."
"He's really self-centered."

Once you've compiled this list, look at each statement and ask yourself:

"Where did my child learn this behavior?"

"Do I do the same thing?"

"Is this a trait I admire but don't have in myself?"

"When did this behavior start? What was going on in the family at that time?"

"Could I be projecting this behavior onto the child? Do I act in similar ways?"

"What is my partner's role in my child's behavior?"

"Whom does this child remind me of?"

"What secret worry of mine does the child make visible?"

"What secret family problem does this child make visible?"

Answering these questions may help you identify the source of some of your dissatisfaction. It could be that your child mirrors some of your faults or the faults of another family member, and your reaction may be laden with excess baggage. Or you could be projecting onto the child some faults that really belong to others.

Next, try to get some insight into family dynamics. Could it be that the Left-Out Child is resenting the amount of time you spend with a brother or sister? Is the child unwittingly trying to balance out some deficiency in the family? For example, if you are a compulsive overachiever, is your son's lack of interest in school an unconscious attempt to make you relax? If you are always trying to see the bright side of a situation, is your daughter's depression an attempt to round out the picture? Are you and the child polarized? If you say one thing, does your child say the other? Are you using the child as a scapegoat or as a way to take your mind off your own unhappiness? If this child weren't such a source of unhappiness for you, what would you be worrying about?

Next, figure out what you want from your child. The way to do this is to look at your list of critical comments and write down the behavior that would correct the problem. For example, if you wrote, "I don't like the way she dresses," the corrected behavior might be, "I want her to dress more conservatively. I want her to be a better reflection of me."

Finally, look at your criticisms and wishes and after each item ask yourself, "Is this an issue I can let go of in order to ease the tension between us?" Some things are worth arguing about and others are not. If your daughter's manner of dress is not causing problems at school or in her personal life, it might be better to drop the matter. Improving your relationship is more important than imposing a dress code.

Once you've gone through this drill, let your child know that you would like to get together and talk. If your child balks at the idea, be patient and ask again another time. If the child still refuses, put your thoughts in a letter or wait for another opportunity.

✽ Realignment Session with a Left-Out Child

1. **Begin by summarizing your relationship.** This is your chance to state objectively how the two of you have been getting along. Stick to your part of the process. Don't blame or recount old hurts. Don't ask for an apology or remind your child of his or her faults. Simply give a brief description of your side of the relationship. Here are some examples:

"Our relationship has not been very good over the past two years. I'd like to talk about what I've done and apologize to you for it."

"Many times during your life I've taken out on you my frustration with others."

"I have been angry at you when I was really angry at myself or at other people."

"I have given a lot more time and attention to your brother than I have to you. I'd like to change that and have the two of us be closer. I'm willing to make some changes."

"I became a parent before I had the best of information. As a result, I've made a lot of mistakes. I yelled at you when I shouldn't have. I hit you when I shouldn't have. I've called you names when I shouldn't have. I ignored you when I didn't know how to help you. There were times when I didn't listen to you or consider your feelings."

"When I married your father, you and I got off to a bad start. I was jealous of your relationship with him. And, because I'd never been a parent before, I didn't know what to expect of a teenage girl. My expectations were far too high. I was used to living alone. I ended up being too strict with you, and I regret it."

"When I began dating Susan, I didn't think about how hard that must have been for you. I was blind to your needs. I'm sorry I was so insensitive. You must have felt abandoned."

"It was hard for me to feel close to you. Your personality is very different from mine. You are more dramatic and emotional. I tend to be much more subdued. In many ways, you remind me of your father, and you know I had a hard time getting along with him. There were times when I wasn't able to overcome these differences between us, and you must have felt unloved. It's been easier for me to get along with your brother and older sister, and I think you've sensed that."

2. **Apologize for your part in the estrangement.** In order to make amends, you need to apologize for your mistakes. Be honest and brief.

"I'm sorry that I turned my back on you. You needed me and I wasn't there."

"I apologize for all the times I yelled at you. I feel really bad about it."

"I wish I could take back every bad name I called you. It must have hurt you very much. I'm sorry."

"I'm sorry that I didn't pay as much attention to you as I did your sister. You deserved more from me."

"I'm sorry that you had to absorb so much of my anger. It wasn't fair."

"I'm sorry for all the hostility you witnessed. It must have been hard living in this family."

"I deeply regret the time I hit you and hurt you. I wish I could go back and do it differently. I was out of control. I feel very ashamed."

"I was unfair to you. I apologize."

"I'm sorry it has been hard for me to appreciate all your wonderful qualities. I've been too preoccupied with the way you are like your father. I've overlooked many appealing things about you. I've allowed my problems with your dad to color our relationship. I'm truly sorry for that."

3. **Let the child know that he or she is not to blame.** Even though the child had a part to play in the drama, you as an adult have to bear the brunt of the responsibility.

"I blamed you when I was at fault."

"I don't blame you for being so angry at me. I didn't treat you fairly."

"You're not to blame for the divorce. The problem was between me and your mother. You were an innocent bystander."

"You couldn't help the fact that you look and act like your father. You are his daughter! You are as much a part of him as you are a part of me!"

"It's not your fault we didn't get along. It was my fault. I was too angry and frustrated to be a good parent. I felt overwhelmed."

"You were not the reason why your stepmother and I broke up."

"I'm going to be less demanding about your homework. You're old enough to be responsible for your own work. I'll be here to help if you ask me, but I won't be on your case about it."

"I'd like to come down and visit you in California. It's been a long time since we've spent time together. Would spring vacation be okay?"

It will take patience and perseverance to make these changes, and it is likely that you will make some mistakes. Also, your child is likely to test your resolve. For instance, it would be normal for your child to increase the behaviors you find so annoying in an unconscious attempt to get you to return to the old style of relating. There is comfort in old routines—even destructive ones. You will need a lot of support to weather this transition period.

As a part of your effort to treat your child more positively, make an effort to get reacquainted. For example, a colleague of mine made an agreement with his son to go to the movies once a week. One week he got to choose the movie. The next week, it was his son's turn. They both saw a lot of movies they wouldn't have seen otherwise and gained new appreciation for each other's point of view.

If you've not been attending your child's school events, now is the time to do it. I can't tell you how many adults have complained to me, "My parents never saw me play ball." "My father never came to one of my concerts." "My parents didn't come to my high school graduation." "When I went away to college, they stuck me on a bus." Your child will know by your actions whether he or she is important to you.

✂ A Parent's Success Story

Maria was a single parent with two children. Her 15-year-old daughter, Midge, lived with her. Her 20-year-old son was in the armed services. When she started counseling sessions with me, Maria led a bleak life. She wasn't dating and she hated her job. She spent much of her time watching soap operas, which she taped during the day so she could see them at night. Although she was an attractive woman, she did little to play up her good looks.

With little to look forward to each day, Maria became overly reliant on her daughter. She was lonesome when Midge was away from home and felt jealous when she spent time with her friends. She restricted her daughter's activities far more than was necessary and made her daughter feel guilty for having a life of her own. Another problem was the fact that Midge did more parenting of her mother than her mother did of her. Midge was always counseling her mother and giving her advice on how to live her life.

The first stage of Maria's therapy was to help her see how desperately lonely she was, which she had covered up by compulsive eating and by her TV addiction. She needed to face up to the pain that was causing her to rely so heavily on her daughter. She spent the first six months in therapy talking about her unhappiness, exploring her past, and making connections between the way she was treated as a child and the way she was now treating herself. There were many striking parallels.

The next stage of her therapy was to take a cold, hard look at her life and start making some changes. Her goal was to enrich her life so that she had something she wanted to do each day. Toward this end, I had her identify three people she'd like to know better and develop a simple plan for spending more time with them. In a few months, one of these women had become a much better friend.

We looked at her work life next. Maria was a capable woman locked into a low-paying, dead-end job. I suggested she read the want ads each morning to get a sense of what jobs might interest her. On her own, she signed up for a job counseling seminar, which helped her choose a goal of becoming a physical therapist. She followed up on this interest by enrolling in a two-year certificate program at a local community college.

So far, none of this work focused directly on her relationship with her daughter, Midge. But by addressing the root cause of the problem—her impoverished life—changes started happening automatically. For example, ten months into her therapy, Maria no longer allowed Midge to give her unsolicited advice. She had too much self-esteem to allow her daughter to run her life. A few months later, she began allowing Midge more freedom to be with friends.

Maria was further able to release her daughter from responsibility for her welfare by making positive comments around her, such as: "I really am enjoying going to school." "I look forward to evenings alone so I can get some of my schoolwork done." "I had a great lunch with my friends today." "I don't have time to watch my soaps tonight because I'm too busy. There's so much I want to do."

In a year, Maria had become a more nurturing, caring, freedom-giving parent. Because she had taken courageous steps to change her own life, she was able to allow her daughter to become more independent, without having to carry a lifetime burden of guilt.

There was a final crisis Maria had to overcome. A few months before Midge was scheduled to leave for college, Maria became quite agitated. The thought of her daughter's leaving home for good stimulated waves of anxiety. Together, we developed a plan to help her weather the rocky transition. First of all, to find an additional source of support, Maria joined Overeaters Anonymous. Second, she became more active in her church by accepting a volunteer position with a fair amount of responsibility. Finally, she stepped up her search for a job as a physical therapist and was eventually hired by a nearby clinic. This added effort raised her self-esteem to the point where her daughter's leaving home no longer loomed as a threat. She had the feeling that both she and her daughter were heading into a promising future.

15

Victory Laps

88

As you read the preceding chapters you may have found yourself
wondering, "Is it worth it to go to all this effort to explore the past
and change my relationships? What rewards lie at the end of the
journey?" The best way for me to answer these questions is to share
the stories of two of my clients who are well on their way to recovery.
In the beginning of the book I went into some detail about people
who were suffering from emotional incest. Now you'll have a chance
to see how two people resolved their difficulties.

The two stories in this final chapter are fairly representative.
One is about a man who had to protect himself from an invasive
mother, and the other is about a woman who was enmeshed with her
adoring father. Through the process described in this book, they've
been able to get a clear understanding of what went wrong in their
families and to overcome most of their emotional problems. With
courage and persistence they've healed the wounds of enmeshment.

88 Evan: "I came out fighting!"

"My mother claims I came out fighting," Evan announced ten
minutes into our first session, "and I believe she's right. That's how
I survived childhood. Subconsciously, I knew that if I was going to
come out of it alive, if I wasn't going to be smothered, I was going to
have to fight for my life."

Evan was a 40-year-old postal clerk. I always looked forward to
my sessions with him because he was such a good worker. He was
eager to understand his problems and was more than ready to resolve
them. He just needed some help in doing it.

He homed in on his mother as the source of his problems that very first session. Unlike other clients, his recovery was not impeded by much denial. "My mother's the kind of person who comes at you from all directions," he said. "She is so persistent, so incessant. She interfered in every aspect of my life. She told me what I could or couldn't do. She passed judgment on my friends. She passed judgment on everything I did. And she would pick, pick, pick." With no brothers or sisters to run interference for him, he had to bear the full brunt of her overbearing personality.

He was aware that one of the more subtle ways she manipulated him was by being an overzealous mother. "She smothered me by taking too good care of me," he told me. "When I'd go off to play tennis with my high school team, everything would be ready for me. She would have bleached and pressed my tennis shorts, bought me new balls, even polished my tennis shoes! She insisted on doing everything for me, which crippled me and made me dependent."

Evan's father was not much help in shielding him from his mother. He was a Shadow Man, letting his wife rule the roost. The only way his father rebelled was by having affairs with other women. His father's passivity left Evan with only one line of defense—his anger. He was always defying his mother and talking back to her. He told me one day that he would have talked back to her even if she had threatened to kill him: "There was no stopping me."

Many times a client can isolate one key event in his life that sums up his relationship with a parent, one moment that encapsulates their entire interaction. This was true for Evan: "When I was growing up, there were no locks in the house—not even on the bathroom door. One day when I was twelve years old, I was soaking in the bathtub, and my mother came in without knocking. She saw me sitting there and didn't even apologize or ask if I minded she be in there. She just proceeded to lift her dress and sit down on the stool. That was it. I stood up stark naked and screamed out at her, 'Get out! Get out! Get out!' I yelled so loud that my father came running in to see what was the matter. He quickly figured out what was going on and got my mother out of the bathroom. It's a good thing, because I was mad enough to attack her."

At first it may seem that Evan was coping reasonably well with his mother. He did not allow her to run his life, and he was managing to hold on to his sense of self. However, he had to be overly aggressive to maintain his identity, and over time his anger crystallized into permanent form; it became a permanent fixture of his personality. In later years, he would unwittingly associate with people who provoked his anger. In Evan's words: "The very thing that helped me break loose from my mother kept me in a bind, because I was always angry." His primary task was to let go of a coping tool that had outlasted its usefulness.

Where his anger proved the greatest liability was in his love relationships. From the beginning, he was unconsciously attracted to women who ignored his needs and triggered his anger. Women, in short, who were very much like his mother. "If a woman would be there for me," he said candidly, "I would throw her overboard. I couldn't handle the intimacy."

For many years he avoided marriage altogether. Then, when he was 27 years old, he married a woman named Carmen. "Carmen would croak to hear me say this," he told me, "but she and my mother are very much alike. They are both withholding, critical, and smothering." It wasn't long before Evan and Carmen were fighting like cats and dogs, a situation that felt both familiar and frustrating to Evan. "For five and a half years we fought with each other," he said. "I felt she was trying to castrate me, and she felt she had taken up residence with the devil. After the sixth year of this hell, we threw in the towel."

Evan's second marriage turned out to be a variation on the theme—another angry, withholding woman; another endless series of fights. It, too, ended in divorce. After one particularly bitter argument with ex-wife number two, he sat up all night and took a hard look at himself. He told himself, "This is all feeling very, very familiar. You won't stop getting into these messes unless you figure this out." Right then and there he decided to sign up for therapy.

During one of my sessions with Evan, I asked him if he could identify the overriding message he had learned from his mother. "That's simple," he replied. "Don't be happy, and don't be reason-able. Charge into everything with rage." For the remainder of the session he talked about the way this unspoken commandment had ruled his life. Then he wisely concluded, "I won't be fully recovered until I can say to myself, 'I have a right to be happy. I have the capacity to be reasonable.'"

A few months later, Evan began to show some interest in learning new tools for dealing with his mother. In the twenty-five years since leaving home, he'd added only one coping tool: avoid-ance. He'd seen his mother twice in the previous ten years and had talked to her only a couple of times on the phone. He had found it a tremendous relief to put physical distance between them. Now, however, he was beginning to realize that avoidance wasn't a permanent solution: it just meant he'd been putting other women in his mother's place. Perhaps dealing with his mother directly would help him get a better handle on his anger.

Christmas was approaching, so he decided to initiate contact with his mother over the holidays. His eventual plan was to invite her to spend a weekend with him at his house. "I'm not going to her house," he told me. "I'm not that crazy. Ten feet into her house, and it's just the way it was thirty years ago. If she comes here, I have at least some hope of staying an adult."

The week before his mother was due to show up, he talked to me at length about how he wanted to treat her. "My mother does all of two things," he told me. "She bitches and she moans. I need to think of how I'm going to deal with that." He decided that he wanted to be firm yet reasonable. He wanted to stand up for himself without succumbing to rage. "The visit will be a success," he decided, "if I don't raise my voice at her and if I don't swear. Those two things alone would be a momentous breakthrough." To help him further his goal, I coached him in the art of the Ten-Second Confrontation until he felt confident in its use.

After Christmas, I heard the results. True to form, his mother had started complaining the moment she stepped off the airplane. Her plane had been late taking off, and she had barely made the connecting flight at O'Hare. Even before Evan had time to collect his mother's luggage, he had had more of her grousing than he could stomach. He felt all the old familiar signs of impending rage. His face was flushing, and his jaws were clenched. He felt like flinging her baggage against the wall and leaving her stranded at the airport.

To counter this melodramatic response, he took a deep breath and chanted to himself over and over, like a mantra, "You have the right to be happy. You have the capacity to be reasonable. You have the right to be happy. You have the capacity to be reasonable." Once more in control, he escorted his mother to a quiet corner of the airport and said to her quite bluntly, "Mother, it's Christmas. It's a time to be happy. I will not listen any longer to your complaints. When you have something positive to say, I'm ready to listen."

His mother was stunned. She took in a deep breath and started to berate him: "You've got your nerve . . ."

"Mother, I mean it," he said, asserting himself in the same calm but forceful manner. "I'm going to go get the car. You wait out front.

I'll expect you to be in a good mood when I pick you up. Otherwise, I'm shipping you back to New York."

This time his mother was shocked into silence. She waited by her bags with an angry look on her face and didn't say a word all the way home.

"Remember," Evan told her as he carried her bags into his house, "when you have something nice to say, I'm ready to listen."

His mother sulked for the remainder of the day, but she surprised Evan by coming down to breakfast the next morning willing to talk. The visit was not a great one—in fact it was very difficult for Evan to have his mother in his house—but he never lost his temper. When he shared this news with me, I could see his relief. "I wasn't sure I could do it," he said. "It was real close. But I made it."

It wasn't long before this breakthrough was reflected in other areas of Evan's life. One evening, in the middle of a violent argument over the phone with his first wife, Carmen, a thought floated across his mind: *I don't need to be fighting with this woman.* He had the sudden sensation that a rubber band was breaking inside him, and he knew with a certainty that he would never fight with her again. He interrupted the conversation. "I'm not going to fight about this, Carmen. I don't have the energy for it. Call me when you're ready to discuss this calmly." Then he hung up the phone. His ex-wife immediately called him back, and Evan calmly repeated the same statement to her, hung up the phone, then took the phone off the hook so she would have time to cool off.

Shortly after the encounter with Carmen, Evan started dating a woman in her early thirties named Stacy, who was very unlike his first two wives. He met her at a friend's wedding. He remembers leaving the wedding thinking to himself, "That was a very nice woman. I really enjoyed talking with her." Soon he was seeing her on a regular basis.

One day he tried to explain to me how Stacy was different from the other women he'd been with: "Stacy has her junk like all other human beings, but you couldn't send her to hell—she would air-condition the place. The only time she's unreasonable is when I'm being reasonable, and it's safe for her to do it. There's a conscious decision there on both our parts. We're a very sane partnership."

Evan married Stacy some months later and discovered that he now had a potent ally in his campaign to realign his relationship with his mother. He told me about an incident that took place at their wedding reception. During dinner, his mother got into what he calls a "blue funk." "Mother can't stand much happiness," he told me, "and there was a lot of happiness going on at our wedding. First thing I knew, Mother was sitting all alone at a table, pouting. I pointed her out to Stacy, and Stacy marched right over to her. She got down on her knees so she could talk to my mother at eye level and said to her, 'Mom, this is our wedding day, and I want you to be happy for us. If you want me to do for you, I'll do whatever you need to have done, but you're going to have to tell me what it is that you want. Now, what do you want?'" Evan's mother replied in an uncharacteristically meek tone of voice, "I'd like a Margarita, please." And Stacy said, "Well, I'd be happy to get you one."

This mixture of firmness and kindness turned out to be a winning combination. From that day on, whenever Evan's mother started getting unreasonable, either Stacy or Evan would firmly redraw the boundaries for her. They wouldn't put her down or get angry with her; they just let her know what they would and would not accept. For the first time in his life, Evan was able to be around his mother and feel like a sane human being.

It's been four years since my last session with Evan, but a few weeks ago he called me to ask if he could come in for a single session. When I look back on that visit, I see it as a victory lap. He walked into my office with a big grin on his face and brought me up-to-date. He was still happily married to Stacy, he told me, and he was doing well on his job. But the big news was that he and his wife had recently had a baby. He was a first-time father at the age of 46. He said to me, "I now know what happiness is."

Toward the end of the session, I asked him how he was handling his anger. He told me that whenever he starts to get mad, which he still is prone to do sometimes, he tells himself, "Evan, be reasonable. You're doing it again." When he starts to get upset, he takes one full step backward and puts his brain into gear. "If I start to fire off, I try to pull it together and reason it out. I don't have my temper licked entirely. I'm still working on it. But ninety-five percent of the time, I'm successful. And I'm learning to forgive myself for the other five percent. I've come a long way."

✂ Diana: "My father always told me, 'You'll never let me down.'"

Diana's story is quite different from Evan's. Instead of fighting to break free from a critical mother, Diana had to let go of a fantasy bond with an adoring father. This proved to be a two-step process. First, she had to recognize that there was something wrong with her relationship with her father. Until she was 30 years old, she looked back on her early years with him as the happiest time of her life. Second, she had to struggle to diminish his prominence in her life. It was harder for Diana to let go of her father than it was for Evan to free himself from his mother: Evan felt he had everything to gain from the endeavor; Diana was afraid that she had something to lose.

When Diana was born, her mother and father were in their middle forties and had two teenage sons. With such a large age gap between Diana and her older brothers, she was treated more like an only child than one of three. She describes her mother as being attractive, loving, and kind and her father as being funny, warm, and kindhearted. She got along well with her mother, but she was even more attached to her father.

One of the first stories Diana told me about her father was the time he was driving home from work and happened to see a fawn standing by the road, hovering by the dead body of its mother. He rescued the fawn, wrapping it up in his jacket. He drove home and presented the baby deer to Diana. There were tears in his eyes as he handed her the bundle. I remember thinking to myself as Diana told me this story, "This could be the opening to a Disney movie."

Diana's happy and carefree childhood came to an abrupt end later that year when her mother was killed in a car accident. Diana's grief was matched by her father's desolation. She remembers weekly visits to the cemetery, where her father would cry and cry. She would put her little arms around his broad shoulders and do her best to console him. Twenty-five years later she would reflect on this scene and wonder why it was she who had been doing the comforting, not her father. But at the time, taking care of him seemed the expected thing to do.

In the years that followed, Diana and her father became very close. Her two older brothers were now living on their own, so father and daughter set up household together. They went bike riding together, read together, traveled together, cooked together, shopped together, and washed dishes together. When Diana's father had to work late at his office, he didn't hire a babysitter—he took Diana along with him and set up a cot for her beside his desk. She remembers falling asleep blissfully watching him work on his papers. The love her father had once spread out to a wife and two sons was now being channeled into her.

Diana has wonderful memories of the first Christmas after her mother's death, a time when her father happened to be making very little money. To bring joy to her life, he scrimped and saved and went into debt to buy her hundreds of dollars worth of toys and new clothes. He was so excited by the gifts, he couldn't sleep all Christmas Eve. When he heard Diana get up in the middle of the night, he went to her room and told her she could open up all her gifts right then and there. They went downstairs together at three in the morning. Her father turned on the light, and Diana saw a tree heaped with presents. She remembers feeling overwhelmed with love and happiness.

Six months later, Diana's father started dating a woman named Laura, who worked in his office. A year later, they got married. Diana never got along very well with Laura. "I got the feeling I was in her way," she told me. "She made sure I had clean clothes and that there was food on the table, but she showed little affection. At the time, I thought she just didn't know how to be a mother, because she had no children of her own. But now I suspect she was jealous of the relationship between me and my father."

It wasn't long after the marriage that Diana's father began to fade into the background and allow Laura to rule the household. He was a good man but a decidedly passive one. For Diana, the transition was abrupt and painful. Her stepmother's moods seemed totally unpredictable. One day Diana would be yelled at for leaving a sock on her bedroom floor; another day, her stepmother would say nothing about it. There were no clear rules in the household, so Diana never knew what to expect and was in constant fear of getting into trouble.

What bothered her even more, however, was when her stepmother denied her access to her father. "My father and stepmother would be discussing something, and I would be sitting close to my Dad, as usual," Diana told me. "Laura would see me sitting there and tell me to go away. 'This is not for your ears,' she would say. 'This is between my husband and me.' I would go away feeling crushed and humiliated."

When there was conflict between Diana and her stepmother, her father never stood up for her. Instead, he kept urging her to "be a good girl. Don't cause any trouble. Do what Laura asks." He showed his love for Diana on the sly. For example, he would buy her presents, but make her promise to keep them hidden. Instead of openly spending time with his daughter, he would slip out of the house with her when his wife wasn't looking.

One of the most memorable events in Diana's life (one that was as significant to her as Evan's screaming fit in the bathtub was for him) took place during one of these secret assignations. One Saturday her father offered to go over to a neighbor's house to help him repair his furnace. Just before leaving, he went up to Diana's room and told her where he was going so she could join him there later. When Diana arrived at the neighbor's house, her father was alone in the basement. Apparently, the neighbor had gone shopping for parts to the furnace. Diana looked at her father and saw there were tears in his eyes. "What's the matter, Daddy?" she asked him. He hugged her close to him and said, "What have I gotten us into, Diana? What have I gotten us into?" He clung to her and cried and cried about how miserable he was. "Nothing seems right anymore. Why did I ever remarry?"

When Diana told me this story, I was deeply moved. I said to her, "You know, as I was listening to you, I was trying to imagine what it would be like to be a thirteen-year-old girl caught up in her father's arms listening to such an intimate confession. He seduced you with a level of intimacy far beyond your years. Thirteen-year-olds are not supposed to comfort their fathers. They're not supposed to hear how unhappy their fathers are in their marriages. That exchange must have given you emotional stretch marks!"

Diana laughed at my comment, but there were tears in her eyes. "You're right," she said. "I don't think I've ever felt that close to anyone. Not before. Not after. It was an epiphany."

"The kind of bond you had with your father was like Krazy Glue," I said.

"Yeah," she laughed through her tears, "it's the stuff that sticks pianos to ceilings. I've been stuck to my father for thirty years!"

The secret alliance Diana had with her father continued until tragedy struck once again: her father died of a heart attack. "I've never experienced such acute devastation," she told me. "I can't begin to describe how painful it was. Total, gut-wrenching agony.

Far, far worse than when my mother died. It was like banging my head against a brick wall. I had no tools. No one to help me. It was like my skin had been ripped off me."

Given all the trauma in her childhood, it's no wonder that Diana went through some tough times in her young adult years. She left home at 18 to go to college, but dropped out of school during the first semester. She didn't have enough sense of direction to take advantage of what she was learning. Soon after that she was sexually abused by an uncle, and slept with dozens of men—three of them older, married men. At times she felt as if she were two completely different people: the "daddy's little girl" of old, who was sweet and good and compliant, and "Diana," a wanton and wayward woman. There was no safe middle ground.

After five tempestuous years, Diana did a sudden about-face and went from a life of debauchery to a life of discipline and celibacy. She abandoned her odd assortment of boyfriends and moved in with a favorite aunt. There, she met a kind man from her hometown and married him a few months later.

Diana managed to steer a fairly straight course for the first years of her marriage. She and her husband had two little boys and became deeply involved in antiwar activities. The "good" side of her was in ascendance. Then, without warning, in the sixth year of her marriage she found herself romantically and physically attracted to a married man and became involved in a damaging affair. The affair soon took over her life. She dreamed about her lover at night and looked for an excuse to see him every day. She was so torn apart by the double life she was leading that she finally sought professional help.

It was in group therapy that Diana first glimpsed her hidden anger at her father. A member of the group asked her one day why her father had allowed his second wife to rule the household. "If my father had caved in like that," said the woman, "I'd have been furious! What a jerk!" These candid remarks made Diana question her father's devotion. Why *hadn't* he taken better care of her? Why had he shown his love for her only in secret? Slowly, Diana began to feel some of her hidden rage. Her anger began to build until a few months later she was shaking her fists at the sky and yelling, "How could you do that to me?"

Evan, the man in the preceding portrait, had to learn to control his anger. Diana needed to reclaim hers. When Diana finally got in touch with her repressed rage, a deep split inside her began to heal. She no longer felt as if she were part good and part evil. She was neither a sweet, smiling "daddy's girl" nor a loathsome whore. She was an ordinary human being with both angry and loving thoughts. She felt more unified and whole.

As Diana was working on resolving the relationship with her father, she experienced a gradual recommitment to her marriage. She finally saw her affair for what it was—an unconscious re-creation of her secret trysts with her father. She had been blindly searching for the emotional intensity she had experienced as a little girl when she had been the intimate partner of an older man, an experience that could only be matched by those first heady weeks of a furtive affair.

During one session with me, Diana talked about the affair. Her comments centered on one aspect of the relationship that stood out in her mind as an almost exact duplication of her childhood experience. She told me she frequently met her lover in a room in the basement of the building where he worked. He would cling to her with tears in his eyes and cry about the agony of having such strong feelings for her but being married to another woman. Diana realized with a shudder that these scenes were almost identical to the furnace-room scene with her father when he had cried about his unhappiness at being married to her stepmother. I assured her that to her unconscious mind, the difference between the two events was nonexistent, which helped explain the obsessive nature of the affair.

Diana continued to be attracted to other men throughout the course of her therapy, but her insights kept her from acting on her impulses. When she felt drawn to a man, she was able to hold herself back. For example, at one point she found herself attracted to a neighbor whose daughter had died a tragic death. As she helped out with plans for the young woman's funeral, she found herself totally consumed with love for the father. She found the urge to connect with him almost unbearable. She wanted to talk with him and hold him and comfort him in his grief.

Then she had the sudden realization that she was once again trying to relive the past; this time she was trying to recreate the role with her father when she had comforted him about her mother's death. At that point, she had a stern talk with herself: "You don't even know this man! What on earth are you doing! You're jeopardizing your marriage for some guy you don't even know! This is crazy! The whole reason you're getting pulled into this is because this is how you dealt with your father's grief—by rescuing him. Now let go!"

Having made this decision, Diana felt depressed; she felt she was losing something irreplaceable. After a few days, however, her depression lifted, and she found a new respect for herself. She had made a choice. She was in control of her emotions. She was no longer held hostage to feelings of twenty years ago. She said to herself, "You're playing a different role now, Diana. You have choices."

When Diana related this epic struggle to me, I told her that just because she'd done the work of reexperiencing the past, she wouldn't be able to cut it off entirely. She would still find herself attracted to men outside her marriage; she would still feel some of the old, familiar pulls. But now she would be able to delineate; she would be able to separate the past from the present. She would be able to make better choices—just as she had done in this particular instance—choices that would be better for her and for her whole family. I said to her, "Your attraction to your neighbor and your decision not to act on your impulses is exactly what the healing process is all about."

A few weeks later, Diana came to my office with a dream she wanted to share. It had felt very significant to her. In her dream she had been at her father's funeral, looking down into the ground at his coffin. She watched as load after load of dirt was dumped on top of it. She told me she had felt strangely peaceful while this was happening, as if his burial was long overdue.

The dream had been so moving to her that she had awakened in the middle of the night. As she lay in the dark, two things happened simultaneously. One, she felt a powerful attraction to her sleeping husband. She looked over at him and felt more at one with him than she had at any other time in her marriage. Two, she had the strange sensation that her relationship with her father was finally assuming the proper proportions. "I felt as if I had finally buried him," she said. "But I also felt that his image—his countenance—was burning more brightly in my life than it had for years. But this time, it wasn't a blaze lighting up the whole room. It was a candle over in the corner, where it belonged."

88 Back to the Self

It is a joy to see Evan and Diana today. They are two people representing countless others who have had the courage and the dedication to alter the course of their lives. Are they free from struggle? Of course not. But they address life's difficulties with the wisdom and confidence that comes from being a whole person.

The struggles they went through are representative of the healing journey of the Chosen Child. First, they both had to learn how to shore up the boundaries between themselves and their parents, boundaries that had been missing in childhood. Evan had to learn how to keep his mother at bay without compromising his integrity or triggering his rage; Diana had to find a way to love and value her father without denying his weaknesses or allowing him to play an overly large role in her life. By realigning these relationships, they were able to restore a sense of balance within themselves.

Second, they needed to see how their history as Chosen Children was reflected in their present-day lives. Even had to see how he was choosing women who resembled his mother so that he could stay locked in his anger. Diana had to realize that she was falling in love with men outside her marriage so that she could re-create the clandestine nature of her involvement with her father. Once these insights had a chance to settle in, they were translated into changed behavior. Evan and Diana no longer kept repeating the same painful mistakes. They were free from much of the destructive influence of the past.

Finally, having looked at the past and restructured the present, they both came to the awareness that they had the capacity to be happy, fully functioning human beings. They learned that they were indeed special—not because a parent saw them that way, but because they were loving, whole human beings. Their hard work had enabled them to experience joy in their lives and to be loving and supportive parents to their own children. Their journey had taken them full circle—back to their original, undivided selves.

I hope this book has added to your understanding of your childhood and given you enough concrete advice and incentive to resolve your difficulties. You may want to reread the book at a later time in your life. It will mark your progress as well as map out future growth.

I want to reiterate that change takes time and patience. It rarely happens the way I think it should, and it pays little attention to the timetable I have in mind. It's always slower and more difficult than I would like. While I'm in the middle of my struggles, I rarely feel as if I'm making much headway. It's only when I look back on my life that I can see the consistent growth.

My parting advice to you is to follow the suggestions in this book that make the most sense to you, and then allow them time to bear fruit. If you would like additional help, by all means search out a knowledgeable and reliable therapist. I am certain that your efforts to work through the unprocessed events of the past will be fully rewarded.

If you would like to write to me about your experiences, I encourage you to do so. Writing is good therapy, and I'm an interested reader.

Best wishes on your journey.

Notes

8̈8̈

CHAPTER 1

1. (p. 8) Salvador Minuchin, noted family therapist, refers to the estranged family as the "disengaged" family—his term for the psychological isolation that results from overly rigid boundaries between individuals and family subgroups. He uses the term *enmeshment* to refer to the blurring of psychological boundaries, which results in a loss of autonomy in family members.

2. (p. 8) The term *emotional incest* comes from the pioneering work of Pia Mellody, a nationally recognized authority on co-dependence, who first delineated this area of parental abuse. The term is appropriate when a parent's emotional invasiveness is severe. A child has a right not to expect sexual invasion or *psychological* invasion from a parent.

3. (p. 11) Salvador Minuchin, through his dedicated work with families, has developed "Structural Family Therapy," a process that defines and reinforces subgroups within the family. Making a clear distinction between subgroups is a key to recovering from emotional incest and restoring healthy relationships within a family. Family subgroups are defined in chapter 7. Strengthening the boundaries between these subgroups is one of the underlying ideas in the subsequent recovery chapters. For further information about Structural Family Therapy, refer to Minuchin's book, *Families and Family Therapy* (Cambridge, Mass.: Harvard University Press, 1974).

CHAPTER 2

1. (p. 22) Lynn Hoffman, *Foundations of Family Therapy* (New York: Basic Books, Inc., 1981), p. 110.

2. (p. 23) To further explore the area of emotional sexual abuse, I suggest you read Pia Mellody's book, *Facing Co-dependence* (San Francisco: Harper & Row, 1989).

CHAPTER 3

1. (p. 28) Pat Conroy, *The Prince of Tides* (New York: Bantam Books, 1986), p. 110.

CHAPTER 4

1. (p. 58) Minuchin, Salvador, *Families and Family Therapy*, pp. 7–9.

2. (p. 68) *Favorite Fairy Tales*, edited by Jennifer Mulherin (New York: Grosset and Dunlap, 1983), p. 63.

CHAPTER 6

1. (p. 86) U.S. Bureau of the Census, *Statistical Abstract of the US: 1988 (108th ed.), Washington, D.C., 1987*. Further indication of the rapid rise in single-parent families is found in the June 1987 edition of the magazine *American Demographics* (p. 70), which reports a near *doubling* of single-parent families from 1970 to 1986.

CHAPTER 8

1. (p. 117) This aphorism comes from the title of John Gray's book, *What You Can Feel, You Can Heal* (Mill Valley, California: HEART Publishing, 1984).

2. (p. 119) Harvey Jackins, *The Human Side of Human Beings, The Theory of Re-Evaluation Counseling* (Seattle: Rational Island Publishing, 1963).

3. (p. 130) For more information about second order change, see Watzlawick, P.; J. Weakland; and R. Fisch, *Change: Principles of Problem Formation and Problem Resolution* (New York: Norton, 1974). The old adage "give a man a fish and he goes without hunger one day; but teach him to fish and he will never hunger again" is another example of second order change. If you merely give a person a fish, this addresses the immediate symptom—hunger. But if you teach him to fish, you change the process or system that causes the hunger. Think of first order change as a stopgap measure. Second order change corrects the underlying problem.

CHAPTER 9

1. (p. 143) In developing the outline of this autobiographical exercise, I drew on my work with Pia Mellody, who has done an excellent job of categorizing the various facets of abuse and neglect.

2. (p. 152) The idea of diagramming the interpersonal dynamics of one's family is credited to Murray Bowen, a well-known family therapist.

CHAPTER 10

1. (p. 161) Andrew Ferber, Marilyn Mendelsohn, and Augustus Napier, *The Book of Family Therapy* (Boston: Houghton Mifflin Co., 1973), p. 456.

2. (p. 180) This is an adaptation of a Gestalt therapy model developed by Fritz Perls.

3. (p. 182) Philip Guerin, Leo Fay, Susan Burden, Judith Gilbert Kautto, *The Evaluation and Treatment of Marital Conflict* (New York: Basic Books, 1987).

CHAPTER 12

1. (p. 197) In my work with couples, I have been greatly influenced by my work and training with Harville Hendrix, a nationally recognized marital therapist and the author of *Getting the Love You Want: A Guide for Couples* (New York: Henry Holt & Co., 1988). I strongly recommend this book for couples and individuals who wish to understand and improve their love relationships.

Suggested Reading

❀

Campbell, Susan, *The Couple's Journey*. San Luis Obispo, CA: Impact Publishers, 1980.

Elkind, David, *The Hurried Child*. Reading, MA: Addison-Wesley Publishing, 1981.

Faber, Adele and Elaine Mazlish, *Siblings Without Rivalry: How to Help Your Children Live Together So You Can Live Too*. New York, NY: Norton Publishers, 1987.

Forward, Susan, *Toxic Parents*. New York, NY: Bantam Books, 1989.

Gray, John, *What You Can Feel, You Can Heal*. Mill Valley, CA: HEART Publishing, 1984.

Hendrix, Harville, *Getting the Love You Want: A Guide for Couples*. New York, NY: Henry Holt & Co., 1988.

Jackins, Harvey, *The Human Side of Human Beings. The Theory of Re-Evaluation Counseling*. Seattle, WA: Rational Island Publishing, 1963.

Mellody, Pia, A. Miller and K. Miller, *Facing Co-dependence*. San Francisco, CA: Harper & Row, 1989.

Minuchin, Salvador, *Families and Family Therapy*. Cambridge, MA: Harvard University Press, 1974.

Minuchin, Salvador, *Family Kaleidoscope*. Cambridge, MA: Harvard University Press, 1984.

Pearsall, P., *Super Marital Sex*. New York, NY: Doubleday, 1987.

Popkin, Michael, *Active Parenting*. San Francisco, CA: Harper & Row, 1987.
"The Family Therapy Networker." Subscription Service, 8528 Bradford Rd., Silver Spring, MD 20901.

INDEX

About the Authors

DR. PATRICIA LOVE grew up in Sistersville, West Virginia, and received her doctorate in counseling from West Virginia University. She is a Licensed Professional Counselor, and a Clinical Member/Approved Supervisor in the American Association for Marriage and Family Therapy. She is a charter member of the Imago Institute and is a trainer and clinician in Imago Relationship Therapy. Dr. Love currently resides in Austin, Texas, where she continues to write, practice, and consult, promoting the concept of family reconciliation and healthy family functioning.

JO ROBINSON is a freelance writer living in Portland, Oregon. Previous collaborative works include: *Getting the Love You Want: A Guide for Couples* by Dr. Harville Hendrix; *Full House* with Karen Anderson; and *Unplug the Christmas Machine* with Jean Staeheli.